Music in Advertising

Commercial Sounds in Media Communication
and Other Settings

MUSIC IN ADVERTISING

Commercial Sounds in Media Communication
and Other Settings

Edited by:

Nicolai Graakjær & Christian Jantzen

AALBORG **UNIVERSITY PRESS**

Stafford Library
Columbia College
1001 Rogers Street
Columbia, MO 65216

Music in Advertising
Commercial Sounds in Media Communication and other Settings
Edited by Nicolai Graakjær & Christian Jantzen

© Aalborg University Press, 2009

Cover: ZUCCEZ
Photo on frontpage by Gabriel Bouys (AFP)
Layout: Anblik Grafisk, Lars Pedersen
Review by Morten Michelsen, Associate Professor, University of Copenhagen

Printed by Narayana Press, Gylling 2009
ISBN: 978-87-7307-965-2

Distribution:
Aalborg University Press
Niels Jernes Vej 6B
9220 Aalborg
Denmark
Phone: (+45) 99 40 71 40, Fax: (+45) 96 35 00 76
E-mail: aauf@forlag.aau.dk
www.forlag.aau.dk

The production of this book was made possible by a grant from the Danish Research Council (SHF/FKK) for the research program "Aesthetics in Market Communication" (2004-2009) and by a sponsorship from the Department of Communication & Psychology (Aalborg University).

All rights reserved. No part of this book may be reprinted or reproduced or utilized in any form or by any electronic, mechanical, or other means, now known or hereafter invented, including photocopying and recording, or in any information storage or retrieval system, without permission in writing from the publishers, except for reviews and short excerpts in scholarly publications.

Contents

Introduction — 7
Music for commercial purposes
Nicolai Graakjær and Christian Jantzen

Chapter 1: Mapping research on music in TV commercials — 13
Nicolai Graakjær and Christian Jantzen

Chapter 2: Music in TV commercials — 53
Formats, frequencies, and tendencies
Nicolai Graakjær

Chapter 3: Making sense of music in advertising research — 75
An interpretive model of the interaction between music and image
Matthias Bode

Chapter 4: The JYSK jingle — 99
On the use of pre-existing music as a musical brand
Nicolai Graakjær

Chapter 5: Music videos and TV commercials — 121
Similarities and differences
Erkki Pekkilä

Chapter 6: On the commercialization of Shostakovich's 'Waltz No. 2' — 141
A case study of textual, contextual and intertextual meaning of music
Anders Bonde

Chapter 7:	Relevant… but for whom? On the commercial (ab)use of music on television Nicolai Graakjær and Christian Jantzen	169
Chapter 8:	Watch this! Yearn for that! Stay tuned! The use of channel music as a promotional tool in television programming Nicolai Graakjær and Christian Jantzen	183
Chapter 9:	Functions of sound in web advertising Iben Jessen and Nicolai Graakjær	195
Chapter 10:	The soundtrack of sales Music in Swedish radio commercials Alf Björnberg	223
Chapter 11:	Music for shopping Supplementary sounds of consumption Nicolai Graakjær and Christian Jantzen	237
Chapter 12:	Producing corporate sounds An interview with Karsten Kjems and Søren Holme on *sonic branding*® Nicolai Graakjær and Christian Jantzen	259
Chapter 13:	The musical ready-made On the ontology of music and musical structures in film A preliminary study Martin Knakkergaard	275

INTRODUCTION
Music for Commercial Purposes

Nicolai Graakjær and Christian Jantzen

THE SOUND OF MONEY

It is a simple fact that most music of today is composed, performed, produced, distributed, sold and bought, stored and listened to for some commercial purpose. More 'noble', e.g. artistic intentions may prevail, but modern music is always actively seeking an audience, so that the artist, the record company, the event organiser, the sales outlet or some other party may prosper. In modern capitalist economies, the cultural field of aesthetics is inevitably entangled with a commercial field of financing, production and sales. Furthermore, the social and especially the technological development of such economies imply that music is increasingly utilized for the main purpose of selling. What are being sold, are not merely records or performances, but also – and ever more so – quite 'unmusical' goods ranging from detergents to customer services.

This volume is about the use of music in commercial settings outside its 'proper' field of cultural production and reception: e.g. music in TV- and radio-commercials, in web-ads or in shops. This kind of music is also actively – sometimes even desperately – seeking an audience. But a defining characteristic of this use of music might be that it is not primarily intended for active listening. Only very few, if any, compilations of music for TV-commercials exist. At best, music in these commercial settings is to be heard. When remembered, it should help the hearer to recall the overall message of the commercial (e.g. the brand name), not the artist nor the composer. In this realm, catchy sounds are crafted not to sell records, but to promote the sales of other products and services. The prime function of this music is to make money outside the music industry – for advertising agencies, producers of other consumer goods, department stores, etc.

In this respect music for commercial settings is functional music *per se*. It only exists to serve some 'non-musical' function. Our everyday life of consumption is filled with tunes of popular music, and commercially instigated sounds undoubtedly make up a fair proportion of the melodies, songs and jingles we encounter on a daily basis, whether we enter public space, go shopping, listen to the car radio, browse the Internet or watch television at home. Crafting such sounds has hence become a significant industry of its own with a very considerable annual turnover.

But perhaps because we as consumers hear such sounds when we are preoccupied with doing something *else* – often something slightly more important or interesting – the output of this industry goes by and large unnoticed. The fact that functional music does not count for much in our awareness may misleadingly make us assume that is does not count for much at all. But actually music for commercials settings makes us remember specific messages, watch particular programmes and prefer some brands above other ones. In addition, it helps us relax in stressing shopping situations and stimulates our consumer appetites in other contexts.

Furthermore, the fact that we only rarely listen attentively to this music may just as misleadingly make us assume that the crafting of these sounds is an aesthetically simple matter. While such an assumption may be true from the perspective of elite culture (but is obviously highly debatable from a popular music perspective), it is definitely false when it comes to aesthetic structure and aesthetic effect. Regardless of its cultural value, music for commercial settings is structurally just as complex as many (or perhaps most) other kinds of music. And this music counts for something in the life of its involuntary audiences as well as the advertised products, precisely because it generates aesthetic effects, if not similar then comparable to those elicited by more valued phenomena. It might even be argued that advertising music has historical significance by developing its own short formats and devices (e.g. jingles), which again have become recycled and re-used in cultural settings outside the realm of commerce.

SCOPE OF THIS BOOK

With this volume, we want to draw attention to the aesthetic features of music in commercial settings: i.e. to those structural characteristics that, in an often unnoticeable manner, gives this kind of music a commercial impact in the decision-making of consumers and on the bottom-line of companies. We argue that this type of functional music is extremely suited for exploring the persuasive impact that music may have beyond all those well known qualities of classical as well as popular music such as the ability to entertain, edify and purify its audience.

A secondary goal is to raise the readers' awareness of the unnoticed commercial motives, which underlie much music exposure in the media. We claim that researchers as well as critics of music and media are presently too ignorant of these motives. But television programming is driven by an urge to attract large audiences and 'sell' them to advertisers. Entertainment in general and music programmes in particular are means to reach this goal. At the same time, music programmes of all sorts are targets for the record industry wanting to expose their 'products' (i.e. artists) in a natural setting for an audience without having to pay for it. A third indicator of this entanglement is the fact that channels use the same musical devices as the advertising industry to attract audiences, grab the publics' attention and affect memory of the message.

A tertiary goal is to call for closer cooperation and mutual inspiration between distinct traditions of research to develop the study of music for commercial settings. A divide in methodology, research history, academic background and periodicals has practically and mentally blocked the possibility of establishing a platform for communication. This divide is not only a matter of great differences in perspective between the major agents in this field: musicology, advertising research (and market communication) and media research. These agents also seem internally divided. To the outsider it looks as if musicology has been preoccupied with a futile discussion between researchers in favour of studying other kinds of music than those belonging to the realm of "autonomic art" and those opposed to this idea. And in research on advertising and market communication, an even more useless quarrel between experimentalists and those in favour of qualitative methods seems to split the field. In media studies, music – and sound in general – is neglected in favour of verbal language and visual perception.

This volume does not pretend to succeed in uniting these different perspectives. The chapters are authored by researchers coming from mainly the musicological and media studies traditions. It is nonetheless our hope that the contributions will be relevant also to readers outside these traditions, so that an interdisciplinary forum for research in music for commercial purposes might be established in the future.

STRUCTURE OF THE BOOK

The book consists of three sections and a final chapter discussing the ontological status of music in audiovisual texts. The first six chapters all deal with topics related to music in 'ordinary' TV commercials. The volume starts with presenting a survey of previous research on music in TV commercials, followed by a quantitative analysis of diachronic developments in the use of music in TV commercials. Chapter 3 presents a model of how the relationship between music and the visuals may be interpreted. The next three chapters present case analyses of the use of pre-existing music in a commercial, the relationship between music in commercials and music videos and the transformation of musical meaning in commercials, film and documentary.

The second section investigates music for commercial purposes on television outside the space of commercial breaks. Chapter 7 discusses phenomena like product placement and 'puppeting', which might mislead the viewers and damage the channel's reliability. The use of techniques from music in commercials in profiling a channel's own programmes is discussed in chapter 8.

The third section studies music for commercial purposes in other media and other settings than television: on the radio, on the Internet and in shops and malls. Chapter 12 is an interview with practitioners on acoustic branding. The final chapter raises the question whether music in commercials or in films really *is* "music" at all.

This book is, to our knowledge, the first anthology of articles focussing solely on music in commercial messages and settings. The chapters are structured to give a sample of the many themes and topics involved in studying this issue. But these chapters do in no way present a complete picture of the field, not even from the perspective of musicology and/or media studies. As indicated by the research survey in Chapter 1, the results from previous studies remain inconclusive in many respects. Musicology still needs to integrate insights from advertising research (and vice versa) and many topics of mutual interdisciplinary interest need as yet to be addressed. The social and technological changes in producing, distributing and receiving music will beyond doubt perpetually generate new forms of and platforms for utilizing music for non-musical functions, safeguarding this field from going out of fashion. It is hence our hope that this volume will inspire to further studies and future research collaboration.

Acknowledgements

This idea to publish this volume originates from a symposium on music in advertising held at Aalborg University in the summer of 2006. A research grant from the Danish Research Council for the Humanities (Forskningsrådet for Kultur og Kommunikation) donated to a project on *Marketing and Aesthetics* (2004-2009) made it possible to arrange this symposium. Participants came from the Scandinavian countries, Germany and the United Kingdom. In editing this volume, we have added new contributions to articles based on some of the presentations given at this symposium.

We want to thank FKK for the original grant and the Department of Communication & Psychology (Aalborg University) for funding this publication. But first and foremost, we want to express our gratitude to the contributors for their years of patience.

MAPPING RESEARCH ON MUSIC IN TV COMMERCIALS

Nicolai Graakjær and Christian Jantzen

A FIELD OF PERPETUAL NEW BEGINNINGS

The first impression one gets when taking stock of research in music in advertising, is the scarcity of research initiatives. Relatively few books and articles have been published on this issue over the last four decades and almost every publication in this field will welcome its reader with regretting the lack of prior contributions to the field. The following list of examples spanning a period of almost thirty years is by no means exhaustive, but it will give the reader some idea of how general the tendency to bemoan the state of affairs within research in music for commercials is:

> "There is a lack of existing published research that concentrates on any such related topic [music as a commercial element]" (Wintle 1978: 7).

> "[R]esearch carried out on television advertising in Italy [...] continues to take no account whatsoever of the musical elements present in television advertising" (Ala & Ghezzi 1985: 406).

> "Regarding the effects and not least the functions of advertising music, much research remains to be done" (Steiner-Hall 1987: 11).

> "There is a clear need for a better understanding of nonverbal communication in advertising" (Hecker & Stewart 1988: 4).

> "Because music is pervasive in commercials, its power to communicate warrants more systematic study" (Stout, Leckenby & Hecker 1990: 888).

> "Research in advertising music hardly exists and the few contributions available are very difficult to access" (Bjurström & Lilliestam 1993: 7).

> "Serious research contributions on the relation between music and image in commercials are barely existing" (Helms 1994: 5).

> "Because so little literature has been published on the relation between the effects of music and the imagery, this contribution will deal with various research attempts" (Leo 1999: 12).

> "Indeed, music in television advertising is a surprisingly under-researched area of study, one which has the potential to shed many insights into the consequences of how sound and image are combined" (Negus & Street 2002: 248).

> "The influence of music upon cognitive and affective response to advertising has received less attention than it may deserve" (Oakes 2007: 38).

Apparently, music in advertising is not a well-attended field of research, even though this kind of music is among the most frequent musical phenomena to which people in present western societies are exposed. Apart from research in advertising music being scarce, the quotations also indicate that the field is fragmented. It is striking that new contributions almost never quote previous ones. Only rarely does new research develop ideas and concepts presented in earlier publications. This generates the impression of a field of research that perpetually starts all over again.

The main ambition of this chapter is therefore once and for all to get done with new beginnings. We want to show that a body of knowledge exists that may be exploited in a prospective way by future research in this field. These insights come from research traditions that apply different methodologies, rely on different concepts and terminology, refer to their own specific histories, hold sometimes wildly divergent opinions on whether music in advertising is the solution or a menace, and use distinct publication outlets. They are moreover often written in different tongues and have usually been unaware or ignorant of related topics and concepts in other traditions and languages. For research to 'take off' and not merely begin, it seems obvious to present an overview of what all these 'old beginnings' have amounted to. We hence intend to map the themes that previous research has dealt with and to present major contributions that have explored and developed these themes.

The two major traditions in this field are musicology on the one hand and advertising research and market communication on the other. The first tradition is preoccupied with aesthetical, historical and sociological aspects of music. It has a predominantly interpretive approach to its subject although quantitative methods are not stigmatized. The second tradition is dominated by quantitative and experimental approaches focussing on what a message psychologically affects in viewers/listeners. Merely a handful of qualitative or interpretive contributions in adverti-sing and marketing, interested in the meaning (and not the effect) of music and commercials for consumers, have contributed to the field (Scott 1990, Jacke, Jünger & Zurstiege 2000, Andersen 2001, Bode 2004, Holbrook 2004). Their point of reference has typically been interpretive research in other fields of market communication, advertising studies and consumer behaviour rather than contributions from musicology. Musicology and the 'experimentalists' have mutually ignored one another, presuming that the doings on the other side of the fence were of little importance. It is nonetheless our claim that musicologists, 'experimentalists' and 'interpretivists' can learn from each other. It might even be so, that problems in one tradition have been solved in one of the others or that findings from divergent perspectives are mutually supportive.

CONSTRUCTING AN OVERVIEW

Our overview is based on a review of 84 contributions in English, German and Scandinavian languages published between 1966 and 2008. Our database has registered publications in these languages dealing with music in TV commercials. Commercial music in other media (e.g. radio and Internet) as well as other settings (e.g. shops) is not included. In our overview, we will not comment on all contributions in our database, nor does this database pretend to be complete, because contributions in Roman, Slavic and other languages are omitted (cf. Graakjær 2008, for an extended research review). We have translated all citations from non-English sources.

A majority of the contributions in our database deal with music in television commercials from musicological perspectives. 51 publications out of a total of 84 are written by musicologists and/or published in musicological journals. This number might be the result of a bias caused by the fact that we come from musicologist and interpretive traditions and hence have been ignorant of some important periodicals and agendas in the 'experimentalist' tradition.

The earliest contributions in our database are in German language (Ritscher 1966, Jungheinrich 1969, Motte-Haber 1972a, 1972b, 1973), and German musicologists quantitatively dominated the field well into the 1980s. Since then, the German interest in the field seems to have declined. There are no significant Anglo-Saxon musicological contributions before the late 1980s, and musicological contributions in English were only sporadically published in the early 1990s (Huron 1989, Cook 1994). The introduction of commercial television in Scandinavia in the late 1980s seems to have triggered a short-lasting interest in music in television commercials (e.g. Klempe 1991, 1992, 1993, Bjurström & Lilliestam 1993, Raunsbjerg 1993).

It is interesting to observe that German contributions are rarely quoted in non-German publications (and vice versa). Actually, especially in the musicological tradition, cross citations are sparse in non-German contributions, which no doubt explains why many contributions start out with proclaiming (another) 'new' beginning (see above). The 'experimentalist' tradition seems more conscious of its own history.

In systematizing the contributions in our database, we have identified seven main themes developed by musicologists. These themes will structure our overview. They concern the impact of commercial music on society, the impact of society on commercial music, the functions of music in commercials, the frequency of music and music forms in commercials, the definition of formats of music in commercials, the contribution of music to the creation of meaning and, finally, the production process.

Two arguments can justify our choice to structure our overview based on themes from musicology. Firstly, these contributions are numerically dominant in our database, and hence quantitatively represent the largest part of the body of knowledge. Secondly, a number of review articles already exist within the advertising research and market communication tradition (Yoon 1993, Vihn 1994, Bode 2004, Bullerjahn 2006, Oakes 2007), whereas a map of the musicological contributions is still missing. Our original intention was therefore to restrict our overview to musicological contributions only. Because mutual inspiration between the main traditions is needed, we realized that this modest ambition was patently futile or indeed might prove counterproductive. We have hence supplemented our overview with publications from the other tradition wherever this seemed relevant. We are painstakingly aware of the bias created by this choice, and we invite researchers from the advertising studies and marketing communication perspective(s) to draw an alternative map based on the main themes in their tradition. As a service to readers who might be in demand of a brief account of major contributions from 'experimentalists', we supply a table giving a survey of 26 experimental contributions in a chronological order specifying the scope (the variables) and design (quality of the stimuli and the number of respondents) of the research (Table 1). Advertising research has, apart from the four interpretive studies mentioned above, also contributed with two important quantitative, non-experimental studies (Olsen 1994, Murray & Murray 1996) to be discussed below, and a seminal review article by Bullerjahn (2006) mapping the state of the art in this field as well as presenting an analysis of quantitative data.

Table 1. A survey of experimental research on music in TV commercials presented in a chronological order.

Contribution	Independent variable	Dependent variable	Stimuli	Respondents
Wintle 1978	Supporting and contradicting music	Emotion, meaning	Constructed	120 undergraduate students
Aaker & Bruzzone 1985	Music, no music	Irritation (attitude toward ad)	Real	780 households

continued on the next page ...

Park & Young 1986	Involvement	Attitude toward brand	Constructed	120 women (21-60 y.o.)
Stout & Rust 1986	Music, no music	Recall, attitude, emotion	Real (?)	60 women
Paltschik & Lindqvist 1987	Feelings aroused, sex, TV-exposure, former experience	Recall	Real	76 students
Macklin 1988	Jingle, background music, no music	Attitude toward ad and brand, product choice, behavioral intent, recall	Constructed	75 children (average 57 months)
Stout & Leckenby 1988	Mode, tempo, melody, music versus no music	Recall, behavioural intent, attitude, emotion	Real and constructed	1498 respondents (90 % female)
Witt 1989	Mode, pitch, metre, rhythm, tempo, melody, style, Instrumentation, duration of spot and music, known music	Recall, attitude towards ad and brand	Real and constructed	750 respondents
Tauchnitz 1990	Emotional evaluation of music	Emotional evaluation of brand, brandawareness	Real and constructed	67 (?) students (average age 24 y.o.)
Tom 1990	Hit music, parody of hit music, original music	Recall	Constructed	151 students
Stewart, Farmer & Stannard 1990	Exposure, time, cue	Recall	Real	2856 respondents (18-54 y.o.)
Stout, Leckenby & Hecker 1990	Tempo, volume, mode melody	Attitude toward ad and brand, emotion	Real (?)	1200 respondents (18-54 y.o.)
Gorn, Goldberg, Chattopadhyay, & Litvack 1991	Music, information, music+ information	Recall, Belief, Attitude toward ad and product, product choice	Constructed	176 elderly (60-84 y.o.)

continued on the next page ...

MacInnis & Park 1991	Fit, indexicality, involvement	Attitude toward ad and brand, emotions, attention	Constructed	178 undergraduate women
Yoon 1993	Familiarity, liking	Attention, recall Attitude, evaluation of brand, skin conductance	Real	105 students
Hung 1994	Congruity	Attitude toward ad and brand, brand perception, meaning	Real and constructed	569 students (in 2 experiments)
Middlestadt, Fishbein & Chan 1994	Music versus no music	Attitude toward ad and behaviour, beliefs	Constructed	97 undergraduate students
Bozman & Mueling 1994	Liked, disliked, neutral music, involvement	Attitude toward brand	Constructed	210 undergraduate students
Vihn 1994	Emotional evaluation of music and visuals, attitude towards music and visuals	Emotional evaluation of ad and brand, attitude towards ad and brand, behavioural intent	Real and constructed	163 respondents (124 repondents 1-30 y.o and 39 respondents 60+ y.o)
Hitchon, Duckler & Thorson 1994	Ambiguity, complexity	Attitude toward ad and brand	Constructed	102 undergraduate students
Olsen 1997	Music, silence, interstimulus interval	Recall, attitudes to ad elements	Constructed	744 (3 experiments)
Stewart & Punj 1998	Exposure, time, cue	Recall	Real	745 responendets (18-54 y.o.)
Hahn & Hwang 1999	Tempo, Known background music, ressource-match	Recall, attitude toward ad and brand, emotion	Constructed	249 undergraduates (2 experiments)
Hung 2000	Congruity	Meaning	Real and Constructed	134 students (25-44 y.o.)

continued on the next page ...

| Hung 2001 | Congruity | Music images and emotions, Ad images and emotions, meaning | Constructed | 102 students (18-22 y.o.) |
| Shen & Chen 2006 | Congruity, attention | Recall, attitude toward ad | Constructed | 130 students (average 23 y.o.) |

THE IMPACT OF MUSIC IN COMMERCIALS ON SOCIETY

Almost all of the early German contributions are preoccupied with the implications of music in TV commercials for the appreciation of "ordinary" music (i.e. classical music), for the well-being of listeners/viewers or for society at large. The perspective is critical, often based on Marxist notions of ideology (cf. Marx & Engels 1970) and inspired by Freudo-Marxist theories of "false needs" and "surrogate gratifications", which dominated the German intellectual climate in the 1970s (cf. Haug 1986). This particular perspective is not yet manifest in our database's earliest contribution, Ritscher (1966). But by having a non-specific psychoanalytical approach, the author claims that music in commercials is efficient by appealing to the more unconscious strata of the self – or the *id* in Freudian terminology. By stressing how music in commercials affect the "primitive person" more than the conscious "I-person" (ibid.: 82), this contribution seems inspired by the fear of "subliminal seduction" of the 1950s (Packard 1960). By blocking consciousness, music might threaten the audience's psychological well-being.

The various publications by Motte-Haber (1972a, 1972b, 1973) are clearly informed by a Marxist perspective. She claims that the use of classical music in commercials leads to a "destruction of musical meaning" (1973: 178), not because the original piece has been re-arranged but simply because it is utilized commercially. Commercial music thus transforms "art to the lowest stage of non-art" (1972a: 153), and leads to "musical illiteracy" (Gertich & Motte-Haber 1987: 59). The similarities with Haug are apparent in Motte-Haber's claim that "music in industrial settings solves aesthetic and moral discomfort" (1972a: 129) and that the melody becomes an automatic, positive trigger for a product once it has "eaten itself into memory" (1972b: 147). Music functions ideologically by making listeners forget the harsh reality of production, thereby turning them into helpless prey for consumer society. Motte-Haber's position is reflected in other German contributions. Schmidt (1983: 95) states that music is "debased to the role of a harlot" in commercials, and Fehling (1980: 88) maintains that functional music by its non-rational effects manipulates its listeners and hence is "a threat to individuals' mental health". These claims are not backed by empirical research – experimental or ethnographic – and concrete examples of the aesthetic mechanisms bringing about such dangerous effects are largely absent.

THE IMPACT OF SOCIETY ON MUSIC IN COMMERCIALS

The concerns of those early German contributions quoted above apparently went out of fashion in the late 1980s (for an exception, see Allan 2005). Our database has no registrations of contributions on this issue after 1995. Since the early 1990s though there has been a slight interest in the reverse issue: the impact of society and cultural change on the music being used in commercials.

Cook (1994) asserts that the coming of postmodernism has changed musical practice: "Traditionally, musicians compose with notes, rhythms, and perhaps timbres. Only with postmodernism has the idea of 'composing with styles' or 'composing with genres' emerged" (ibid.: 35). This claim is followed by the following statement: "But composing with styles or genres is one of the most basic musical techniques found in television commercials" (ibid.), implying that the practice of advertising and marketing itself historically might have been a presage of the coming of postmodernity (cf. also Firat, Dholakia & Venkatesh 1995). In a similar vein, Andersen (2001) registers changes in the functioning of music in adverts caused by postmodern culture: e.g. the music becomes more prone to irony, parody and pastiche and intertextual references become more pronounced.

In his contribution on "world music", Taylor (2000) discusses how an authentic non-western music style is being rehashed in commercials to represent an idealized image of exotic environments. Music thus contributes to the creation of a "hyperreal simulacrum": i.e. a copy for which there is no 'original referent' (Baudrillard 1994). The melodies heard do not refer to a particular opus or to a specific style. It is merely "style-like". Pekkilä (1998) has utilized the same concept in his analysis of the transformations involved in using classical music commercially.

THE FUNCTIONS OF MUSIC IN COMMERCIALS

Some early German contributions, though, have stressed the importance of understanding *how* music in commercials actually works and *what* kind of phenomenon it basically is (Jungheinrich 1969, Meissner 1974, Rösing 1975, Schmitt 1976). The first systematic approach to these questions is Helms (1981) who identifies three main functions of music in commercials as well as typical music forms that serve these functions. Firstly music may contribute to drawing attention to the overall message. This function is typically served by a fanfare, signalling that something interesting is about to happen. Secondly, music may enhance the learning and remembering of the message. Jingles, signature tunes and composed songs may increase the audience's chance of understanding and memorizing the message. Thirdly, music helps in constructing an attractive impression for the message or the product. Pre-existing classical or popular music is presumed to be specially suited for bringing about this branding effect.

Helms' contribution differs from those quoted above by being based on 'objective' registration of different forms and formats. Furthermore, the author's personal opinions on whether this kind of music is lamentable or even dangerous are with few exceptions absent. That this line of research has been seminal is demonstrated by the fact that it was picked up by other researchers (e.g. Rösing 1982, Steiner-Hall 1987). Rösing (1982) claims that music gives important non-verbal clues for understanding the overall meaning of the advertisement. Music provides additional information on the message at three levels. At the illustrative level, music as a 'sound image' can represent extra-musical events. The temporality of music can imitate movement, while the sound of music can represent the acoustic aspects of objects represented in the commercial. At the second level, association, stereotypical music styles and genres can activate culturally formed schemes or interpretational frames for identifying the setting or action depicted in the commercial. The third level, the emotional one, helps the audience in interpreting whether the visuals of the advertisement should be understood in a positive (e.g. joy or love) or negative vein (e.g. mourning or loss).

The significance of Rösing's contribution is that it points to the role of music in the construction of the overall meaning of the audio-visual message, a perspective explored more meticulously in later research on popular music (e.g. Cook 1998, Tagg & Clarida 2003). Steiner-Hall's contribution (1987) is on the other hand pre-occupied with the functions of music for market communication: i.e. which effects does music generate in the audience? The three functions identified by Helms (1981) are further specified in 10 functions each exemplified by a short case analysis:

1. Grabbing attention and enhancing memory
2. Generating a positive mood
3. Increasing arousal/excitement
4. Reducing tension
5. Triggering or enhancing associations
6. Illustrating or showing the product's effect
7. Commentating or interpreting the plot
8. Solving dramaturgical conflicts
9. Instigating the positive evaluation of the commercial
10. Being a motive for buying the product

These functions make good sense and many of the examples are illustrative. A musicological objection, though, against Steiner-Hall's study is that it describes *that* commercials may function in specific ways, but not *how* and *why* it aesthetically brings about this effect. In fact, this study's scope resembles the 'experimentalist' perspective, although the methodologies vary considerably. This remark also goes for Leo (1999), the only study that explicitly has taken up Steiner-Halls' research (more on this study below).

Huron (1989), one of the earliest Anglo-Saxon contributions in our database, proposes another categorization. This essay identifies six functions and classifies them historically. The first and oldest function, derived from *Vaudeville*, is "entertainment", which serves to engage the attention. The second function is claimed to originate from film and functions to create "continuity" between each cut. The jingle is perceived as an example of the third function, which serves to increase the product's "memorability". "Lyrical language" is the fourth function, which comprises emotional, non-rational arguments that are believed to be more efficient when sung instead of spoken. The two last functions, "targeting" and "authority establishment", are presumed to be closely related. The stylistic properties of music lend authority to the advert and the product. Huron presents an array of inspiring claims, but many of these remain undocumented.

One of the seminal contributions to the field, Bjurström & Lilliestam (1993), presents five functions of music in commercials:

1. Creating a mood or background for the advert
2. Illustrating or emphasizing the dialogue or the plot
3. Signalling the beginning or end of the commercial spot
4. Emphasizing certain features or associations related to the product
5. Supporting memory of the product or the advert

These five functions elaborate those described by Helms (1981), Rösing (1982) and Huron (1989) in a more systematic way. This can be illustrated in the following model (Table 2).

This model illustrates how some of the early classifications can be seen to relate to Bjurström & Lilliestam. Helms as well as Rösing lack at least one function in Bjurström & Lilliestam's list. In both cases, at least one of the author's functions covers several functions in Bjurström & Lilliestam. As for Huron, it seems straightforward to compare the first three functions with Bjurström & Lilliestam. The fourth function is more difficult to place, indicating that this function's definition might lack precision. The last two functions should perhaps be re-named to only one function. Regarding Bjurström & Lilliestam, the first four functions point to the text-internal contribution of music to meaning creation in the commercial (which of course might decisively affect the audience). Only the fifth function is text-external, implying the cognitive and emotional effect of music on the audience.

Table 2. A comparison of four classifications of the music's function in commercials based on Bjurström & Lilliestam (1993).

Helms (1981)	Rösing (1982)	Huron (1989)	Bjurström & Lilliestam (1993)
	2. The associative level 3. The emotional level	(4. Lyrical language)	1. Creating mood & background
1. Drawing attention to the overall message	1. The illustrative level	2. Continuity	2. Emphasizing plot & dialogue
(1. Drawing attention to the overall message)		1. Entertainment	3. Signalling beginning and end
3. Creating an attractive image	2. The associative level	5. Targeting 6. Authority Establishment	4. Emphasizing features and associations
2. Enhancing learning and memory	3. The emotional level	3. Memorability (4. Lyrical language)	5. Supporting memory

The functions are numbered in the order in which they were presented in this chapter. The brackets indicate that an extended definition of a function also may cover another of Bjurström & Lilliestam's functions.

Bjurström & Lilliestam's classification also presents a more condensed account of many of the functions presented by Steiner-Hall (1987). Although this last mentioned classification lists twice as many functions as Bjurström & Lilliestam, at least two of these additional functions are merely specifications of Bjurström & Lilliestam as interpreting the plot (function 7) and solving a conflict (function 8) are contained in Bjurström & Lilliestam's second function. The last two functions in Steiner-Hall are hardly specific for music, but rather for the overall significance of the advert to which music contributes. Only functions 3 and 4 – increase or decrease of tension/arousal – are lacking in Bjurström & Lilliestam (cf. Kafitz 1977, Krommes 1996, Bullerjahn 2006, for more on this issue). They could be an additional extra-textual function (i.e. a sixth function in a classification taking Bjurström & Lilliestam as its point of reference). This extra function points at the importance of music in generating neurophysiologic change in the audience, thereby creating a "present moment" and tuning them in on the 'right' way of receiving the message (cf. Pfaff 2006, Stern 2004).

Bjurström & Lilliestam's contribution has two additional advantages compared to most of the other classifications discussed. In the first place, the authors discuss the relationship between functions and different music forms in considerable detail. And, in the second place, this research is based on solid quantitative research on the frequency of the different forms of music in commercials (more on this below). Two contributions from the interpretive perspective on market communication also classifying various functions (Scott 1990, Andersen 2001) lack both these qualities. Scott (1990) identifies eight functions:

1. Creating contrasts by means of dissonance/consonance
2. Representing or emphasizing motion
3. Enhancing learning and memory by means of rhythm and repetition
4. Supporting the plot: music as narrative
5. 'Locating': music represents the location depicted
6. Structuring time
7. Forging identifications: music enables identification with the style, genre or values
8. Making a personal appeal: musical ethos

This categorization adds little to those quoted above, but symptomatic for the lack of cross-citation in this field, Scott quotes none of the authors mentioned above. In his contribution, Andersen (2001) has elaborated Scott's classification by pointing at three supplementary functions, which he believes might be typical for newer, more postmodern adverts: music as intertextual reference, music as irony and music as mediator. Just like Scott, Andersen's account lacks empirical underpinning, so it is an open question whether these additional functions are widespread and representative or not.

COMPARING FORMS OF MUSIC IN COMMERCIALS

Collecting samples of commercials is a necessity for finding out how frequently music is utilized in adverts, which forms and formats of music prevail in commercials, how widespread specific aesthetic devices may be and (potentially) which functions the use of specific music formats actually serve. A fair amount of the contributions in our database relies on such samples, 18 out of 84. But the manner, in which these samples are collected vary widely. Steiner-Hall's study, quoted above, is for example partly based on two series of spots for two different products, collected over a non-specified period of time. Some large-scale samples, though, are collected within a short and well-defined period of time. Here is a list of the most significant contributions:

- 1765 commercials on 4 national and international commercial channels during 16 randomly chosen days in 1992 (Bjurström & Lilliestam 1993)
- 2 samples of 336 and 193 commercials (a total of 529) on 4 major U.S. networks and 4 Dominican channels during a period of two weeks (Murray & Murray 1996)
- 2 samples of 368 and 264 commercials (a total of 632) on 7 national commercial channels with an interval of 2 years, November 1996 and 1998 (Leo 1999)
- 441 commercials on 2 major national public service channels in a period of three weeks in Spring 1998 (Czypionka 1999)
- 4 samples of 210, 275, 397 and 564 commercials (a total of 1446) on 1 national public service channel with an interval of 4 years, April 1992, 1996, 2000 and 2004 (Graakjær 2008)

These studies are highly representative and have good reliability. Collecting such samples may furthermore prevent the researcher from predominantly focusing on special or unique phenomena, thus neglecting more ordinary forms of music. They are crucial for "good classification": for constructing an exhaustive typology of mutually exclusive forms or formats (Laskey, Day & Crask 1989). Other large-scale sample collections fail to specify either the period in which the commercials were collected and/or the channels on which they were exposed (Aaker & Bruzzone 1985, Stewart & Furse 1986, Moser 1987, Appelbaum & Halliburton 1993, Krommes 1996). And, some samples do not indicate the number of commercials collected, only stating that their study is based on "all commercials shown" within a specific period or on hundreds of randomly selected ones (e.g. Helms 1981, Rösing 1982, Greckel 1987, Tauchnitz 1990, Lønstrup 2004, Bullerjahn 2006). These last two groups may be in danger of over-interpreting the significance of unique phenomena, overlooking less conspicuous phenomena and misinterpreting the frequency of music in advertising or the dominance of certain forms.

Almost all of the studies quoted are of a synchronic nature. They take stock of how commercials sound at a given moment in time on particular channels, and they utilize these data to quantify the frequency of music in advertising and the distribution of various forms in the sample. Two groups of contributions expand this synchronic perspective. The first group consists of sample collections that allow for comparative studies. Bjurström & Lilliestam (1993) have sampled commercials from national as well as international channels: two Swedish commercial stations as well as MTV and Eurosport (two international, commercial channels). This leads to the interesting observation that music is more pronounced in Eurosport spots and less on MTV compared to the two Swedish studies. In comparing their U.S. and Dominican samples, Murray & Murray (1996) can point at intercultural differences. The Dominican adverts utilize music more frequently, and the use of Latin music in locally produced commercials is much more pronounced than in internationally produced ones. Generally, intercultural comparisons are still blatantly absent in this field (other exceptions are Haguchi 1998, Shen & Chen 2006, Haguchi 2007).

The second group consists of studies, which combine a synchronic approach with a diachronic one. Only two such large-scale studies exist. The first, Leo (1999), consisting of two samples with two years interval is hardly suited for documenting significant changes in the frequency of the use of music or in the distribution of forms. The second, Graakjær (2008), consists of four samples collected with four years interval, and is hence able to demonstrate how the use of music has changed in a period of 12 years. Results from this study will be presented in Chapter two of this volume. It would be interesting to see this study replicated in other national settings in order to initialize diachronic comparative studies of the development of commercials – e.g. for analyzing the role of cultural globalization in changing national advertisements.

Future large-scale sample studies could also help clarifying the potential relationships between music forms and the products being advertised.

This issue is still under-researched, despite many more or less qualified guesses about possible relationships having been presented (e.g. Bjurström & Lilliestam 1993: 54, on the need for high profiled music use in certain products; Leo 1999: 42, on the absence of music in adverts for financial products; Krommes 1996, on the differences between emotional and informational appeals).

Forms of music in commercials

Most of the studies relying on sample collection utilize this data for measuring the frequency of music use in TV commercials *and* for quantifying the distribution between various forms of music. The studies document that music is present in many adverts. The figures vary remarkably from 42% in Stewart & Furse (1986) to 99% in Lønstrup (2004), but most studies indicate that between 80 and 90% of all commercials use music. The absence of music in a commercial or even of sound in all or most of its duration might thus have a significant effect on attitudes and recall, as pointed out by experimental studies (Aaker & Bruzzone 1985, Stout & Rust 1986, Olsen 1995, 1997). Olsen (1994) is a survey study on creative directors' opinion of the functions of silence in adverts. The respondents assume that absence of music might positively affect the attention paid to the spot. This device might potentially also improve the conveying of information.

Furthermore, these sample-studies invalidate the claim that the use – or as some would say: abuse – of classical music, contrary to the concerns in some of the early German contributions, should be dominant in adverts. Nonetheless, the utilization of pre-existing music in commercials has generated several interesting publications. Springer (1992) has researched the rhetorical dimensions of this kind of music. In a single case study, Raunsbjerg (1993) has presented an analysis of how this kind of music interacts with the rest of the text in a specific advert (more on this study below). Pekkilä (1998) has analyzed the transformations implied in using classical music commercially. Tota (2001) also studied the implications of using this kind of "second hand music". The author points out how the exposure to the abbreviated and 'amputated' version of the musical piece in the television spot may affect the listener's appreciation of the 'original' piece later on. This contribution proposes interesting perspectives on hybridization and "the career" of a musical piece from opus to cliché (for more on this issue, see Chapter four in the present volume). Taylor (2000) differs from the other contributions mentioned by analyzing a style and not an opus: i.e. "world music" utilized to create an exotic ambience in the ad. The author points out that in the case of this particular style, commercials more often use originally composed music resembling an authentic pre-existing genre than the real stuff. The outcome of this fabricated music is claimed to be "affectively flat" (ibid.: 183).

Graakjær (2008: 235) has proposed different subcategories of "pre-existence" and "originality": namely pre-existing known opus music, pre-existing known genre music, and "pre-existing unknown" music. The last category consists of rare specimens of music first becoming known to the public by being used in a commercial. In comparison with Tota (2001), this indicates the possibility of music having different "careers". What and how music is "known" seems in this classification to rely on the knowledge structure of the general public. In a similar vein, music composed specifically for a commercial could be divided in three subcategories (Graakjær 2008: 237): original opus music (creating an acoustic brand), original genre music (originating from a producer's catalogue) and music of unknown origin. The commercial music described in Taylor (2000) would qualify as original genre music.

Seminal experimental contributions to understanding the impact of pre-existing music come from authors working within the *Knowledge Activation* framework, not least North & Hargreaves (2006). Although these two authors do not specifically focus on pre-existing music in commercials, the authors claim that a fit between associations attached to the music and the values and attitudes attached to the product by consumers enhances decision-making. This clarifies (some of) the motives for advertisers to opt for this kind of music. "Sophisticated classical music in an advertisement for perfume", for example, might have a positive influence (ibid.: 113). The trick is that music activates culturally determined knowledge structures in the audience (for more on this issue, see Chapter 11 in the present volume). Further experimental contributions to this "fit" are Park & Young (1986), MacInnis & Park (1991), Areni & Kim (1993).

Studies based on sample collections also show that even though many different forms of music occur in commercials, "background music" is the most frequent one. But the absence of common criteria for sample collection renders comparisons between sample-studies difficult when it comes to discussing the frequency of specific formats and genres. Sometimes, a study uses various criteria to classify music. An example of this is Leo (1999), who mixes musical formats (categories such as "song/jingle" and "background") with musical genres (categories such as "classical", "pop-classical", "rock/beat", "jazz" and "film music-like"). Whereas a categorization based on musical genres may provide important insights into the (ab)use of (types of) pre-existing music in commercials, a classification by musical formats may tell something about the text internal as well as external functioning of music in commercials. In classifications like Leo's, these two separate issues are entangled.

The studies furthermore disagree on how to define the various formats, and the lack of precise definitions often impedes replication: e.g. a significant category in terms of quantity such as "background music" is defined differently by Ritscher (1966), Helms (1981), Bjurström & Lilliestam (1993) and Leo (1999). And to make matters worse, because there is no universal agreement on what "music" really *is* (cf. Nattiez 1990), researchers might disagree on what qualifies as "music" in commercials and which sounds are "non-musical" effects or mere noise.

In both matters, we agree with Bjurström & Lilliestam. In regard to "music", they claim that sound patterns with "a clearly identifiable rhythmic and harmonic structure" should usually be considered music (ibid.: 36). However, rhythmic structure should be considered an indispensable condition for "music", whereas harmonic structure is not. This implies that the rhythmic barking of a dog in an advert should be considered music, whereas the sounds produced by the destruction of a violin should be labelled a non-musical effect (for an alternative discussion on the ontological status of musical sounds in audiovisual texts, see Chapter 13 in the present volume). Other contributions, though, have considered melody to be the most distinctive element in qualifying a sound pattern as music (e.g. Helms 1981, Wüsthoff 1999).

In qualifying "background music", Bjurström & Lilliestam propose a negative definition: this form of music is not distinct (ibid.: 81f). In purely musical terms, indistinct music resembles "muzak" by having a neutral, non-intrusive character: i.e. medium tempo, neutral harmony, only instrumental sounds, a positive mood, few and small melodic oscillations. When it comes to the role of music in the overall 'sound image', music is very much in the background. The auditory side of the commercial will be dominated by speak (dialogue or voice-over) and by diegetic or extra-diegetic non-musical sounds. Because the music is often "weak", it is difficult to describe and analyze.

In the words of Ritscher (1966: 142), "distinct music", on the other hand, is the earliest contribution in our database, characterized by having *Prägnanz* ("conciseness") because either the melody, rhythm, harmony, dynamics or the instrumentation is pronounced, thus allowing a figure – or *Gestalt* – to emerge. Distinctiveness might furthermore be defined in terms of "markedness" (Hatten 1987, Monelle 1992). In its strict sense, a marked musical event "conflicts with stylistic expectations" (Monelle 1992: 271), so "markedness" is an internal feature of the musical structure. But in an extended sense, "markedness" could also be understood as "a comparatively significant event in a universe of lesser significance" (ibid.: 269). This significance could then be "related to the context" (ibid.: 270), in the case of commercial music this implies the "universe" of other spots in the same commercial break as well as the "universe" of other audio-visual elements in the same advert. Distinctive music either makes the spot stand out compared to other commercials or makes the music a pronounced feature of a spot's overall audio-visual structure.

Many contributions in our database discuss one or several distinctive formats. The following model gives an overview of contributions on this issue (Table 3):

Table 3. An overview of contributions on musical formats
in TV commercials, based on Graakjær (2008).

Main category of formats	Sub-category of formats	Main contributions
Indistinctive formats		Ritscher 1966, Helms 1981, Park & Young 1986, Yalch & Spangenberg 1988, Stewart & Furse 1986, Stout & Leckenby 1988, Kellaris & Cox 1989, Kellaris, Cox & Cox 1993, Bjurström & Lilliestam 1993, Krommes 1996, Leo 1999, Hung 2000, Zhu & Meyers-Levy 2005, Graakjær 2008
Distinctive formats		
	Short-duration formats	
	Jingle	Riethmüller 1973, Teixera 1974, Helms 1981, Ala & Ghezzi 1985, Miller 1985, Steiner-Hall 1987, Macklin 1988, Edel 1988, Huron 1989, Karmen 1989, Scott 1990, Wallace 1991, Yalch 1991, Bjurström & Lilliestam 1993, Krommes 1996, Pekkilä 1997, Rule 1997, Fischer 1997, Cook 1998, Leo 1999, Wüsthoff 1999, Andersen 2001, Karmen 2005, Graakjær 2008
	Emblem	Riethmüller 1973, Graakjær 2008
	Long-duration formats	
	Song	Helms 1981, Rösing 1982, MacInnis & Park 1991, Krommes 1996, Pekkilä 1997, Leo 1999, Graakjær 2008
	Melody	Helms 1981, Steiner-Hall 1987, Witt 1989, Cook 1998, Krommes 1996, Graakjær 2008
	Groove	Graakjær 2008

The formats in this categorization are inspired by general research on popular music (Tagg 1982, Middleton 1990, Tagg 1987, Björnberg 2000, Tagg & Clarida 2003) and are actually represented in the sample analyzed by Graakjær (2008). Short-duration formats only last for a few seconds, while long-duration formats may accompany the visuals throughout all or most of the spot. Looking at the mere distribution of publications dealing with these formats, it is evident that most studies in our database deal with the most well-known and also most frequent formats: i.e. indistinct or "background" music (56% of all commercials in Krommes 1996; 35% of all commercials in Leo 1999) and jingles (21% of all commercials in Krommes 1996; 18% in Graakjær's 2004-sample of national commercials). Some minor formats are only discussed by one or very few authors. They are represented in Graakjær's, but with (very) low frequency: in 2004 4% of the national commercials used grooves and only 0.4% used emblems. This perhaps explains why these formats have hitherto been neglected. They may simply have been overlooked in smaller-scale sample studies. Formats like song and melody are somewhat more frequent, and so is research on these.

We will focus exclusively on contributions on the jingle. In our database, we have registered 24 publications dealing with this format. This interest should come as no surprise as the jingle is often conceived as *the* musical format of commercials (e.g. Andersen 2001: 149). Some authors may even misleadingly label *all* music in commercials as "jingles" (e.g. Miller 1985). A jingle is a coherent and clearly delimited short-format with a distinct musical structure and a well-defined placement within the overall audio-visual structure. This placement is typically in connection to the logo or slogan near the end, or, quite opposite, it is in the beginning of the television spot. Contrary to the emblem, the jingle consists of at least two "musemes" (Tagg 1982). In an early contribution, Ala & Ghezzi (1985), define the jingle as a brief "musical incident", typically characterized by being "conceived on a pentatonic base [...] one of the oldest and most widely diffused musical systems in the world [...] extremely suitable for mass medium [...] the remainder are mainly based on the first five notes of the major scale" (ibid.: 413).

The jingle is believed to be extremely suited for drawing attention to the verbal message (slogan, logo) or to signal the start of the spot. And, its distinctiveness and short duration are considered to have a positive mnemonic effect (cf. Huron 1989). A number of musicological contributions have dealt with this format, but there is considerable disagreement on how to define the difference between a jingle and other formats (e.g.

Helms 1981, Bjurström & Lilliestam 1993, Leo 1999, Graakjær 2008), and whether a jingle's placement is most frequently at the beginning (Krommes 1996: 442; Wüsthoff 1999: 25) or at the end of a commercial (Ala & Ghezzi 1985: 413, Graakjær 2008: 292).

The significance of this format has generated books and articles by practitioners on how to craft a perfect jingle (Teixeira 1974, Miller 1985, Edel 1988, Karmen 1989, Rule 1997, Wüsthoff 1999, Karmen 2005). The alleged positive effect for advertisers of utilizing jingles has also attracted the attention of experimental researchers. Macklin (1988) studied the effects of the jingle on attitudes towards the ad and brand, on the formation of product preferences and on recall-effects. Wallace (1991) and Yalch (1991) focused on this last issue in their studies on the efficiency of the jingle as a mnemonic device.

These experimental studies point at correspondences between formats and functions, a suggestion initially made by Helms (1981). Krommes (1996) has pointed out that music may be a seminal device in generating emotional, aesthetic and attitudinal effects, but also that it may be detrimental in adverts communicating 'rational' information. In the case of 'high involvement' products, music may actually reduce recall. The author has not tested these claims empirically, but it seems obvious that Krommes has primarily been thinking of pronounced, distinct music. A format like the jingle might quite possibly generate attention, increase arousal (awareness) and foster recollection of the sound image (at the potential loss of information).

Compared to Bjurström & Lilliestam's (1993) functions (cf. Table 2), the jingle could hence be said to signal the beginning or the end of the commercial (function 3) and to support memory (function 5). It is quite possible that other distinctive formats like song and melody help emphasizing features and associations (function 4). As pointed out by Bjurström & Lilliestam, indistinct music supports the creation of mood and background. But this format also helps establishing continuity in the visual material, thus contributing to emphasizing plot and dialogue (function 2). And when it comes to Steiner-Hall's two physiological functions – i.e. increasing or decreasing arousal – the jingle may very well generate the first effect, while indistinct, non-profiled music as well as melodies may possibly bring about the second effect. More empirical research is needed to make such correspondences plausible.

THE ROLE OF MUSIC IN THE CREATION OF AN OVERALL MEANING

Sample studies may give important clues on the frequency of music and the distribution of musical formats and genres in commercials and experimental studies may inform us on how aesthetic and communicative factors effect the audience. But case studies, understood as the detailed textual analysis of the aesthetic structure, may provide us with a deep understanding of the process of signification: i.e. on how meaning is generated. They might even prove useful in researching how effects are produced neuroaesthetically (cf. Ramachandran & Hirstein 1999). In a few contributions, large-scale sample studies, uncovering the features to investigate, are the stepping-stone for such case studies in the form of text analysis (cf. Steiner-Hall 1987, Leo 1999, Graakjær 2008). But single case studies are still rare in the field of commercial music, even though this line of research might be one of the most widespread in musicology at large. We only found two contributions of this kind in our database (Raunsbjerg 1993, Pekkilä 1997).

These two contributions employ their analytical approach to shed light on the question of how music relates to other structural features and sign systems in creating an overall meaning of the text. This issue is no doubt of seminal importance for understanding the meaning of an audio-visual text, but it has been largely ignored in most media and film studies. Here, music is often treated rather haphazardly (if at all). Musicology could be criticized for showing a similar neglect of the visual aspects of the text, so the articles by Raunsbjerg and Pekkilä are rare exceptions in that they address musical, visual as well as verbal aspects of the text. Inspired by Larsen (1988), one of the few film researchers taking an active interest in the role of music, Raunsbjerg (1993) presents a detailed analysis of how a pre-existing opus of Muddy Waters brings about continuity in the sequence of images and emphasizes certain aspects in these images thus guiding the audience towards a 'proper' understanding of the text, a Levi's commercial. Pekkilä (1997) analyzes music composed specifically for a Wrigley advert, and the author argues that the role of music is crucial in conveying the impression of the text as a unified whole. The significance of this contribution is moreover that it (just like Pekkilä 1998) compares commercials with music videos. Although this might seem like an obvious research item, it is nonetheless a road less taken (for more on this issue, see Chapter 5 in the present volume).

Three other researchers have contributed to studying the role of music in signification, albeit not in the form of single-case studies (Klempe 1991, 1992, 1993, Cook 1994, Bode 2004). Klempe's studies claim that style is the key concept for understanding the interplay between music, visuals and verbal text, and commercial music is considered uniquely suited for demonstrating this point, because it is targeted towards a very broad audience. Commercials for Coca-Cola are utilized to show the formation of a specific style. This is done in a convincing manner, but the publication as a whole is more stylistically oriented than focused on music in commercials. Cook (1994) also investigates commercials to illustrate a point of general importance to musicology: i.e. the very process of signification. By comparing the role of music in four different adverts, Cook argues that music in itself does not have meaning (denotation), but that it works on a connotative level by interpreting what is being said and shown at the verbal and visual strata of the text. By being imbued with such connotative qualities, music has the potential of constructing or negotiating meaning by interacting "with the story line, the voice-over, and the pictures" (ibid.: 30) (for more on this issue, see Chapter 6 in the present volume). Meaning thus "emerges" from interactions in specific contexts, a concept that is further developed in Cook (1998) and – from a quantitative perspective – in Hung (2000, 2001).

Inspired by Scott (1990), Bode (2004) is one of the rare representatives of the interpretive approach to advertising research. The book contains a detailed critique of quantitative and experimental contributions to the field, arguing for the advantages of hermeneutic and cultural perspectives. The author's main ambition, though, is to present a theoretical model of the intricate relationships between a commercial's visual/verbal strata and the music, thereby illuminating the role of music in a "socio-cultural system of signification" (ibid.: 21). The construction of this model, which is not derived from textual analysis, is based on a figure/ground dichotomy. When music is the figure, the images serve "to visualize the music", whereas music "musicalizes the image" when the visuals are the figure (ibid.: 408). This model is still in need of empirical verification (e.g. by a large-scale sample study) or single-case analysis (for more on this model, see Chapter 3 in the present volume).

With the exception of Klempe (1991, 1992, 1993), all contributions in this paragraph are inspired by semiology. The authors hence share a conception of music as a connotative sign system, unable to denote specific meanings but highly suitable for generating associations. Some of the authors (Raunsbjerg 1993, Pekkilä 1997, Pekkilä 1998, Bode 2004) adhere to classical semiological notions, derived from Barthes (1977), on how different sign systems relate to one another: i.e. either by specifying each others' meaning ("anchorage") or by supplementing one layer of meaning with another one ("relay"). Bode (2004), but especially Cook (1994), supplements this traditional perspective with a newer "poststructuralist" version, informed by Cultural Studies (e.g. Hall 1980). Meaning is not solely the result of text internal processes of signification, but also – and perhaps foremost – of the text being embedded in a larger social and cultural context of free-floating signifiers. Signification is thus a result of perpetual negotiations constructing temporary meanings.

Interestingly, the inspiration from audience-response theory is blatantly absent from these contributions (Eco 1997, Iser 1994): i.e. the issue of how "model or implicit listeners/viewers" create meanings from the interplay between music and other sign systems (Tota 2001 is the only contribution in our database utilizing this concept). Equally absent are considerations on how actual listeners/viewers use these texts in their own making sense of everyday life and media contents. Such a media ethnographic perspective is one way in which the issue of signification could be developed in future research. Another – and quite different – way to go is applying Peircean semiotics to the issue of meaning generation or "semiosis" (e.g. Tagg & Clarida 2003). This would create a realist (instead of nominalist) foundation for understanding the interplay of signs, which in its turn could be related to a phenomenological position as well as to the upcoming field of neuroaesthetics mentioned above.

The production perspective

The books written by and for practitioners make up the larger part of contributions on the production of music for advertising. Some publications resemble "do-it-yourself-books" (e.g. Teixeira 1974, Young & Young 1977, Lockhart & Weissman 1982, Baldwin 1982, Woodward 1982, White 1986, Edel 1988, Garrard 1988, Karmen 1989, Fisher 1997, Zager 2003), others are interviews with informed professionals and may provide the outsider with insight in this universe (e.g. Miller 1985, Weiner 1992, Rule 1997, Fitzgerald 1999). Wüsthoff (1999) is a rare example of a publication by a practitioner explicitly addressing topics and themes relevant for musicological research. Research on how music for commercials is produced is still sparse. This issue involves important questions for gaining a fuller understanding of why commercial music sounds the way it does. At what stage in the production process does music become a matter of serious consideration for the advertiser and the advertising agency: Is music first added at the final stage or is it an integral part of the concept from the beginning? How do the people involved in producing commercial music view their own role? How do they go about producing the music? How are they educated? And how do they collaborate with other professional groups (e.g. creative writers, art directors etc.)? Which role does music in television commercials play for the acoustic branding of a product or a company?

The answers given in existing studies are at some points still inconclusive, and little is known in regard to the last question (for more on this issue, see Chapter 12 in the present volume). As for the first question, interview surveys by Leo (1999) and Helms (1981) showed that music was considered an important aspect of the production process, and that considerations about which music to select or compose were made in the initial stages of the process. This finding is at odds with Dunbar (1990) whose interviews suggested a hierarchical order of production: first words, then pictures and finally music: "[Music] is used in a very haphazard and unplanned way. Too often, a television film is finished before anyone even asks about music" (ibid.: 210). This state of affairs is confirmed in interviews with Danish practitioners (Eigtved 1999, Nørbæk 1994).

To date, no observation studies of the routines, organizational procedures or the division of work amongst different professions exist. Future research could get inspiration from media sociological studies of e.g. news production (e.g. Schlesinger 1978, Gans 1979, Golding & Elliott 1979). The research literature as well as contributions from practitioners point out that the most important quality for working in this business is a well-developed intuitive sense of which emotions, moods and associations a particular musical expression might elicit (cf. Rule 1997: 69, Fitzgerald 1999: 366). These studies also indicate that the profession is 'self-made' to a large extent: i.e. not academically trained, and that experience is considered crucial (cf. Helms 1981: 140, Miller 1985: 52, Weiner 1992: 59, Leo 1999: 21). It remains to be seen whether this 'amateurism' is going to survive. The last decade's digital revolution may already have significantly altered the profile of the people working in this profession. The increasing awareness of the importance of acoustic branding for business could furthermore lead to an upgrading of the profession's skills in regard to strategic communication as well as knowledge of consumer psychology and aesthetics.

Recently Klein (2008a) has published an article on one of the potential implications of this increased awareness. By analyzing the operations of Coca Cola and Pepsi, the author demonstrates how the urge for a distinct acoustic brand leads to a merging of music and commerce, thus influencing music culture as a whole. This contribution thus points back at the theme that opened our overview: The impact of commercial music on society. In Klein's perspective this impact might not only be ideological but also economical: it may decisively alter the structure of music industry e.g. by cutting out the record companies and by supporting certain artists thus potentially narrowing down the range of music available to listeners (cf. Klein 2008b).

A MAP OF RESEARCH THEMES, TOPICS AND CONTRIBUTIONS

A simple but productive way to create an overview is to regard the themes and topics as aspects of a communication process. Music in television commercials is produced in order to reach an audience in an aesthetically pleasant, socially meaningful and psychologically efficient manner. The commercial is exposed in a medium, which poses certain technical, economical, juridical and other constraints on the message. The commercial is furthermore produced and received in a social context. We can thus draw a map of the research discussed above based on these five factors: production, text (or message), audience, media and social context (Table 4). In this map, a "theme" refers to a general aspect of a factor, and a "topic" relates to a specific aspect of a theme. Our overview has identified seven themes and a number of related topics (an eighth theme has been added to the model, to capture topics relating to the audience). These themes and topics have emerged from our research review. By being structured according to the factors of the communication process, additional themes not sufficiently covered by existing research come to the fore. Such new themes uncover blind spots in the current perspectives. As for the single contributions: they may very well deal with various themes and topics. A contribution will thus be listed under all those themes and topics to which it contributes significantly.

Table 4. A map of the distribution of significant research contributions seen from a communicative perspective.

Communicative factors	Themes and topics	Significant contributions
Production	The production process	
	The status of music	Dunbar 1990, Helms 1981, Leo 1999
	The sociology of production	–
	'Professionalism'	Helms 1981, Weiner 1992, Miller 1985, Rule 1997, Fitzgerald 1999, Leo 1999
	Commercials and acoustic branding	Klein 2008a

continued on the next page ...

Text	The functions of music	Helms 1981, Rösing 1982, Steiner-Hall 1987, Huron 1989, Scott 1990, Bjurström & Lilliestam 1993, Andersen 2001
	The frequency of music (forms)	
	Synchronic studies	Helms 1981, Rösing 1982, Aaker & Bruzzone 1985, Stewart & Furse 1996, Bjurström & Lilliestam 1993, Krommes 1996, Murray & Murray 1996, Leo 1999, Czypionka 1999, Lønstrup 2004, Bullerjahn 2006, Graakjær 2008
	Comparative studies	Bjurström & Lilliestam 1993, Murray & Murray 1996
	Diachronic studies	Leo 1999, Graakjær 2008
	The forms of music	
	'Non-music'	Aaker & Bruzzone 1985, Stout & Furse 1986, Olsen 1997
	Pre-existing music	Springer 1992, Raunsbjerg 1993, Park & Young 1986, MacInnes & Park 1991, Areni & Kim 1993, Pekkilä 1998, Taylor 2000, Tota 2001, North & Hargreaves 2006, Graakjær 2008
	Indistinct music	(See Table 3)
	Distinct music	(See Table 3)
	Music and meaning	Klempe 1992, Raunsbjerg 1993, Cook 1994, Pekkilä 1997, Bode 2004
Audience	Use and response	
	Effect studies	(See Table 1)
	'Audience-response' theory	Tota 2001
	Ethnographies of use	–
Media		Pekkilä 1998

continued on the next page ...

Social context	Music's impact on society	Motte-Haber 1972a, 1972b, 1973, Fehling 1980, Schmidt 1983, Gertich & Motte-Haber 1987
	Society's impact on music	Cook 1994, Pekkilä 1998, Taylor 2000, Andersen 2001, Klein 2008b

First and foremost, this map shows that the contributions are distributed remarkably uneven. Most publications investigate either textual features or audience effects (cf. Table 1). Whereas studies of effect may deal with textual features (but only as a single factor, cf. Bullerjahn 2006), musicological studies apparently eschew the issue of whether music might contribute to the effect. Surprisingly, also the issue of how music might contribute to signification, i.e. the production of textual meaning, is a road less taken (in the present volume Chapters 4, 5 and 6 elaborate on this topic). Music is an element of the aesthetic structure of commercials *only* because music has – or is presumed to have – a 'positive' effect on the audience. And being such an element it *always* plays a role in signification and in the viewers'/listeners' perception of the meaning or purport of the message. To develop the issues of effect, signification and perception, it seems imperative that musicology engages itself more actively with experimental research, film studies and media psychology. As a minimum, musicologists should explore the use that 'ordinary' members of the audience make of commercials with music: i.e. approaches from media ethnography or qualitative consumer research.

By basing the map on the communication process, it also becomes evident which themes and topics are missing from current research. The topics related to the production factor are not yet sufficiently covered. More specifically, research on how practitioners actually go about creating music for television spots is lacking. Also the topic of how music in commercials relate to acoustic branding is as yet largely absent (for more on this issue, see Chapter 12 in the present volume).

The scattered number of contributions on the social and cultural context of music in commercials is probably caused by the fact that the topics involved often (but not always, cf. Klein 2008b) address issues that engage many more musical phenomena than just music for commercials. Postmodernity would be such an issue. Media concentration, i.e. the merging of media channels, publishing houses, record labels, advertising agencies, etc. and the impact of this on distribution, the public sphere and consumer supply, would be another example of an issue involving many other aspects than merely commercial music (cf. Smith 1998, 1999).

Speaking of media, comparisons between music in TV commercials and commercial music in media such as the Internet or radio are, with few exceptions (e.g. Krommes 1996), absent in our database (Chapters 9 and 10 in the present volume address this topic). We have only registered few contributions dealing with the similarities and differences between TV commercials and music videos, but this topic has certainly not been strange for studies of music videos (e.g. Aufderheide 1986, Kaplan 1987, Goodwin 1993; see also Chapter 5 in the present volume). How the aesthetics of commercial music is employed to profile and 'sell' not just products but also 'ordinary' television programmes to viewers is with the exception of Graakjær (2004) a topic not previously explored (Chapter 8 discusses this issue). The many aesthetical, sociological and economical aspects involved in the "mediatization" of music and the "musicalization" of media for commercial purposes call for a closer cooperation between musicologists and media researchers. One of the topics involved is "music placement": i.e. the use of music as a prop or requisite in film and television programmes with the purpose of selling records or concert events (see Chapter 7 in the present volume).

Coda

The aesthetically intriguing issue at stake in commercials is how to convey a message to a mass audience in the compressed duration of only some 30 seconds. The psychological challenge is to convince viewers/listeners who are not really interested in the importance of the proposition – and sometimes might even be hostile towards the message as well as the messenger. In this respect, music is an important means for getting the message across and creating sympathy, evoking emotions, influencing attitudes and generating recall for the product advertised. Music in commercials moreover produces continuity in the flow of visuals and speak, pinpoints certain aspects of the message, creates relevant associations, suggests a frame for understanding the plot and (perhaps) even involves the audience in the mini-drama evolving on the screen. Understanding what music does aesthetically, rhetorically and psychologically in the field of market communication, i.e. far beyond the realm of "autonomic art", is thus not only a matter of economic interest or of social debate. It also involves issues of a more profound existential nature: e.g. why are certain impulses being experienced as pleasurable, how can contact and understanding be established instantaneously despite physical or mental obstacles, why are certain moments remembered even though they may seem trivial or how are lessons learned and convictions created in manners unnoticed by the 'pupil'? Such issues make music for commercials significant to study. This phenomenon, indeed, points to the fact that music is more than entertaining, exciting, relaxing, purifying or edifying. It is also a tool for persuading. Hence, it is relevant to research this persuasive device in all its industrial, textual, psychological, social and mediated aspects.

REFERENCES

Aaker, D., & Bruzzone, D. (1985). Causes of irritation in advertising. *Journal of Marketing, 49(Spring)*, 47-57.

Ala, N., & Ghezzi, E. (1985). Music and advertising on Italian television. In D. Horn (Ed.), *Popular music perspectives II* (pp. 405-416). Exeter: A. Wheaton & Co.

Allan, D. (2005). An essay on popular music in advertising: The bankruptcy of culture or the marriage of art and commerce? *Advertising & Society Review, 6(1)*, 1-9.

Andersen, L.P. (2001). Reklamens form og indhold [The form and content of advertising]. In F. Hansen, G. Lauritsen, & L. Grønholdt (Eds.), *Kommunikation, mediaplanlægning og reklamestyring. Bind 1 – metoder og modeller* (pp. 118-152). Copenhagen: Samfundslitteratur.

Appelbaum, V., & Halliburton, C. (1993). How to develop international advertising campaigns that work: The example of the European food and beverage sector. *International Journal of Advertising, 12*, 31-43.

Areni, C., & Kim, D. (1993). The influence of background music on shopping behavior: Classical versus top-forty music in a wine store. *Advances in Consumer Research, 20*, 336-340.

Aufderheide, P. (1986). Music videos: The look of the sound. *Journal of Communication, 36(1)*, 57-78.

Baldwin, H. (1982). *Creating effective TV commercials*. Chicago: Crain Books.

Barthes, R. (1977). The rhetoric of the image. In R. Barthes, *Image – music – text* (pp. 32-51). New York: Noonday Press.

Baudrillard, J. (1994). *Simulacra and simulation*. Ann Arbor: University of Michifan Press.

Bjurström, E., & Lilliestam, L. (1993). *Sälj det i toner* [Sell it in tunes]. Stockholm: Konsumentverket.

Björnberg, A. (2000). Structural relationships of music and images in music videos. In R.Middleton (Ed.), *Reading Pop – Approaches to textual analysis in popular music* (pp. 347-378). Oxford: Oxford University Press.

Bode, M. (2004). *Musik in der Werbemittelforschung unter besonderer Berücksichtigung interprativer Verfahren* [Music in advertising research, especially regarding interpretive approaches]. Frankfurt am Main: Peter Lang.

Bozman, C., & Mueling, D. (1994). The directional influence of music backgrounds in television advertising. *Journal of Applied Business Research*, *10(1)*, 14-18.

Bullerjahn, C. (2006). The effectiveness of music in television commercials. In S. Brown, & U. Volgsten (Eds.), *Music and manipulation: On the social uses and social control of music*. (pp. 207-255) Oxford: Berghahn books.

Cook, N. (1994). Music and meaning in the Commercials. *Popular music*, *13(1)*, 27-40.

Cook, N. (1998). *Analysing musical multimedia*. Oxford: Oxford University Press.

Czypionka, A. (1999). Musikalische Repertoirebildung durch Werbung [The formation of musical repertoire by advertising]. In M.L. Schulten (Ed.), *Medien und Musik. Musikalische Sozialisationen 5-15 jähriger* (pp. 198-238). Münster: LIT Verlag.

Dunbar, D. (1990). Music, and advertising. *International Journal of advertising*. *9(3)*, 197-203.

Eco, U. (1979). *The role of the reader*. Indianapolis: University of Indiana Press.

Edel, H. (1988). The jingle business. In G. Martin (Ed.), *1988 making music: The essential guide to writing, performing and recording* (pp. 326-327). London: Barrie & Jenkins.

Eigtved, M. (1989). Klingeling ['Dingleling']. *Opus*, *6/7*, 9-10.

Fehling, R. (1980). Funktionelle Musik – Manipulationsversuch im Gewanden der holden Kunst [Functional music. Attempts at manipulation in the guise of art]. In R. Brinkmann (Ed.), *Musik im Alltag* (pp. 84-95). Mainz: Schott.

Firat, F., Dholakia, N., & Venkatesh, A. (1995). Marketing in a postmodern world. *European Journal of Marketing*, *29(1)*, 40-56.

Fisher, G. (1997). *How to make money scoring soundtracks and jingles*. Emeryville: Mix Books.

Fitzgerald, J. (1999). Music in advertising: The creation of an Australian TV commercial. In T. Mitchell, & P. Doyle (Eds.), *Changing sounds: New directions and configurations in popular music* (pp. 365-368). University of Sydney: IASPM.

Gans, H. 1979. Deciding What's News. New York: Vintage Books

Garrard, M. (1988). Creating a commercial. In G. Martin (Ed.), *1988 making music: The essential guide to writing, performing and recording*. (pp. 328-329). London: Barrie & Jenkins.

Gertich, F., & Motte-Haber, H. (1987). Werbung aus musikpsychologischer Sicht [Advertising from the perspective of music psychology]. *Musikerziehung, XI(4)*, 155-160.

Golding, P. & Elliott, P. (1979). Making the News. London: Longman.

Goodwin, A. (1993). *Dancing in the distracting factory – music television and popular culture*. London: Routledge.

Gorn, G. (1982). The effects of music in advertising on choice behaviour: A classical conditioning approach. *Journal of Marketing, 46(1)*, 94-101.

Gorn, G., Goldberg, M., Chattopadhyay, A., & Litvack, D. (1991). Music and information in commercials: Their effects with an elderly sample. *Journal of Advertising Research, 5*, 23-32.

Greckel, W. (1987). Die Verwendung klassischer Musik in der amerikanischen Fernsehwerbung [The use of classical music in American TV commercials]. In E. Ostleitner (Ed.), *Massemedien, Musikpolitik und Musikerziehung* (pp. 195-215). Wien: VVWGÖ.

Graakjær, N. (2004). Nyhedernes musik [The music of news]. *MedieKultur, 37*, 36-46.

Graakjær, N. (2008). Musik i tv-reklamer. En tekstanalytisk undersøgelse [Music in TV commercials. A text analytical approach]. Aalborg Universitet (Dissertation).

Haguchi, H. (1998). Non-domestic music in Japanese TV commercials. In T. Mitsui (Ed.), *Popular music: Intercultural interpretations* (pp. 33-37). Kanazawa: Kanazawa University.

Haguchi, H. (2007). *Non-domestic music in Japanese television commercials*. Paper at AAS Annual Meeting, Boston, March.

Hahn, M., & Hwang, I. (1999). Effects of tempo and familiarity of background music on message processing in TV advertising: A resource-matching perspective. *Psychology and Marketing, 16(8)*, 659-675.

Hall, S. (1980). Encoding/decoding. In S. Hall et al. (Eds.) *Culture, media, language*. (pp. 107-116). London: Unwin Hyman.

Hatten, R. (1987). Style, motivation and markedness. In Th. Sebeok, & J. Umiker-Sebeok (Eds.), *The semiotic web* (pp. 408-429). Amsterdam: Mouton de Gruyter.

Haug, W.F. (1986). *Critique of commodity aesthetics: Appearance, sexuality and advertising in capitalist society*. Minneapolis: University of Minnesota Press.

Hecker, S., & Stewart, D. (Eds.). (1988). *Nonverbal communication in advertising*. Lexington, MA: Lexington Books.

Helms, S. (1981). *Musik in der Werbung* [Music in advertising]. Wiesbaden: Breitkopf & Härtel.

Helms, S. (1994). Musik und Werbung – Theorien und Tatsachen [Music and advertising – Theories and facts]. *Musik und Unterricht, 29*, 4-8.

Hitchon, J., Duckler, P., & Thorson, E. (1994). Effects of ambiguity and complexity on consumer response to music video commercials. *Journal of Broadcasting & Electronic Media, 38(3)*, 289-304.

Holbrook, M. (2004). Ambi-diegetic music in films as a product-design and -placement strategy: The sweet smell of success. *Marketing theory, 4(3)*, 171-185.

Hung, K. (1994). An empirical investigation of the impact of music on brand perception in television commercials. Ann Arbor: UMI (Dissertation).

Hung, K. (2000). Narrative music in congruent and incongruent TV advertising. *Journal of Advertising, 29(1)*, 25-34.

Hung, K. (2001). Framing meaning perceptions with music: The case of teaser ads. *Journal of Advertising, 30(3)*, 39-49.

Huron, D. (1989). Music in advertising: An analytical paradigm. *Musical Quarterly, 73*, 557-574.

Iser, W. (1994). *Die Akt des Lesens. Theorie ästhetischer Wirkung* [The act of reading. Theory on aesthetic effect]. Stuttgard: UTB.

Jacke, Chr., Jünger, S., & Zurstiege, G. (2000). Aufdringliche Geschichten – Zum Verhältnis von Musik und Werbung. [Importunate stories – On the relationship between music and advertising]. In H. Rösing, & Th. Phleps (Eds.), *Populäre Musik im Kulturwissenschaftlichen Diskurs* (pp. 25-42). Karben: CODA Musikservice + Verlag.

Jungheinrich, H.-K. (1969). Hörmassage – Musik in der Werbung [Auditory massage. Music in advertising]. *Musica, 23(6)*, 559-561.

Kafitz, W. (1977). Der Einfluss der musikalischen Stimulierung auf die Werbewirkung [The influence of musical stimulation of the effect of advertising]. Saarbrücken (Dissertation).

Kaplan, A. E. (1987). *Rocking around the clock: Music television, postmodernism and consumer Culture*. London: Routledge.

Karmen, S. (1989). *Through the jingle jungle. The art and business of making music for commercials*. New York: Billboard Books.

Karmen, S. (2005). *Who killed the jingle? How a unique American art form disappeared*. Milwaukee: Hal Leonard.

Kellaris, J., & Cox, A. (1989). The effects of background music in advertising: A reassessment. *Journal of Consumer Research, 16(June)*, 113-118.

Kellaris, J. & Cox, A., & Cox, D. (1993). The effect of background music on ad processing: A contingency explanation. *Journal of Marketing, 57(October)*, 114-125.

Klein, B. (2008a). In perfect harmony: Popular music and cola advertising. *Popular Music and Society, 31(1)*, 1-20.

Klein, B. (2008b). 'The new radio': Music licensing as a response to industry woe. *Media, Culture & Society, 30(4)*, 463-478.

Klempe, H. (1991). Musical stylistic analysis and its applicability in the understanding of advertising music. *Studia Muicologica Norvegica, 17*, 113-124.

Klempe, H. (1992). En stil-analytisk innfallsvinkel til forståelsen av musikken i Reklameuttrykket [A stylistic perspective for understanding the music in advertising]. Universitetet i Trondheim (Dissertation).

Klempe, H. (1993). Music, text and image in commercials for Coca-Cola. In J. Corner (Ed.), *Communication studies: Introductory reader; 4th ed.* (pp. 245-272). London: Routledge.

Krommes, R. (1996). Musik in der Fernseh- und Rundfunkwerbung [Music in TV and radio commercials]. *Jahrbuch der Absatz- und Verbrauchsforschung, 42*, 406-434.

Larsen, P. (1988). Musik og moderne billedfiktioner [Music and modern visual fictions]. *Kultur og Klasse, 60*, 33-53.

Laskey, H., Day, E., & Crask, M. (1989). Typology of main message strategies for television commercials. *Journal of Advertising, 18(1)*, 36-41.

Leo, H. (1999). *Musik im Fernsehwerbespot* [Music in the TV commercial]. Frankfurt: Peter Lang.

Lønstrup, A. (2004). *Stemmen og øret – studier i vokalitet og auditiv kultur* [The voice and the ear – Studies in vocality and auditive culture]. Århus: Klim.

MacInnis, D., & Park, C.W. (1991). The differential role of characteristics of music on high- and low-involvement consumer's processing of ads. *Journal of Consumer Research, 18(September)*, 161-173.

Macklin, M. (1988). The relationship between music and advertising and children's response: An experimental investigation. In S. Hecker, & D. Stewart (Eds.), *Nonverbal communication in advertising* (pp. 225-252). Lexington, MA: Lexington Books.

Marx, K., & Engels, F. (1970). *The German ideology. Introduction to a critique of political economy.* London: Lawrence & Wishart.

Meissner, R. (1974). *Die Funktion der Musik in der Rundfunk- und Fernsehwerbung* [The function of music in radio and TV commercials]. Technischen Universität Berlin (Dissertation).

Middlestadt, S., & Fishbein, M. (1994). The effect of music on brand attitudes: Affect- or belief-based change? In E. Clark, T. Brock, & D. Stewart (Eds.), *Attention, attitude, and affect in response to advertising* (pp. 149-167). Hillsdale: LEA.

Middleton, R. (1990). *Studying popular music*. Milton Keynes: Open University Press.

Miller, F. (1985). *Music in advertising*. New York: Amsco Publications.

Milliman, R. (1982). Using background music to affect the behavior of supermarket shoppers. *Journal of Marketing, 46(3)*, 86-91.

Monelle, R. (1992). *Linguistics and semiotics in music*. London: Routledge.

Morris, J., & Boone, M. (1998). The effects of music on emotional response, brand attitude, and purchase intent in an emotional advertising condition. *Advances in Consumer Research, 25*, 518-526.

Moser, K. (1987). *Die Rolle der Musik in der Werbung* [The role of music in advertising]. Universität Salzburg (Dissertation).

Motte-Haber, H. (1972a). *Musikpsychologie. Eine Einführung* [Music psychology. An introduction]. Köln: Musikverlag Hans Gerig.

Motte-Haber, H. (1972b). Das singende und klingende Plakat. Werbung durch Musik [The singing and cinging billboard. Advertising through music]. *Sprache im technischen Zeitalter, 42*, 143-153.

Motte-Haber, H. (1973). 'Erkennen sie die Melodie?' Gedanken zur gewaltsamen Zerstörung von Kunstwerken ['Do you recognize the melody?' Thoughts on the violent destruction of art works]. *Musik und Bild, 5*, 178-181.

Murray, N., & Murray, S. (1996). Music and lyrics in commercials: A cross-cultural comparison between commercials run in the Dominican Republic and in the United States. *Journal of Advertising, XXV(2)*, 51-63.

Nattiez, J.-J. (1990). *Music and discourse – toward a semiology of music*. Princeton: Princeton University Press.

Negus, K., & Street, J. (2002). Introduction to 'Music and Television' special issue. *Popular Music, 21(3)*, 245-248.

North, A., & Hargreaves, D. (2006). Music in business environments. In S. Brown, & U. Volgsten (Eds.), *Music and manipulation – on the social uses and control of music* (pp. 103-125). New York: Berghan Books.

Nørbæk, P. (1994). Jimi Hendrix giver kaffen mening [Jimmy Hendrix makes sense of coffee]. *Markedsføring, Uge 20, 18.maj*, 42-43.

Oakes, S. (2007). Evaluating empirical research into music in advertising: A congruity perspective. *Journal of Advertising Research, 47(1)*, 38-50.

Olsen, G.D. (1994). The sounds of silence: Functions and use of silence in television advertising. *Journal of Advertising Research, 34(5)*, 89-95.

Olsen, G.D. (1995). Creating the contrast: The influence of silence and background music on recall and attribute importance. *Journal of Advertising, 24(4)*, 29-44.

Olsen, G. D. (1997). The impact of interstimuli interval and background silence on recall. *Journal of Consumer Research, 23(4)*, 295-303.

Packard, V. (1960). *The hidden persuaders*. Harmondsworth: Penguin.

Park, C., & Young, S. (1986). Consumer response to television commercials: The impact of involvement and background music on brand attitude and formation. *Journal of Marketing Research, 23(1)*, 11-24.

Pekkilä, E. (1997). Connotative meaning and advertising music. *Applied Semiotics, 2(4)*, 119-132.

Pekkilä, E. (1998). On musical signification in television commercials. Les universaux en musique: Actes du quatrième Congrés international sur la signification musicale. *Série esthétique: Nr. 1* (pp. 323-330). Paris: Publications de la Sorbonne.

Pfaff, D. (2006). *Brain Arousal and Information Theory. Neural and Genetic Mechanisms*. Cambridge, MA: Harvard University Press.

Ramachandran, V. S., & Hirstein, W. (1999). The science of art. A neurological theory of aesthetic experience. *Journal of Consciousness Studies, 6(6-7)*, 15-51.

Raunsbjerg, P. (1993). 'Stay cool' – smid bukserne i køleskabet ['Stay cool' – throw your jeans in the fridge]. *Kultur og Klasse, 74*, 109-132.

Riethmüller, A. (1973). Das Tonsignet. Versuch einer Bestimmung seiner Eigenschaften und Aufgaben [The auditory seal. An attempt to specify characteristics and functions]. *Archiv für Musikwissenschaft, XXX(1)*, 69-79.

Ritscher, I. (1966). *Akustische Werbung – Ihre Wirkung und Anwendungsmöglichkeiten* [Acoustic advertising – It's effect and potentials]. Berlin: Duncker & Humblot.

Rösing, H. (1975). Funktion und Bedeutung von Musik in der Werbung [Functions and meaning of music in commercials]. *Archiv für Musikwissenshaft, XXXII(2)*, 139-155.

Rösing, H. (1982). Music in advertising. In D. Horn & Ph. Tagg (Eds.), *Popular Music Perspectives* (pp. 41-51). Gothenburg: IASPM.

Rule, G. (1997). Jingles all the way. Making music for commercials. *Keyboard, March*, 69-75.

Schlesinger, P. (1978). *Putting reality together*. London: Constable.

Schmidt, H.-Chr. (1983). Audiovisuelle Ge- Mis- und Verbrauch von Musik [Audiovisual use, abuse, and consumption of music]. In E. Jost (Ed.), *Komponieren heute – Ästhetische, soziologische und pädagogische Fragen* (pp. 95-107). Mainz: Schott.

Schmitt, R. (1976). Musik in der Werbung – Ein Beitrag zu ihrer Didaktik [Music in advertising. A didactical contribution]. *Musik und Bildung, 8*, 327-331.

Scott, L.M. (1990). Understanding jingles and needledrop: A rhetorical approach to music in advertising. *Journal of Consumer Research. 17 (September)*, 223-236.

Shen, Y.-Ch., & Chen, T.-Ch. (2006). When East meets West: The effect of cultural tone congruity in ad music and message on consumer ad memory and attitude. *International Journal of Advertising, 25(1)*, 51-70.

Smith, J. (1998). *The sounds of commerce – marketing popular film music*. New York: Columbia University Press.

Smith, J. (1999). Selling my heart: Music and cross-promotion in Titanic. In K. Sandler, & G. Studlar (Eds.), *Titanic. Anatomy of a blockbuster* (pp. 46-63). New Brunswick: Rutgers University Press.

Springer, C. (1992). Society's soundtrack: Musical persuasion in television advertising. Ann Arbor: UMI (Dissertation).

Steiner-Hall, D. (1987). *Musik in der Fernsehwerbung* [Music in TV commercials]. Frankfurt: R.G. Fischer Verlag.

Stern, D. (2004). *The present moment in psychotherapy and everyday life*. New York: Norton.

Stewart, D., & Furse, D. (1986). *Effective television commercials – a study of 1000 commercials*. Lexington, MA: Lexington Books.

Stewart, D., Farmer, K., & Stannard, Ch. (1990). Music as a recognition cue in advertising-tracking studies. *Journal of Advertising Research, 30(4)*, 39-48.

Stewart, D., & Punj, G. (1998). Effects of using a nonverbal (musical) cue on recall and playback of television advertising: Implications for advertising tracking. *Journal of Business Research, 42(1)*, 39-51.

Stout, P., & Leckenby, J. (1988). Let the music play: Music as a nonverbal element in television commercials. In S. Hecker & D. Stewart (Eds.), *Nonverbal Communication in Advertising*. Lexington, MA: Lexington Books.

Stout, P., Leckenby, J., & Hecker, S. (1990). Viewer reactions to music in television commercials. *Journalism Quarterly, 67(4)*, 887-898.

Stout, P., & Rust, R. (1986). The effect of music on emotional response to advertising. *Proceedings of the conference. American Academy of advertising* (pp. R82-R84). Lubbock.

Tagg, Ph. (1982). Analyzing popular music: Theory, method and practice. *Popular Music, 2*, 37-67.

Tagg, Ph. (1987). Musicology and the semiotics of popular music. In E. Tarasti (Ed.), *Semiotics of music (Special issue of Semiotica), 66, 1(3)*, 279-298.

Tagg, Ph., & Clarida, B. (2003). *Ten little title tunes*. New York: MMMSP.

Tauchnitz, J. (1990). *Werbung mit Musik* [Advertising with music]. Heidelberg: Physica-Verlag.

Taylor, T. (2000). World music in television ads. *American Music, 18(2)*, 162-192.

Teixeira, A. (1974). *Music to sell by. The craft of jingle writing*. Boston: Berklee Press Publications.

Tom, G. (1990). Marketing with music. *Journal of Consumer Marketing, 7(2)*, 49-53.

Tota, A.L. (2001). 'When Orff meets Guinness': Music in advertising as a form of cultural hybrid. *Poetics, 29*, 109-123.

Wallace, W. (1991). Jingles in advertisements: Can they improve recall? *Advances in Consumer Research, 18*, 239-242.

Weiner, G. (1992). Die Musik die Sie aus der Schokoladenwerbung kennen [The music you know from the chocolate commercial]. *Musik & Theater, 12*, 56-59.

White, H. (1986). *How to produce effective TV commercials*. Lincolnwood: NTC Business books.

Vihn, A.-L. (1994). *Die Wirkung von Musik in der Fernsehwerbung* [The effect of music in television commercials]. St. Gallen (Dissertation).

Wintle, R. (1978). *Emotional impact of music on television commercials*. University of Nebraska (Dissertation).

Witt, F.-J. (1989). Musik in der Werbung [Music in advertising]. *Planung und Analyse, 16(10)*, 377-380.

Woodward, W. (1982). *An insider's guide to advertising music*. New York: Art Direction Books.

Wüsthoff, K. (1999). *Die Rolle der Musik in der Film-, Funk, und Fernsehwerbung 2nd ed.* [The role of music in film, radio and TV commercials]. Kassel: Merseburger.

Yalch, R. (1991). Memory in a jingle jungle: Music as a mnemonic device in communicating advertising slogans. *Journal of Applied Psychology, 76(2)*, 268-275.

Yalch, R., & Spangenberg, E. (1988). An environmental psychological study of foreground and background music as retail atmospheric factors. I A. Walle (Ed.), *AMA educators' conference proceedings* (pp. 106-110). Chicago: AMA.

Yoon, S. G. (1993). *The role of music in television commercials: The effects of familiarity with and feeling toward background music on attention, attitude, and evaluation of the brand*. University of Texas, Austin (Dissertation).

Young, J., & Young, J. (1977). *Succeeding in the big world of music*. Boston: Little Brown And Co.

Zager, M. (2003). *Writing music for television and radio commercials: A manual for composers and students*. Lanham: Scarecrow Press.

Zhu, R., & Meyers-Levy, J. (2005). Distinguishing between the meanings of music: When background music affects product perceptions. *Journal of Marketing Research, 42(3)*, 333-345.

MUSIC IN TV COMMERCIALS
Formats, frequencies, and tendencies

Nicolai Graakjær

INTRODUCTION

Diachronic research analysing developments of music in TV commercials is practically non-existing. Indeed opinions on the tendencies of commercial music are prevalent but, characteristically, these views are not supported by empirical research. In best case, they present plausible assumptions and, in worst case, they present misleading guesswork. Also synchronic studies investigating similarities and differences in samples of commercials are few, and this applies in particular for commercials produced in different countries (see Bjurström & Lilliestam 1993, Appelbaum & Halliburton 1993, Murray & Murray 1996).

Nevertheless, the relevance of diachronic and synchronic studies should be obvious. From an overall perspective, diachronic studies are helpful in providing insights into the production and reproduction of musical codes and into what could be coined the 'musical mother tongue' of western societies. However, this alleged musical mother tongue is a very complex phenomenon which cannot be dealt with here. Instead, more specific levels of diachronic analysis will be offered, and especially the *prevalence of musical formats* is investigated in further detail. Potentially, this might avoid what could be called the *fallacy of ethnocentricity*. This *fallacy* will be illustrated and discussed below, but, by way of introduction, it has to do with relatively small samples of commercials forming the basis of rather wide-ranging or even universal claims concerning, for example, the relationships between specific products and specific musical genres, specific placements of particular musical formats, and specific historical changes in the use of music. An associated phenomenon in the research on music in TV commercials is what might be called the *attractiveness of particularity bias*. Thus, it seems that *unusual* (extraordinary, attention-grabbing) cases are frequently analysed at the expense of the *usual* (ordinary, mainstream) ones. With a synchronic analysis of the frequency of specific musical formats, a bias such as this may be detected and avoided. Finally, diachronic analysis may also shed light on the way in which music is handled and understood from a producer's point of view. The prevalence of distinctive music formats seems particularly indicative of the producers' awareness of the potential of music (see chapter 12, this volume for more on the producer perspective).

Method

The fact that synchronic and diachronic analyses are so relatively rare may very well be an effect of the difficulties in collecting an appropriate sample. The sample used in the present study consists of a total number of 1446 TV commercials broadcasted on the Danish TV channel TV 2.[1] These commercials embody comparable samples of newly broadcasted commercials in the month of April from four volumes (1992, 1996, 2000 and 2004). The four volumes all consist of both nationally and internationally produced commercials, and apart from volume 1992, nationally produced commercials are differentiated in commercials for regional and national broadcasting (cf. figure 1 below). Because they form a relatively homogeneous and representative material, the analysis will concentrate on the nationally produced commercials. As TV 2 is the market leader, close to all Danish produced commercials broadcasted nationally for the first time in four volumes of the month of April are represented. As it will be discussed in further detail below, the chosen sample is not easily comparable to other samples, but it has proved almost impossible to set up sample criteria matching with more than one previous study.

The analysis of the sample is characterised by two strategies. On the one hand, an attempt is made to *quantify* the prevalence of music formats; on the other hand, an attempt is made to *qualify* this prevalence. In other words, the quantification is based on categories, which, to a considerable extent, are subjective, which is evident throughout the analysis: from the determination of 'music' to the delimiting of each specific musical format and its degree of distinctiveness. Distinctiveness will be an important focus of the analysis, as this concept seems to be the most reliable measure for changes of music in TV commercials. The categorization of distinctiveness thus allows for so-called 'good' classification in the following sense:

> "A 'good' classification scheme, or typology, should meet certain requirements. Any typology should be mutually exclusive and exhaustive; all creative strategies should be able to be categorized in one, but only one, category. Furthermore, the typology should capture meaningful differences between creative executions while remaining parsimonious […]. Finally, a typology should be operational; creative strategies should be able to be consistently categorized according to the rules for classification" (Laskey, Day & Crask 1989: 36).

The purpose of quantitative analysis is to *indicate* possible changes in the sample material, but due to the rather small number of commercials analysed, any proper statistical analysis will not be effectuated. Reliability of the study is substantiated by the intention of analysing all commercials in a similar way and in addition by propounding the method of analysis (as much as space permits).

DISTRIBUTION OF MUSIC IN TV COMMERCIALS

On the most general level, it appears that 1273 out of 1446 commercials contain music[2], which corresponds to 88%. Figure 1 illustrates the distribution of music in the four volumes.

As implied, how to further qualify this enumeration is importunate: No previous diachronic studies exist and when it comes to synchronic studies, comparisons are rendered difficult because of great variety in the criteria for sampling.[6] But scrutinizing previous synchronic research, nonetheless gives some indication of emerging tendencies (see figure 2).

Figure 1. Overview of TV commercials with music

		1992	1996	2000	2004
Number of newly broadcasted commercials in Denmark, TV 2, month of April. / With music	Total	210 /158 75,2%	275 / 222 80,7%	397 / 367 92,4%	564 / 526 93,3%
	National	176 / 128 72,7%	121 / 89 73,6%	177 / 153 86,4%	222 / 201 90,5%
	Regional[3]	...[4]	78 / 59 75,6%	128 / 124 96,9%	263 / 248 94,3%
	International	34 / 30 88,2%	76 / 74 97,4%	92 / 90 97,8%	79 / 77 97,5%

The enumerations listed in figure 2 all provide precise information on the number of commercials examined as well as on most criteria for sampling. In other studies, like the ones listed figure 3, the distribution of music in commercials is only roughly estimated, potentially diminishing the reliability of the enumerations (see figure 3).

All together, these specifications and estimates indicate a tendency of music being part of an increasing percentage of TV commercials (until 2004, at least). This tendency emerges from my own diachronic study, but is confirmed by the bulk of other synchronic research quoted. It is beyond the range of this chapter to examine in any detail whether national deviations from this general tendency exist, as suggested by the specifications by Murray & Murray 1996 (cf. the difference between commercials from The Dominican Republic and commercials from USA). In the following section, the issue of the mere prevalence of music will be elaborated, and a pertinent question will be: *how* does music appear in TV commercials.

Figure 2. List of specifications of TV commercials with music

Author	Sample criteria	Number of commercials	Sample year	Percentage with music
Aaker & Bruzzone 1985	Prime time network commercials	524	1985(?)	51,7%[7]
Stewart & Furse 1986	Representative selection of commercials tested during the period by RSC[8]	1059	1980-1983	42,3%[9]
Moser 1987	All produced in Austria	515	1984	80%
Appelbaum & Halliburton 1993[10]	International, French, North American, British, German	213	1987-1991	77,8-89,3%
Bjurström & Lilliestam 1993	16 randomly chosen days. Four different, Swedish and International, TV channels	1765	1992	88%
Murray & Murray 1996	All U.S. commercials broadcasted on four different major U.S. networks (every day in two weeks between 8pm and 10pm)	336	1994	84,5%
Murray & Murray 1996	All Dominican commercials broadcasted on four different Dominican networks (every day in two weeks between 8pm and 10pm)	193	1994	94,3%
Krommes 1996	Randomly chosen from four different German TV channels	201	1995(?)	88,6%
Czypionka 1999	All commercials broadcasted on ARD and ZDF between 6pm and 8pm (May 18th – June 6th).	441	1999(?)	78%[11]
Leo 1999	All commercials on 7 German private TV channels in November	368	1996	82%
Leo 1999	All commercials on 7 German private TV channels in November	264	1998	84%

Figure 3. List of estimates of TV commercials with music

Author	Reference	Percentage with music
Meissner 1974	'All TV-commercials'	65%
Schmitt 1976	'All TV-commercials'	66%
Helms 1981	'Spring / Summer of 1979'	80%
Rösing 1982	'All TV commercials'	65%
Steiner-Hall 1987	'All TV commercials'	70%
Greckel 1987	'A few hundreds'	60-70%
Huron 1989	"…sixty billion broadcast advertising hours encountered by North Americans each year"	75%
Tauchnitz 1990	'All TV commercials'	80%
Lønstrup 2004	All TV commercials broadcasted on TV 2 on October 17th and 19th in 1994 between 7 and 11 pm	95-99%
Bullerjahn 2006	'Advertisements screened internationally'	90%
Allan 2007	'Commercials in prime time TV'	86%[12]

CATEGORIES OF MUSIC

When viewing TV commercials, a simple experience is that some music seems to attract attention while other music does not. In the following, the concept of *distinctiveness* is introduced as a way to differentiate between musical expressions in TV commercials. This concept is offered as an assessment of the degree to which music attracts attention.[13] Three interrelated dimensions constitute distinctiveness and figure 4 gives an overview and classification of these dimensions:

Figure 4. Overview of analytical dimensions

CONTEXT
The spreading of the music outside the specific commercial
(e.g. pre-existing or original music).

COTEXT
The relations between the music and other textual elements involved
(i.e. visual and other auditory elements).

TEXT
Structural characteristics of the music involved
(e.g. rhythm, melody, sound, harmony).

'Context' refers to the possible previous uses of a specific piece of music, and two main categories can be identified: Pre-existing music and original music. *Pre-existing music* is music with a history 'outside' the specific commercial: i.e. previously or simultaneously to its appearance in a TV commercial. This kind of music has not been composed with the intent of being part of a commercial (even if it may benefit from such an appearance; cf. chapter 7, this volume). *Original music* is music composed for a specific commercial. Having had no appearance prior to the commercial broadcast, the existence of this music is closely related to the commercial. With a few exceptions (see below), the appearance of pre-existing music is highly distinctive, either because it is well-known and faces its audience with a sort of insistence on *being known*, or because it, in spite of its hitherto rather unknown 'career', faces its audience with a sort of insistence on *becoming known*.[14] Music can furthermore stand out as distinctive by embodying a so-called *musical* or *sonic brand*. In such cases, music is consistently used across different media (TV, radio, Internet) and throughout the given media (e.g. in various TV commercials for the same product). Consistency occurs when the same music accompanies every exposure of the producer (e.g. logo and slogan), and when the music itself is clearly recognizable: i.e. identical or only indistinctly modified in different media or the various commercials for the same brand.

'Cotext' refers to the placing of music within the commercial. A high degree of distinctiveness is apparent in commercials with music in eye-catching places, like in the beginning (as a kind of attention-grabber) or towards the end (as a kind of winding up). Also the relation of music to text, picture and voice-over is of importance, and distinctive music is either the sole auditory expression, or it is arranged in an intricate connection with text, moving picture and voice-over. Here, the exact synchronization of different audio and visual elements becomes seminal. While all textual elements are obviously occurring simultaneously, specific synchronized interactions or synch-points may occur, which may be crucial for signification (as noted by Chion 1994, Cook 1998).

The dimension of 'text' draws attention to the characteristics of the musical expression. Distinctiveness is the effect of a particular musical expression being dissimilar to music in other contemporary commercials. Thus, synchronic analysis is necessary for assessing structural distinctiveness: In one period, a structure can stand out as distinctive while in another it cannot. A source of inspiration when it comes to the analysis of structural distinctiveness is Burns (1987). Burns offers "a framework of categories to facilitate what might be called hook analysis of pop records" and a hook is defined as "a musical or lyrical phrase that stands out and is easily remembered" (Burns 1987: 17,1). Burns' presentation of various hooks makes it seem evident that an absolute and universal definition of the specific musical expression functioning as a hook cannot be given; an insight similar to the one offered explicitly here concerning distinctive commercial music. As is the case with hooks, the distinctive structure of music in commercials is assessable by scrutinizing the various aspects of musical expression, such as melody, rhythm, harmony, sound, etc. When it comes to understanding of distinctive music in TV comercials, this kind of analysis will not suffice, though. The actual audiovisual framing and embedding of music (cf. the dimension of cotext) may also be highly consequential in generating distinctiveness.

To sum up, distinctiveness is a quality, which may be assessed by scrutinizing the musical text and its textual embedding. In the following, distinctiveness is used in a somewhat crude manner, in that only high and low degree of distinctiveness – i.e. the poles on a continuum – will be discussed. Figure 5 presents an overview of the degree of distinctiveness matched with the relation between the music heard and the advertised product:

Figure 5. Relationship between music and product

Relationship between music and product	Typical category of product	Origin of music	Degree of distinctiveness
Music *as* product (*Coincidence*)	Music (CD, concerts)	Pre-existing	High
Music *as part of* product (*Coherence*)	Films (Cinema, DVD)	Pre-existing	Low
Music *as linked to* the product (*Arranged connection*)	All (other than music, films…)	Pre-existing (or Original)	High
Music *as loosely coupled with* product (*incidental connection*)	All (other than music, films…)	Original (or Pre-existing)	Low

In commercials with *music as product* – where music and product coincides – high distinctiveness is safeguarded because of the career of the music (usually a well-known artist is shown, and the music is/has been broadcasted on radio) and because the music is exposed without too many other distracting auditory elements. In general, only a voice-over of few words is present, and the visual parts are structured on the basis of musical expressions: e.g. the artist dancing and gesticulating in time with the music – not unlike the 'visualised music' of many music videos.

In commercials with *music as part of the product*, distinctiveness is predominantly low. Normally, music performs a supportive role, for instance in the presentation of main characters, situations and scenery from movie pictures. In both categories, pre-existing music will typically be prevalent.

In the two remaining categories – *music as linked to the product* and *music as loosely coupled with the product* – there is no previous connection between music and product. Music is used in the commercial with the only obvious purpose of contributing to the advertising of the product, and both pre-existing and original music are to be found. In the category of music as *loosely coupled with the product*, the music appears in a quite haphazard fashion, as it apparently has no 'intention' to *be known* or to *become known* to its audience. Only rarely will this music be pre-existing (thus 'original music' in brackets in figure 5) and if it is, it will most likely occur as an incidental part of a narrative (which by the way is a widespread function of music in motion pictures). Examples of other appearances of music in this category are original music for voice-overs, presenters, dramas and testimonials (see Stigel 2001 for definitions of these commercial formats). In such cases, music often comes in the guise of the format *vamp*, defined here as a repeated instrumental accompaniment (i.e. without melodic features). Vamps are in some respects similar to the musical format of a *groove*: e.g. the repeating and non-melodic characteristics. But, unlike grooves, vamps lack distinction of rhythm and sound. A vamp is characterised by being a short harmonic sequence (a turnaround), functioning in specific musical genres by defining tempo and harmony for an approaching soloist voice (cf. the saying 'vamp till ready'). In commercials, vamps are commonly subdued, and it will have no particular synch-points with text, speak and pictures. Thus a displacement of half a second will not affect on the meaning structure of the commercial as a whole.

In the category of music as *linked to the product*, music appears purposely organized and overall distinctive. If this particular piece of music is replaced by another piece or if the music is displaced by half a second or so, this will alter the meaning of the commercial substantially. When pre-existing music is being used, it enters the audiovisual composition with clear reference to its career and its particular structure: for instance by letting its structure form the basis of the whole sequence of pictures and/or by playing ingeniously on the possible lyrics of a song (for an obvious example see chapter 4, this volume). Original music acquires distinctiveness by means of its particular structure and salient interaction. *Music linked to the product* lends itself to musical branding. Original music is most frequent in this category (thus 'pre-existing music' in brackets in figure 5), and this may have to do with original music being much more controllable, which is seminal to the process of branding. Unknown and unforeseen past, present and possible future appearances of pre-existing music could easily compromise the brand value of the specific piece of music.

In figure 6, the distribution of the different categories in commercials produced in Denmark is shown.

Figure 6. TV commercials with music

Regional broadcast

Relationship between music and product	1996 N=59	2000 N=124	2004 N=248
Music *as* product (*Coincidence*)	1,7% 1	3,2% 4	3,2% 8
Music *as part of* product (*Coherence*)	1,7% 1	2,4% 3	1,6% 4
Music *as linked to* the product (*Arranged connection*)	32,2% 19	12,9% 16	33,1% 82
Music *as loosely coupled with* product (*Incidental connection*)	64,4% 38	81,5% 101	62,1% 154

National broadcast

Relationship between music and product	1992 N=133	1996 N=89	2000 N=153	2004 N=196
Music *as* product (*Coincidence*)	10,9% 14	2,2% 2	7,8% 12	7% 14
Music *as part of* product (*Coherence*)		2,2% 2	4,6% 7	8,9% 18
Music *as linked to* the product (*Arranged connection*)	39,1% 50	39,3% 35	45,8% 70	46,8% 94
Music *as loosely coupled with* product (*Incidental connection*)	50% 64	56,2% 50	41,8% 64	37,3% 75

This figure illustrates that the categories *music as linked to product* and *music as loosely coupled with product* are the most common. But two other tendencies are indicated. Firstly, a comparison of nationally and regionally broadcasted commercials points to a higher occurrence of distinctive music in national commercials. This is probably caused by the fact that nationally broadcasted commercials generally represent more expensive and well-crafted productions, implying that music too might have come to the producers' attention. Secondly, it points to an increase in commercials with distinctive music. In particular, this is apparent in the category of *music as linked to the product*, where music, as described, is a focal element when it comes to signifying meaning and attracting attention. The following section will focus on the category of *music as linked to the product*. The issue of how this linkage is musically articulated will be pivotal.

SPECIFICATION OF DISTINCTIVE MUSIC FORMATS

An overview of a number of musical formats in TV commercials is presented in figure 7. The particular selection of formats is partly deduced from the four volumes analysed and partly inspired by existing literature (e.g. Helms 1981, Krommes 1996, and Leo 1999). The typology in figure 7 differs somewhat from those in existing literature, in that the volumes analysed feature formats that might not have been particularly notable or even existing in previous studies. Groove and emblem are obvious examples. Thus, typologies put forward in previous studies are not perfectly comparable to the one presented here.

An exemplification of the somewhat imprecise nature of the previous overview of typologies is Leo 1999. In Leos account, the following formats and frequencies are affirmed: "Background music: 35%, song/jingle: 16%, classical: 10%, classic pop: 6%, film music-like: 2%, jazz: 4%, rock//beat, 5%, ethnic: 4%" (Leo 1999: 38, my translation). At least three analytical perspectives are confused, namely musical formats (*song/jingle*), functions (e.g. *background music*) and genres (e.g. *classical*). In Krommes, the typology is less ambiguous, by not taking account of musical genres. However, this typology is on the other hand rather undifferentiated in that it only comprises three formats of which one is defined by several sub-formats: "…14,4% a signature motif, 20,4% a jingle, a commercial song or a pop-song and 53,2% background music" (Krommes 1996: 425, my translation).

Figure 7. Typology of musical formats in the category of 'Music linked to product'

Format	Text	Cotext	Context
Tune	Longer accompanied melody	Throughout the commercial. Privileged auditory exposition	Pre-existing or original
Song	Longer accompanied and sung melody	Throughout the Commercial. Privileged auditory exposition.	Pre-existing or original
Groove	Repetitious turn of phrase. Distinct via rhythm and sound	Throughout the commercial. At specific points: Exposed without other sounds, and often synchronized with picture	Typically original
Jingle	Short, rounded melodic motif	Synchronized with logo presentation at the end and/or beginning	Typically original
Emblem	A short-lived musical sound	Synchronized with logo presentation at the end and/or the beginning	Typically original

A distinctive feature in the formats presented in figure 7 is *duration*: some musical expressions have a short duration in the commercial, while others have a long duration (e.g. throughout most or the entire commercial). A *groove* belongs to the latter grouping, and grooves typically last throughout the entire commercial. As already hinted at, the distinctiveness of grooves emanate from the *sound* and *feeling* of a specific predominantly rhythmic configuration (cf. the dimension of 'structure') which stands out of its own accord, unlike the indistinctive structuring of *vamps*. Moreover, grooves are typically arranged in detailed synchronization with the visual parts of the commercial, thus generating interaction at the 'cotext' level. Finally, grooves are often very effective in increasing intensity towards a peaking round off: e.g. in the presentation of logo and/or slogan. Song and melody are also formats of long-duration. What distinguishes them in particular from the groove is the presence of melody either sung or played by instrument.

Emblems and *jingles* are the formats of short duration; *emblems* representing a relatively recent development and the *jingles* embodying commercial music *par excellence*. The history of jingles is long and, colloquially, this format often signifies commercial music as such. Here, the jingle is defined as a short, rounded, predominantly melodic motif. Its distinctiveness is conveyed by an effortlessly remembered and easily recognisable structure and also by being synchronized with logo and/or slogan. The definition is partly etymologically inspired, in that the term was originally used to denote the shrilling and clinking sound of small objects of metal (e.g. coins in a pocket or a bunch of keys). A commercial jingle is hence short, pithy and potentially instrumental.

Emblems are also short musical formats but compared to the jingle, the emblem lacks melody and it is often even shorter than the jingle; typically with a duration of only a second or so. Moreover, emblems are defined as presenting only one museme (in the sense discussed in Tagg 1979), whereas jingles present at least two musemes. An emblem can furthermore be defined as an *object of sound*, and the emblem attains distinctiveness by way of its *sound* and an intricate synchronization with the logo.[15] It is the exact idiom of the sound (cf. instrumentation, phasing, delay, panning, timbre, etc.) that matters when analysing distinctiveness. The apparently recent advent of emblems in TV commercials – suggested in the material analysed (see figure 8 below) – may be an indication of producers' increased awareness of the importance of sound in commercials. Thus, all commercial formats may have sound as at least one of the distinctive dimensions of expression.

FREQUENCIES OF DISTINCTIVE MUSIC FORMATS

When looking closer into frequencies of the formats discussed, the distribution in figure 8 emerges.

Apparently, a shift from song to jingle as the most common format has occurred. This, together with the advent of emblems, leads to the following assumption: *More TV commercials with music* (noted above) are not tantamount to *more music in TV commercials*. On the contrary, it could very well be that music has been increasingly distributed in more well-dosed and refined ways.

Continuing the discussion on jingles, the following remark from a previous study is noteworthy: "What does seem clear is that music's role in commercials has definitively shifted from the level of the two-second jingle to that of the thirty-second background score" (Bullerjahn 2006: 232). In the light of the present study, this shift does not seem all that clear but further examination of this issue is difficult because the study referred to, does not specify its sample.

Figure 8. Frequencies of distinctive music formats

Regional broadcast

	1996 N=19	2000 N=16	2004 N=82
Tune	21,1% 4	31,2% 5	31,7% 26
Song	26,3% 5	50% 8	19,5% 16
Groove		6,3% 1	13,4% 11
Jingle	52,6% 10	6,3% 1	35,4 % 29
Emblem		6,3% 1	

National broadcast

	1992 N=50	1996 N=35	2000 N=70	2004 N=94
Tune	34% 17	31,4% 11	10% 7	30,9% 29
Song	42% 21	37,1% 13	28,6% 20	16% 15
Groove	4% 2	2,9% 1	7,1% 5	10,6% 10
Jingle	20% 10	28,6% 10	44,3% 31	41,5% 39
Emblem			10% 7	1,1% 1

Another issue worth mentioning is the placement of the jingle. For instance it has been stated that "…it is logical, that mostly jingles are placed in the beginning of the commercials" (Krommes 1996: 442, my translation). Again, the present sample material indicates otherwise, as shown in figure 9.

Figure 9. Overview of placements of jingles.

	1992 N=10	1996 N=20	2000 N=32	2004 N=68
In the beginning			15,6 % 5	1,5 % 1
In the beginning and at the end		5 % 1	28,1 % 9	11,8 % 8
After a little while and at the end				8,8 % 6
Close to the end			6,3 % 2	
At the end	100 % 10	95 % 19	50 % 16	78 % 53

It seems reasonable to suggest, that in fact *most jingles are placed at the end* of the commercial (98 jingles out of 130 are placed exclusively at the end). A possible explanation (apart from dissimilarities of the sample material involved) for this result is the increase of the commercial format *drama* (Stigel 2001), in which a jingle often appears as an emphasizing, *punch-line*-like, device at the end of the commercial together with slogan and logo. The empirical material referred to by Krommes might not have contained many commercials of this type in question, simply because it was not (yet) in vogue at the time when the sample was collected.

Finally, an observation made by Lønstrup (2004) must be shortly commented on. Regarding the issue of whether jingles are sung or not, Lønstrup identifies: "…an increase in the use of vocal in commercial music" (Lønstrup 2004: 191). This observation seems misguided. Apart from the fact, that Lønstrup's sample material does not lend itself to diachronic conclusions, the present study indicates the very opposite: namely that there is a decrease in the use of vocals in commercial music. This is apparent in the shift from song to jingle, and it is also supported by diachronic changes in the prevalence of vocal in jingles as figure 10 indicates.

Figure 10. Overview of the prevalence of vocal in jingles (all TV commercials in the sample).

	1992 N=10	1996 N=20	2000 N=32	2004 N=68
With vocal[16]	100 % 10	55 % 11	31,3 % 10	19,1 % 13
Instrumental		45 % 9	68,7 % 22	80,9 % 55

One possible explanation for the waning of vocals in TV commercials could be that verbalised praising of products and producers are increasingly regarded as both old-fashioned und unreliable. Audiences as well as producers supposedly favour more sophisticated and evocative commercial approaches (Bullerjahn 2006, Karmen 2005).

Conclusion

This study has indicated an increase of Danish commercials with music over the last two decades. Furthermore, it has indicated a tendency towards an increasingly distinctive use of music, particularly in commercials broadcasted nationally. When it comes to musical formats, jingles and emblems – the short formats of music in commercials – seem to gain ground at the expense of longer formats, especially the song.

A few, highly interesting issues, which the present chapter has not studied meticulously, remain: 1) Are there any regularities in combining the use of music with particular products? 2) Is there any regularity in combining the use of music with particular commercial formats? The sample material at hand shows no clear regularities, but tentatively it can be argued that for instance song and instrumental tune occur more often than groove and emblem in products for children (e.g. toys, magazines, some foods and beverages). Moreover, it is remarkable how distinctiveness is wide-spread *not least* in advertising financial products (e.g. banks, insurance companies, mortgage providers), in that is has often been contended that these particular commercials are characterized by the very absence of music (e.g. Leo 1999). When it comes to commercial formats there seems to be a correlation between dramas and jingles, whereas music is typically absent in presenters and testimonials.

Notes

1. TV 2 is the most seen channel in Denmark, and it is the only nationwide channel broadcasting commercials. It is on TV 2 that Danes view close to half of the TV commercials they view in total (the other half is viewed on a larger number of international channels). In 2004, the ordinary Danish viewer saw 23 TV commercials per day and 12 out of these were viewed on TV 2 (cf. http://www.mediesekretariatet.dk/bilag/rtv/diverserekl/tvreklamerogboern.pdf).
2. 'Music' is here defined as auditory expressions, either rendered by conventionally approved musical instruments (hereunder singing and whistling (but not chirping of birds)), and/or rendered in a musical fashion by non-musical auditory objects (e.g. car horns tooting a melody).
3. TV 2 is divided into eight regions, and only a limited number of viewers will get to see the individual commercials (a few commercials are broadcasted in all regions presenting different versions of the same commercial, but for the most part each regional commercial is obviously associated with the particular region by way of a specific regional product).
4. In volume 1992, regional commercials are not available.
5. It is important to stress, that the enumeration primarily highlights *differences* between the four volumes. The differences then *indicate* a development. Possibly, other intervening volumes would compromise this indication, but this cannot be investigated at present.
6. Criteria involve place and time (country, channel, season, day of week, etc.), as well as size of the sample. Also the category 'music' should of course be of relevance in this respect but often studies do not explicitly define this category. This is yet another reason why comparisons can only be tentative.
7. The exact percentage is not clearly stated, but 51,7% is based on an addition of two numbers of commercials mentioned here: "Overall, the 163 commercials coded as containing music had a below average irritation score (4.5), and those 108 commercials using a jingle or adapting an old tune had an even lower irritation level (4.0)" (Aaker & Bruzzone 1985: 56). Also, it is unclear in what year the commercials were broadcasted (1985 is presumed).
8. Abbreviation of Research Systems Association. There is no specific reference to criteria of sampling regarding for instance time and place of production (only criteria for the selection of subjects for experimentation are described (cf. Steart & Furse 1986: 165f)), and this comes forth as symptomatic of the interest in the effect of TV commercials. Only, is it pointed out that they make up "…a representative set of commercials tested by the firm [RSC] during the period of 1980-83" (Stewart & Furse 1986: 21). Presumably, the commercials are produced and broadcasted in North America during the stated period of time.
9. It is not clear whether the specified formats of music (cf. Stewart & Furse 1986: 152) are

to be added (amounting to 59,6%) or whether they represent different overlapping analytical perspectives. In all probability, the latter is the case, as it is the interpretation of several sources (cf. Yalch 1991: 268, North and Hargreaves 1997: 268 and not least Stewart, Farmer and Stannard 1990: 39).

10 This sample is not exactly representative of the general distribution of music in that it has been selected with the purpose of studying exceptional ('creative') commercials. Thus, most of the commercials are collected from *The Lürzer Archiv*, allegedly presenting a compilation of 'the best advertisements in the world'.

11 The sample consists of broadcasted commercials and when leaving out of account commercials with more than one appearance, the sample consists of 186 unique commercials. Once again, the sample year 1999 is presumed.

12 Apparently, the estimate is based on an exact specification (Allan 2007: 17), but due to a lack of precise specifications in Allan 2007 (which refers to an unpublished paper from 2006), the percentage is listed as an estimate.

13 Other ways of differentiating between musical expressions in TV commercials are available, and one is the prevalent distinction between background and foreground music (see chapter 3 in this volume). For several reasons, though, distinctions like the one just referred to are deselected in favour of the concept of distinctiveness (see Graakjær 2006 for a specific critique of the use of 'background' and 'foreground music').

14 Typically in form of more or less calculated *music placement*. For instance pre-existing music can be placed in a commercial with the producer intent of having the music becoming known and attractive as a product in itself, and/or because of a particular 'hook' that makes the pre-existing music well suited for the given commercial. Whether a piece of music is in fact known to viewers is of course not a simple matter to clarify. However, in the light of the sample material present, it makes sense to speak of pre-existing music as either well-known or not known (see chapter 4,5 and 6 this volume for case studies on the use of pre-existing music).

15 *Sound* is an aesthetic quality gaining prominence as a dimension of expression, alongside the development of musical genres such as jazz, pop and rock. In jazz, sound expresses elements of an idiosyncratic style of a *musician* (more than of a *composer*, typical for traditions of classical music) whereas in pop and rock, sound is the (trade)mark of a *producer*.

16 Included is one occurrence of bird chipping, six occurrences of human whistle and six occurrences of scat-song. All other occurrences present human song (with words).

REFERENCES

Aaker, D., & Bruzzone, D. (1985). Causes of irritation in advertising. *Journal of Marketing*, *49(2)*, 47-57.

Allan, D. (2007). Sound advertising: A review of the experimental evidence on the effects of music in commercials on attention, memory, attitudes and purchase intention. *Journal of Media Psychology, 12(3)*, 1-35. [Assesed 1 October on: www.calstatela.edu/faculty/sfischo/]

Appelbaum, V., & Halliburton, C. (1993). How to develop nternational advertising campaigns that work: The example of the European food and beverage sector. *International Journal of Advertising, 12*, 31-43.

Bjurström, E. & Lilliestam, L. (1993). *Sälj det i toner* [Sell it in tunes]. Stockholm: Konsumentverket.

Bullerjahn, C. (2006). The effectiveness of music in television commercials. In S. Brown & U. Volgsten (Eds.), *Music and manipulation: On the social uses and social control of music* (pp. 207-235). Oxford: Berghahn Books.

Burns, G. (1987). A typology of 'hooks' in popular records. *Popular Music, 6(1)*, 1-20.

Cook, N. (1998). *Analysing musical multimedia*. Oxford: Oxford University Press.

Czypionka, A. (1999). Musikalische Repertoirebildung durch Werbung [The formation of musical repertoire by advertising]. In M.L. Schulten (Ed.), *Medien und Musik. Musikalische Sozialisationen 5-15 jähriger* (pp. 198-238). Münster: LIT Verlag.

Greckel, W. (1987). Die Verwendung klassischer Musik in der amerikanischen Fernsehwerbung [The use of classical music in American TV commercials]. In E. Ostleitner (Ed.), *Massemedien, Musikpolitik und Musikerziehung* (pp. 119-215). Wien: VVWGÖ.

Graakjær, N. (2006). Musical meaning in TV commercials: A case of cheesy music. *Popular Musicology Online, Issue 5*. [http://www.popular-musicology-online.com/issues/05/nicolai-01.html. Accessed 1 May, 2008]

Helms, S. (1981). *Musik in der Werbung* [Music in advertising]. Wiesbaden: Breitkopf and Härtel.

Huron, D. (1989). Music in advertising: An analytical paradigm. *Musical Quarterly, 73*, 557-574.

Karmen, S. (2005). *Who killed the jingle? How a unique American art form disappeared*. Milwaukee: Hal Leonard.

Krommes, R. (1996). Musik in der Fernseh- und Rundfunkwerbung [Music in TV and radio commercials]. *Jahrbuch der Absatz- und Verbrauchsforschung, 42*, 406-434.

Laskey, H., Day, E., & Crask, M. (1989). Typology of main message strategies for television commercials. *Journal of Advertising, 18(1)*, 36-41.

Leo, H. (1999). *Musik im Fernsehwerbespot* [Music in the TV commercial]. Frankfurt: Peter Lang.

Lønstrup, A. (2004). *Stemmen og øret – studier i vokalitet og auditiv kultur* [The voice and the ear. Studies in vocality and auditive culture]. Århus: Klim.

Meissner, R. (1974). Mendelssohns Söhnlein-Musik in der Fernsehwerbung [Mendelssohn's *Söhnlein*-music in TV commercials]. *Musik und Bildung, VI*, 305-309.

Moser, K. (1987). *Die Rolle der Musik in der Werbung*. [The role of music in advertising]. Universität Salzburg (Dissertation).

Murray, N., & Murray, S. (1996). Music and lyrics in commercials: A cross-cultural comparison between commercials run in the Dominican Republic and in the United States. *Journal of Advertising, XXV(2)*, 51-63.

North, A., & Hargreaves, D. (1997). Music and consumer behaviour. In D. Hargreaves, & A. North (Eds.), *The social psychology of music* (pp. 268-289). Oxford: Oxford University Press.

Rösing, H. (1982). Music in advertising. In D. Horn, & Ph. Tagg (Eds.), *Popular Music Perspectives* (pp. 41-51). Göteborg: IASPM.

Schmitt, R. (1976). Musik in der Werbung – Ein Beitrag zu ihrer Didaktik [Music in advertising. A didactical contribution]. *Musik und Bildung, 8*, 327-331.

Steiner-Hall, D. (1987). *Musik in der Fernsehwerbung* [Music in TV commercials]. Frankfurt: R.G. Fischer Verlag.

Stewart, D. W., & Furse, D. H. (1986). *Effective TV Commercials – A Study of 1000 Commercials*. Lexington: Lexington Books.

Stigel, J. (2001). The Aesthetics of Danish Tv-Spot-Commercials. A Study of Danish TV-Commercials in the 1990'ies. In F. Hansen, & L. Yssing Hansen (Eds.), *Advertising Research in the Nordic Countries* (pp. 327-350). København: Samfundslitteratur.

Tagg, Ph. (1979). *Kojak – 50 seconds of TV music*. Göteborg: Musikvetenskapliga Institutionen.

Tauchnitz, J. (1990). *Werbung mit Musik* [Advertising with music]. Heidelberg: Physica-Verlag.

Yalch, R. (1991). Memory in a jingle jungle: Music as a mnemonic device in communicating advertising slogans. *Journal of Applied Psychology, 76(2)*, 268-275.

Making Sense of Music in Advertising Research

An interpretive model of the interaction between music and image

Matthias Bode

Overture

Social events are (and always have been) accompanied by specific soundtracks. Royal weddings, religious ceremonies, military engagements and sport events unfold to their own rhythm and melody. It should not come as a big surprise that, for centuries, ingenious salespersons have tried to exploit music as a "multi-purpose weapon." Street traders, with the beneficial cooperation of musicians and companies, announced their new products with fanfare starting in the 19th century (McLaren & Prelinger 1998). At the turn of the 20th century, department stores began to organize their own orchestras; in the 1920s, it was not uncommon for their employees to perform in-house musicals to announce recent sales figures and new strategies. IBM became infamous for their own "hymnbook."

Even though scholars may tend to consider the use of music in advertising an innovation made possible by technological advances, the intimate connection between salesmanship and music was established long before the first radio jingles in the 1920s. With the integration of sound and music in the creative departments of advertising agencies in the 1990s, the significance of sound/music design in the commercial field reached new heights. While companies in the 1980s and 1990s focused on visual strategies as key success factors in commercial persuasion, companies are now working with acoustic branding and corporate sound identities to improve their brand equity and strategic market position (Ringe 2005).

Yet, looking at the academic side, advertising research lives in a mute world. Research on music in advertising is fundamentally underdeveloped, fragmentary and contradictory. In this chapter, it is argued that the scientific "overlooking" of the phenomenon of music is not just a failure to realize the market relevancy and ubiquity of music. It is rather a methodological failure in thinking about music and understanding its conceptual foundations. In introducing an innovative approach to music in advertising, I will first outline the existing hurdles towards the scientific subject of "ad music". Within the paradigm of interpretive advertising research, I suggest a new conceptualization of music that goes beyond a naïve stimulus-response research. This allows me to describe a conceptual model which makes sense of the full potentials of a multi-modal advertising rhetoric.

Advertising research on something called "music"

In one of the first monographs on music in advertising, Ingolf Ritscher (1966: 148f) expressed hope that advertising research will soon overcome the exclusive focus on visual ad strategies. His research approach started with the unique qualities of sound, developed subsequent potentials of music, and encompassed the interaction of acoustic, verbal and visual ad elements in commercial communication. He saw the gap quickly diminishing between the elaborated utilization of music in advertising and the lack of scientific analysis. His approach was left without a successor, and forty years later, the gap he described has increased. Contemporary advertising textbooks rarely mention music as a factor on its own, merely relegating music to the category of miscellaneous background aspects such as humor, sex and color. They also tend to describe sound as having a mysterious, extraordinary impact on the human psyche (Tietz & Zentes 1980: 223), subsuming sound under the convenient but misleading label of "musical images" (Kroeber-Riel 1990: 482).

In the few cases of explicit research on ad music in the contemporary advertising literature, theoretical underpinning is based on 19th century psychoacoustic and psychophysiological music psychology, exemplified by scholars such as Helmholtz or Wundt and the empirical American music psychology of the beginning of the 20th century. The methodological procedures are unaltered: musical reception is analyzed experimentally in laboratory environments in which short acoustic stimuli are controlled and modified to detect reaction patterns. Echoing long held criticism of this research stream by scholars as Susanne Langer (1942) or Leonard B. Meyer (1956), Linda M. Scott (1990) was the first advertising academic who expressed the fundamental concern that, in ad research, the basic concept of music as a nonsemantic affective stimulus is the main obstacle for progress in researching music in advertising.

The main fallacies of the concept of music in traditional advertising research can be summarized as follows:

Music as an ahistorical phenomenon: Advertising research is still using the Hevner (1936) and Rigg (1964) experiments from the 1930s to support links between musical elements and effects (e.g. Alpert & Alpert 1990, Bruner 1990, Kellaris & Rice 1993, Morris & Boone 1998). Instruments, their tunings, performance rituals, everyday soundscapes, the availability of music, the media, and the listening modes have all changed over time. However, research on music in advertising insists on universal reactions to timeless music elements. Popular music is most often used in advertising. Like advertising itself, popular music is inherently dynamic. Even when research is on classical music in ads, the observation of Attali (1985: 35) is blatantly obvious: "What is noise to the old order is harmony to the new."

Music as emotional engineering: One of the main qualities of music in advertising is often seen as triggering moods and emotions. In advertising research, this view has the tendency to blur the differences between emotions represented and felt. Hevner and Rigg, even though their research is cited in the literature on music in advertising to suggest otherwise, explicitly point out that their results refer to the identification of emotions and not to experienced emotions (Rigg 1964: 226f). Today, neuro- physiologists and music psychologists share the consensus that music and emotions are always mediated by subjective cognitive processes (Maeß, Kölsch, Gunter & Friederici 2001, Motte-Haber 1982).

Music as acoustic stimuli: Besides research that codes music as absent/present (e.g. Gorn et al. 1991, Park & Young 1986, Stewart, Farmer & Stannard 1990, Olsen 1995), the main approach is to examine the effects of structural musical elements (Alpert & Alpert 1990: 115f). But even the interaction of two controllable elements like tempo and modality (Kellaris

& Kent 1991) exhibits a complexity that is hard to control and to interpret. While the control of all structural elements in music seems to be unfeasible, it also appears to be futile. Structural elements are theoretical artifacts that are useful for analyzing inter musical structures; for most recipients, isolated structural elements are understood as acoustic stimuli and not as music (Serafine 1988).

Music as an abstract artefact: To extract music from its context of production, transmission and consumption means to reduce music to an abstract, fictional, and theoretical entity. The possibility that the same music, heard in a laboratory, on the mp3-player, in a club or in a commercial might be perceived differently is seldom mentioned (see as an exception Macklin 1988: 242). The separation of music from its context impedes research on music in advertising. Thus, one neglected factor is the utilization of interpretive frames by listeners who differentiate between noise and musical experience. The same music phrase heard at home as a neighbor practices the piano or performed in a concert hall is experienced in different ways. The interpretive frame applied to a song used in advertising can reverse the musical experience. Favorite songs, listened to in an ad, can elicit even the most negative feelings.[1]

THE INTERPRETIVE VIEW OF ADVERTISING

From a current musicologist perspective, the consequence of the stated fallacies might seem obvious: in order to improve the research situation, it is time to update a flawed conceptualization of music. Confronted with the main unresolved issues in ad music research, namely the control of contextualized and individual factors in music's impact and the unsatisfying conceptualization of the congruency or fit between music and the ad, the scientific researcher's answer is still: "We have to improve our measurement methods" instead of asking: "What is it that we are actually trying to measure?"

But, luckily, this almost blind belief in scientific measurement is no longer the one and only, undisputable doctrine. Thanks to a small group of Anglo-American consumer researchers who started to voice their dissent in the early 1980s under the label of "interpretive consumer research", new questions and research methods have emerged. Even though this movement intitially faced severe ridicule and contempt from the mainstream research community (Sherry 1991), it has been successful in establishing a research infrastructure of journals and conferences on interpretive consumer research (Arnould & Thompson 2005).

A basic difference between the positivist mainstream and the interpretive paradigm is the refusal of the methodological monism and its single, valid reference point of natural science (Murray & Ozanne 1991). For interpretivists, consumer research should employ methodological pluralism, based on a strong social science and humanities tradition. In line with the more general "interpretive turn" (Rabinow & Sullivan 1979), consumer behavior is integrated into a wider "text" with the aim of reconstructing the subjective negotiation of meanings and understandings.

The main angle to overcome the ontological and epistemological barriers for appreciating the role of music in advertising is *contextuality*. While context is the stumbling block to universal knowledge products in traditional research, it is the constitutive element for meaningful knowledge products in interpretive research (Giddens 1976). When Olson (1986: 281) states that "all meaning is meaning in context", he points out that the scientific (as well as everyday) constraint of the potential multivocality of signs is the link to a certain context. It does not modify the primordial meanings but initially constitutes the relevant meanings of the Marseillaise, played in Rick's Café in the movie "Casablanca" or before a match of the French national soccer team and the framing of a minor mode by the Trip Hop Band Portishead or a Dmitri Shostakovich fugue.

For advertising research, the contextuality also has an impact on the concept of advertising reception. The recipient is no longer the psychological "island of cognitive and affective responses, unconnected to a social world, detached from culture" (Buttle 1991: 97). In the interpretive view, contact with ads is put into effect in a concrete situation: a movie theatre, an unwanted break of the sport coverage on TV, together with friends or alone while doing the dishes. Mick & Buhl (1992) differentiate between a socio-cultural context and the epistemic context of ad reception, encompassing the personal lifeworld of the recipient with his/her own life themes, hopes, ideas and wishes. It exemplifies the endeavor of interpretive consumer research to reach out into everyday life, "where some texts are read differently than others, where some propositions are resisted, where some writers have more authority than others, and where readers are sceptical and products are part of experience." (Scott 1994a: 462). In the end, this contextualized view of the ad negotiation by real human beings is reversing the traditional perspective of advertising research: "what does advertising do to people?" into "what do people do with advertising?" (Lannon 1992). And the interpretive answer is: They negotiate their lives.

On a more concrete level of analysis, the interpretive consumer research model of advertising is most often based on a semiotic perspective, which is also utilized for the analysis of the musical sign system. Here, a modified Saussurian conception of semiotics that I follow understands semiotics (or semiology in his terminology) as "a science which studies the life of signs at the heart of social life" (Saussure 1974: 16). His dyadic sign structure is composed of signifier (basically the sign vehicle or form of the sign) and signified (the mental concept the sign represents). Here, the mental concept or signified stands for the meaning. It is important to note that this meaning conception does not indicate a reified view of meaning as either an essence hidden in the text or an independently existing cognitive representation. Rather, meaning exists only in the semiosis. Meaning is part of a relationship between the sign, other signs and the sign user in a specific socio-cultural context (Fiske 1990: 41). Furthermore, meanings can be differentiated between potential and realized meanings (Livingstone 1993, Lindlof 1988).

Potential meanings are based on an analysis of the ad text. They are created by textual processes, especially formal structures of the advertisement. These textual processes result from two analytical steps. First, a signifier from a referent system is selected. Referent systems constitute a cultural meaning pool that Williamson (1978: 19) describes as "a grist of significance for the ad mill." In a second step, the emergence of new meanings is achieved by a juxtaposition of the product and referent sign. This semanticization of the object (Barthes 1985) is a formal process on the level of signifiers and not on the level of signifieds. This means that there does not have to be a content-based, narrative, causal or logical connection between the signs. *Realized meanings* include the empirical recipient in the analysis and open up the latent structuralist reduction of the text to the post-structuralist power of the reader/recipient (Scott 1992, Elliott &

Ritson 1997). While a post-structuralist view accepts contradictions and ambiguities, it can also run into the danger of fetishizing them. Here, it is assumed that meanings are usually realized in-between an optional space, constrained by the textually induced meaning potentials and the reception context, as well as the subjective textual and social experience.

THE INTERPRETIVE VIEW OF MUSIC

It has been argued that a main deficit in traditional advertising research is the reductive view on music, isolated from its social and cultural embeddedness. The interpretive research starts with a contextualized view of music. Merriam (1964: 32ff) suggested three necessary analytic levels for defining music: An acoustic, a behavioral and a conceptual level. In reference to this framework, music can be defined as the cultural and social structuring of sound, materialized in the process of composing, performing and listening. Besides personal elements, the shared reference to specific cultural conventions is necessary (see also Blacking 1973: 92, Moisala 1995: 17). As a cultural system, music is a form of symbolic expression with meaning potentials (Lull 1987: 141). For understanding the contribution of these expressive potentials of music in the advertising text, it is now necessary to clarify how music can make meanings possible. In line with the interpretive advertising model, a semiotic model of music is developed that can handle the uniqueness of musical meanings.

Although semiotics claims universal applicability, music shows considerable resistance to becoming "readable." The semiotics of music, especially popular music, is one of the least developed fields in semiotics, without consensual terminology, approaches or even agreed on areas (Nettl 1983, Hatten & Henrotte 1988, Monelle 1992, Cumming 2001). It seems that "music and semiotics do not make comfortable bedfellows" (Gronow 1987: c7). The uniqueness of the musical signification process is identified as the main obstacle (Lidov 1986: 577). Different attempts to develop music sign typologies reached a dead end when the linguistic anchor of the iconic, indexical, and symbolic sign structure proved to be restraining (Stefani 1973). A problem is the semantic vagueness of the musical sign. The more musical signs become meaningful, as in iconic sound imitations, the less they are able to stand as a foundation for a general meaning model. They are considered to be semantic enclaves (Kneif 1973: 135).

A promising position regarding this semantic vagueness stems from Langer (1942), who tried to develop a "wordless" semantics that she labeled presentational symbolism in opposition to the discursive symbolism of the verbal language. In this chapter, Langer's basic idea is adopted, without sharing her music philosophy. She coined the expression that music is the "unconsummated symbol" (Langer 1942: 240). To consummate the musical sign system, a contextual semiotic approach that acknowledges the social and cultural dimensions of music is needed. The suggested approach goes beyond acknowledging that music is a context-dependent cultural entity (Bengtsson 1973: 17). In linguistic approaches, contextuality reduces the potential multivocality of signs. They refer to "how" understanding of verbal signs works. In music, contextuality refers to "what" is understood. The fiction of "pure music" only becomes "meaningful music" in a context. Therefore, contextuality is a prerequisite for meanings in music. Only in-between this cue nexus can music be experienced as "real music". Verbal and visual contextualization cues (Gumperz 1982) are the most significant cues. *Verbal cues* can include the title of the song, program-notes, booklets, the performer's name, lyrics, artist statements, liner notes, music criticism, and informal talks about the music. *Visual cues* can include record covers, music videos, performance imagery, visual hooks, corporate design of musicians, the appropriation of music in video games and movies, and associated fashion and body codes (for a detailed discussion, see Bode 2004: 365ff). The musical sign nexus would not be complete without the *sonic cues*. In the interpretive view, the ontological focus is not on the chord, song or the score, but on the materiality of sound as the primary text (Middleton 1990: 220ff). In the performance or in the studio recording, the sonic structure is created. The studio in particular can be classified as one of the most important instruments in popular music (Frith 1996: 233). Recording defines a whole musical aesthetic and makes record producers like Sam Phillips, George Martin, Phil Spector, or Trevor Horn as famous as the musicians they produce. In classical music, the recording first worked as an acoustic snapshot, trying to produce a realist, naturalist representation of an actual performance. This has changed in classical music (most prominently with Glenn Gould in the 1960s) and was always present in 20th century popular music. The sound of the recording defines the aural qualities of the music, which are often not even reproducible in a live performance. The materiality of sonic cues facilitates the "politics of joussiance" (Hawkins 2002: 28), the physical-affective pleasures of popular music. It is argued that this charge of popular music is socially mediated by the dialogical process between the participants of the musical semiosis and not a purely biological process. Meyer (1956: 81) clarified this view in his famous phrase about an often devalued and racialized aspect of music: "Rhythm comes from the mind not the body." And the context of music regulates the norms of physical responsiveness to music. It is a semiotic process in music in which the relevant musical text is an amalgam of inter- and extramusical signs (Cook 1998; Thompson, Graham & Russo 2005).

The contextualization approach is not based on an expert listener, able to actualize the full potential of background information. On the contrary, the less knowledgeable the listener is about the music he/she is listening to, the more existing cues will gain significance: the title of the song, the behavior of the performers, the place the music is performed/broadcasted or how followers look and behave in reaction of the music. In trying to separate music from these cues, research is running in danger of producing research artifacts:

> "I went to high schools and showed pre-selected videos to teen audiences and demanded they give me feedback. Their responses varied from hostility to amity, triggered less by content and more by situational variables such as was the artist hot, had the artist recently appeared in concert locally, or whether there was an avid fan in the classroom." (Lehnerer 1987: 75)

When Lehnerer criticizes the research subjects in focusing on negligible aspects instead of the music, he fails to acknowledge his own conceptual assumption about "pure music". These contextualization cues are not more or less important add-ons (or worse: failures in the assumed reception of music). Neither music nor an interpretation of music is possible without them. They are more or less present in the everyday reception situation and required to constitute the phenomenon of "music alive."

MAKING SENSE OF MUSIC IN ADVERTISING

So far, the interpretive model has focused on verbal and visual elements. The extension with music is overdue and at the same time renders the single mode analysis useless. The integration of sound and music in the analysis of a commercial cannot be reduced to the musical mode when meaningful music is already inherently multi-modal. Furthermore, the inter- and extramusical signs of music interact with the additional visual and verbal elements of the commercial in such a way that the resulting meaning potentials only exist in the space of this comprehensive nexus. They are not hidden in the single modal expressions and cannot be simply added up (Hung 2000).

It is now to be shown how such an approach can advance the main existing problem of traditional advertising research. In the empirical studies, it turned out that the impact of the same piece of music can vary according to the respective integration into a commercial, termed as "fit" or "congruence." MacInnis & Park (1991: 162) define the fit as the "subjective perceptions of the music's relevance or appropriateness to the central ad message." The question of why people perceive a fit and why this perception should be aimed for remained unanswered. Furthermore, the use of music with lyrics in their experiments without any methodological consideration weakened their research. Kellaris, Cox & Cox (1993) tried to further refine the fit concept. They focused on congruent music and product associations. In this way, Chinese music fits to an ad for a Chinese restaurant, but not for a Western restaurant (Mantel & Kellaris 1996).[2]

This approach to analyze the music-spot interactions is fundamentally flawed. First, it is based on an outdated reference model of advertising, presenting basic product information for potential buyers. It denies the relevant dimension of rhetorical figures of expression in modern (and post-modern) advertising (Schrøder 1986, Durand 1987). Even a simple element of irony like Opera music in Nike sports shoe spots is beyond the reach of the fit concept, not to speak of more complex interactions, like Georg Friedrich Händel's "Sarabande" in the martial arts inspired spot "Odyssey" by Jonathan Glazer for Levi's. Second, the fit/congruence concept reduces the complex forms of music-spot interactions to a simple binary "yes" or "no" construct. Thereby, the dynamic changes within the degrees of fit during a commercial are ignored. A simple "before-after" format might play with incongruent (=life without the product) and congruent (=life with the advertised product) music-spot interactions. Furthermore, the whole range of options in utilizing forms of tension, friction, emphasis or contradictions between the different modal expressions cannot be understood with the binary concept. Finally, the lacking concept of music in the congruence model fails to recognize that even within the music mode different forms of fit or congruence are possible. An example is the combination of disparate elements like Drum and Bass music with an old, scratchy phonograph sound or a Heavy Metal song played by a string quartet.

The proposed interaction model, based on the contextualized model of music, starts with Roland Barthes' (1964) analysis of the word-image interaction. He denied the possibility of just "doubling" meanings (like the word "sun" and the image of a sun) as it is implied in the congruence concept. From a semiotic point of view, the formal features of the interactions are relevant for the emergence of new meaning potentials. He differentiated two basic ways of interaction which he called "anchorage" and "relay." With *anchorage*, words basically confine the visual connotations like a vise, while relay describes the process of words opening up the existing visual meanings for new meaning systems. Barthes emphasized the primary function of words to confine or open the visual meanings. In focusing on the music-image interactions it can be argued that the relationships are structurally more ambivalent in terms of primary or secondary functional determination (cf. Larsen 2002: 136). More typical is the mutual interpretation of music and images with two ideal types of modal dominance. As ideal types, they describe functional options in the multimodal interaction that are relevant for a heuristic map for developing meaning potentials. In applying the model to concrete examples, the dynamic aspect has to be incorporated, which then also allows for the analysis of temporal shifts between the interaction modes. Furthermore, the modal consequences for realized meanings have to be considered, as each interaction mode suggests a different interpretive frame for making sense of the concrete commercial. At this point, it is more important to emphasize the theoretical differences in modal dominance.

Figure 1: Modes of music-image interaction

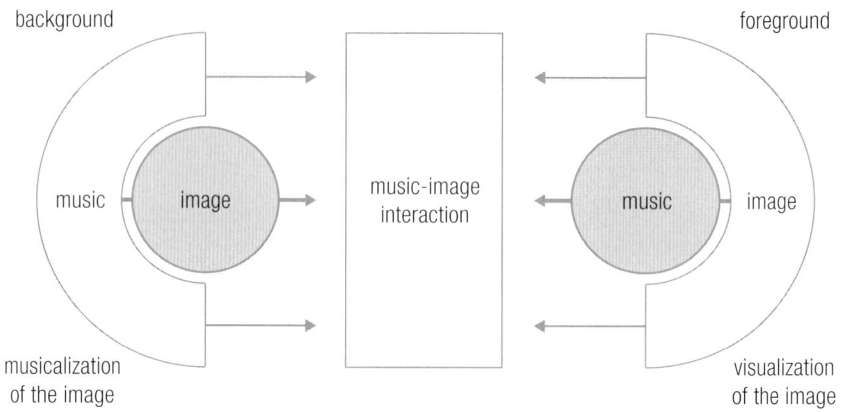

In the *musicalization of the image* mode, music is a background function of the image. In this way, music guides the sign user through the image. It is important to note that the modal dominance is not based on aesthetic but on functional differences. In the background function of music, it is not softness versus loudness that makes the difference. It is rather the function of music leading to the core message which is perceived as to be visual. Here, the theory of musical codes also comes into play (Middleton 1990: 174). The same piece of music can be encoded in a commercial on more abstract or specific code levels (like basic musical norms, styles, genres, sub-genres or idiolects). This coding can guide, but not determine, the decoding process. Based on the available code competence (Stefani 1987), the targeted audiences develop realized meanings, interpreting Aretha Franklin's song "Respect" as a nostalgic soul song in a beer commercial or as a civil rights song in a UN Refugee Agency commercial. For the musicalization function, the relevant code level is typically based on more abstract codes of music. A theoretical reference point for the musicalization function can be found in traditional film music, emphasizing specific aspects of the visual mode and bonding the visual flow (Gorbman 1987). In this way, advertising can utilize the textual experience of the audience that has learned to interpret visuals by the accompanied music. Most importantly, in this interaction mode, music structures the emotional interpretation of the visual mode, it delivers the socio-cultural framing (e.g. time, place) and constitutes the narrative logic (e.g. signaling coming events or closing story lines). In the *emotional framing*, the music guides the interpretation of the emotional states of the actors as well as the intended emotions towards the scenes. Even in a 20 second commercial, the music can emotionally describe the product users, differentiate them from competitor's products and users, characterize the emotional bond between product and user or give a general emotional impression of the potential target group. Most important, the product as the typical protagonist of the commercial can be emotionally positioned by music. In all of these functions, it is not so much the direct emotional impact of music on the listener, but the interpretation of the emotional meanings articulated by the music – image interaction. The *socio-cultural framing* guides the social, economical, historical and cultural position of the depicted scenes. In terms of characterizing the social position of the product and its users, the potential of music is immense. An example is the Pepsi spot "switch" from 1991, in which the rap musician Mc Hammer performs live on stage, and after drinking a non-identified cola turns into crooning the mainstream song "feelings." Only after drinking Pepsi does he switch back into the rap music he started with. As mentioned before, the role of music in positioning a product or company as country-specific by the use of instruments (e.g. accordion=France) or genre (e.g. country music=USA) is very common in commercials. More subtle is the potential of music to express differences and commonalities at the same time. This is used to point out the constant core benefits and history of the product through the development of time by using time-specific genre modifications of the same song. Another example is typical for global companies, articulating the local aspects by locally flavored arrangements with the same melody. Finally, the *narrative* framing localizes the undefined image in time, as in real time by diegetic music or subjective time with non-diegetic music. The music can indicate the position of the visual in the narrative development, indicating the balance, upcoming disorder or final solutions as offered by the product.

To further elaborate the musicalization of the image mode, the theory of film music can be a vital source for advertising research. Advertising not only utilizes the functional repertoire of film music, it is also a specific genre in itself with the structural features of brevity, the dominant persuasion intent and the internal genre conventions and traditions (even in product-specific conventions like the different aesthetics for car and detergent commercials) have to be taken into account.

In the *visualization of the music* mode, music is used in a foregrounding function. Usually, the music is coded on a more concrete level of specific songs. Here, the images guide the sign user through the music by interacting with the acoustic elements and the verbal and visual cues of the music sign nexus. The modal function of images leads to the core message which is perceived to be based on the musical sign system. The theory of film music is a reference point for the musicalization mode; the theory of music video can be used as a reference point for the visualization mode. Actually, music videos and advertising are closely linked, insofar as music videos have the double function entertainment product and commercial for the song and the artist. In the late 1980s, advertisers started to change the aesthetics of commercials to become closer to music videos, trying to fight increasing advertising scepticism and resistance with this entertainment function (Aufderheide 1986, Goldman 1992: 185ff, Englis 1991). Meanwhile, companies like NIKE are even arguing with MTV whether or not their spots should run as part of the programming or as a commercial (Elliott 2001). Also on the practical side, music video directors are often also involved in the production of commercials. The theoretical approach to music videos has long suffered by a "methodological deafness," whereby the visual aspect has dominated research for a long time, neglecting the fundamental visual contextualization cues that have always been present in music, especially in popular music (Frith 1988: 221). More sensitive to the musical sign system are scholars like Goodwin (1993). He suggested the following basic interactions between music and image, which are extended by the multi-modal conception of music:

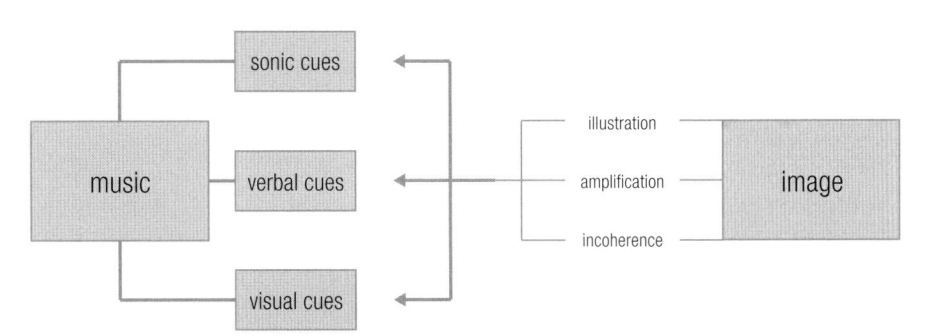

Figure 2: Music-Image interactions in the visualization mode

With *illustration*, the visual narrative signifies the mood and the story of the song, usually in relation to the verbal contextualization cues of the used music. But it is also possible to illustrate musical elements by the rhythm of the editing or light effects responding to the change between vocal and instrumental parts. In commercials, the illustration can emphasize the mood of the song in visualizing the sexiness or dynamics of the song by dancing and physical movements. Pure illustrations of the lyrics are the largest focus in music videos. In commercials, this function is prominent in songs created for an advertisement and in licensed songs in which the lyrics have been modified. An increasing number of commercials, however, try to move beyond pure illustration towards amplification. Adorno & Eisler (1969: 194f) criticized the simple, illustrative relations between music and image in movies in the late 1940, with their most pejorative dictum being "reklameähnlich (like advertising)". They demanded to work with the optional space between parallelism and counterpoint, which they admired in the work of Sergei Eisenstein. Today, advertising is in line with an increased modal sophistication in the TV, movie and videogame worlds, which interact with an increased multimodal competency with the audience (Johnson 2005). As empirical studies on commercials are still more focused on technical categorizations than on aesthetic modes, there are only few approaches to further investigate this development. Supporting examples are the representative study of European commercials in the 1980s by Kloepfer & Landbeck (1991) and the historical study of Danish commercials by Andersen (2004).

With *amplification,* the visuals add new layers of meaning that have an echo with the used music. In advertising research, this mechanism resembles the concept of "resonance" (McQuarrie 1989, McQuarrie & Mick 1992), which is understood as a repetition of elements within the ad that leads to echo one another and a multiplication of realized ad meanings. So far, the interaction of image and words was analyzed as resonance. Examples are the use of the verbal contextualization cues of lyrics, when Wal-Mart amplifies the Patsy Cline phrase "I fall to pieces" by visualizing falling prices or The Hollies lyrics "The air that I breathe" is used in an ad for cough drops. A Danish VW spot used amplification with the song "love is in the air," heard by older people in the traditional VW Golf. The new Golf appears with younger people driving it and listening to a loud Hip Hop-style song. First the older people are annoyed, and then they relax when realizing it is the same song as a cover version. In juxtaposing the two song versions and visualizing the new-old categories by the car and their drivers, VW can emphasize the new car and, at the same time, point out the permanence of the core values that VW Golf stands for.

The final mechanism is *disjuncture.* Here, obliqueness, contradictions and frictions between music and the image open up the text to totally new meaning potentials or to the free floating chain of signifiers. This postmodern aesthetic, typically characterized by intertextuality (O'Donohoe 1997), carnevalesque (Brown, Stevens & Maclaran 1999), bricolage (Scott 1992, Domzal & Kernan 1993), or paradox (Stern 1994) has been an increasing trend in advertising in the late 1980s and 1990s (Goldman 1992, Boutlis 2000). The main emphasis in this area has been on the visual side of advertising. With disjuncture, it also includes the music-image interaction. An example is a Wrangler ad, with David Lynch-like images of a young tramp involving a tension with the original "Wizard of Oz" title song. The intention is for the targeted audience to appreciate the uniqueness of the ad and to appreciate the ambiguity of the text for its own sake rather than to try to find a non-existent, coherent meaning.

In a commercial, these basic mechanisms can be further combined vertically on several layers and horizontally in changing from one mechanism to another one. This proposed interaction model, combining *musicalization* and *visualization* modes, opens inquiry into the potential meanings on the encoding side of commercials as well as the realized meanings on the decoding side of experiencing commercials. It also points out that what is actually interpreted as music depends on the specific multimodal embedding, emphasizing different cues for the same piece of music. A close watch on several interactions reveals a much wider range of options than just a binary fit between music and the ad. The interaction model is a frame which offers a theoretical frame to handle this range of options in the design and analysis of advertising. In advertising creation, it maps a heuristic field of options for meaning potentials. It highlights the importance of focussing on the multimodal interactions in transforming ad strategies into coherent executions. On a procedural level, it facilitates the communication between product managers and ad creatives, as it connects the modern, meaning-based brand management discourse (Allen, Fournier & Miller 2008) with the aesthetic discourse of multimodal creations. In advertising analysis, it offers an integrative framework which emphasizes the necessity of an interdisciplinary analysis of music in advertising.

CODA

Sound and music matter. It is necessary to point out this inane fact because current consumer and advertising research seems soundproof. It is a world of visual spectacle, enchantment, gaze and image. It leaves out the world in which people start the day with a radio alarm clock, commute to work listening to an iPod or the car radio, work to the hum of computers, purchase and share MP3s, consume to the monotonous beat of piped muzak, and relax in the evening listening to music. In avoiding the role of music and sound for so long, consumer research has neglected a part of everyday existence. The rare research on music is inconsistent and conflicting. Here, it was argued that the situation cannot be improved by just pointing out how significant the role of music and sound is in the life of consumers and in making sense in a commercial. What is required is not so much more research, but a different kind of research that avoids the current methodology of annihilating the research object. The current conceptual view is to mix acoustic stimuli with music. To experience and to analyze music, it requires acknowledgement of the contextualized qualities of music as a sonic space embedded in a nexus of inter- and extramusical signs. In realizing the multimodal qualities of music, it should also be clear that further research cannot be focused on a supplementary musical rhetoric in advertising. Instead, taking music seriously means developing an integrative approach to the verbal, visual and sonic world we live in. This research perspective would not stop in really listening to the sound of advertising. It would reach out into the sonification of the consumer experience, where soundscapes shape our sense of being in time and space. In real life, companies already put this thinking into practice, when designing cars, vacuum cleaners, or even potato chips with a specific sound. It is about time to start listening to the rattling, pounding, stomping, honking, and clattering cacophony of the market.

Notes

1   McLaren (1998: 10) describes her encounter with a favorite song after used in an ad with the half ironic, half serious words: "entering a local bagel place, I heard 'Everyday People' in a radio and ... thought of a car commercial. Not Sly Stone. (...) It was as if the song in my head had been swiped. (...) They can take „Revolution" and William Burroughs and KRS-1 and the Verve, but Sly Stone? That's it. Next thing you know they'll be coming for my right arm".

2   It is interesting to note that 55 of the 202 participating subjects had to be excluded from the analysis, as they perceived the music in the actual commercial differently than separately measured in pre-tests.

References

Adorno, Th. W., & Eisler, H. (1969). *Komposition für den Film*. München: Rogner & Bernhard.

Allen, Ch., Fournier, S., & Miller, F. (2008). Brands and their Meaning Makers. In C. Haugtvedt, P. Herr, & F. Kardes (Eds.), *Handbook of Consumer Psychology* (pp. 781-822). Mahwah, NJ: Lawrence Erlbaum Associates.

Alpert, J. I., & Alpert, M. I. (1990). Music influences on mood and purchase intentions. *Psychology and Marketing, 7(2)*, 109-134.

Andersen, L. P. (2004). *The rhetorical strategies of Danish TV advertising. A study of the first fifteen years with special emphasis on genre and irony*. Copenhagen: Copenhagen Busines School Press.

Arnould, E. J., & Thompson, C. J. (2005). Reflections: Consumer culture theory (CCT): Twenty years of research. *Journal of Consumer Research, 31(4)*, 868-882.

Aufderheide, P. (1986). Music videos: The look of the sound. *Journal of Communication, 36(1)*, 57-78.

Barthes, R. (1985). *L'aventure sémiologique* [The semiological adventure]. Paris: Seuil.

Barthes, R. (1964). La rhétorique de l'image [Rhetoric of the image]. *Communications, 4*, 40-51.

Bengtsson, I. (1973). Verstehen – Prolegomena zu einem semiotisch-hermeneutischen Ansatz [Understanding – Prolegomena to a semiotic-hermeneutic essay]. In P. Faltin, & H.-P. Reinecke (Eds.), *Musik und Verstehen. Aufsätze zur semiotischen Theorie, Ästhetik und Soziologie der musikalischen Rezeption* (pp. 11-36). Köln: Volk.

Blacking, J. (1973). *How musical is man?* Seattle: University of Washington Press.

Bode, M. (2004). *Musik in der Werbemittelforschung unter besonderer Berücksichtigung interpretativer Verfahren* [Music in advertising research, especially regarding interpretive approaches]. Frankfurt/Main: Peter Lang.

Boutlis, P. (2000). A theory of postmodern advertising. *International Journal of Advertising, 19(1)*, 3-23.

Brown, S., & Volgsten, U. (Eds.). (2006). *Music and manipulation: On the social uses and social control of music*. New York: Berghahn Books.

Brown, S., Stevens, L., & Maclaran, P. (1999). I can't believe it's not Bakhtin!: Literary theory, postmodern advertising, and the gender agenda. *Journal of Advertising, 28(1)*, 11-24.

Buttle, F. (1991). What do people do with advertising? *International Journal of Advertising, 10*, 95-110.

Cook, N. (1998). *Analysing musical multimedia*. Oxford, New York: London Press.

Cumming, N. (2001). Semiotics [semiology]. In S. Sadie (Ed.), *The new grove dictionary of music and musicians* 23(2nd ed.) (pp. 66-69). London: Macmillan.

Domzal, T. J., & Kernan, J. (1992). Reading advertising: The what and how of product meaning. *The Journal of Consumer Marketing, 9(3)*, 48-64.

Durand, J. (1987). Rhetorical figures in the advertising message. In J. Umiker-Sebeok (Ed.), *Marketing and semiotics: New directions in the study of signs for sale* (pp. 295-318). Berlin: Mouton de Gruyter.

Englis, B. (1991). Music television and its influences on consumers, consumer culture, and the transmission of consumption messages. *Advances in Consumer Research, 18*, 111-114.

Elliott, S. (2001). Advertising: Nike ad blurs into music video. *New York Times*, 10.4.2001.

Elliott, R., & Ritson, M. (1997). Post-structuralism and the dialectics of advertising: discourse, ideology, resistance. In S. Brown and D. Turley (Eds.), *Consumer research: Postcards from the edge* (pp. 190-219). London: Routledge.

Fiske, J. (1990). *Introduction to communication studies* (2nd rev. ed.). London: Routledge.

Frith, S. (1988). Afterword: making sense of video: Pop into the nineties. In S. Frith, *Music for pleasure: Essays in the sociology of pop* (pp. 205-225). Cambridge: Polity Press.

Frith, S. (1996). *Performing rites: On the value of popular music*. Cambridge: Harvard University Press.

Giddens, A. (1976). *New rules of sociological method: A positive critique of interpretative sociologies*. London: Hutchinson.

Goodwin, A. (1993). *Dancing in the distraction factory. Music television and popular culture*. London: Routledge.

Gorbman, C. (1987). *Unheard melodies. Narrative film music*. London: BFI.

Goldman, R. (1992). *Reading ads socially*. London: Routledge.

Gorn, G. J., Goldberg, M. E., Chattopadhyay, A., & Litvack, D. (1991). Music and information in commercials: Their effects with an elderly sample. *Journal of Advertising Research, 31(5)*, 23-32.

Gronow, P. (1987). Music, communication, mass communication. *Degrés: Revue de synthèse à orientation sémiologique, 15(15)*, c1-c30.

Gumperz, J. J. (1982). *Discourse strategies*. Cambridge: Cambridge University Press.

Hatten, R., & Henrotte, G. A. (1988). Recent perspectives on music semiotics. In T. A. Sebeok, & and J. Umiker-Sebeok (Eds.), *The semiotic web 1987* (pp. 421-463). Berlin: Mouton de Gruyter.

Hawkins, S. (2002). *Settling the pop score. Pop texts and identity politics*. Aldershot: Ashgate.

Hevner, K. (1936). Experimental studies of the elements of expression in music. *American Journal of Psychology, 48(April)*, 246-268.

Hung, K. (2000). Narrative music in congruent and incongruent TV advertising. *Journal of Advertising, 29(1)*, 25-34.

Johnson, S. (2005). *Everything bad is good for you: How today's popular culture is actually making us smarter*. New York, NY: Riverhead Books.

Kellaris, J. J., Cox, A., & Cox, D. (1993). The effect of background music on ad processing: A contingency explanation. *Journal of Marketing, 57(4)*, 114-125.

Kellaris, J. J., & Rice, R. (1993). The influence of tempo, loudness, and gender of listener on responses to music. *Psychology & Marketing, 10(1)*, 15-29.

Kellaris, J. J., & Kent, R. (1991). Exploring tempo and modality effects on consumer responses to music. *Advances in Consumer Research, 18*, 243-248.

Kloepfer, R., & Landbeck, H. (1991). *Ästhetik der Werbung. Der Fernsehspot in Europa als Symptom neuer Macht* [Aesthetics of advertising. The TV commercial in Europe as a symptom of new power]. Frankfurt/Main: Fischer.

Kneif, T. (1973). Musik und Zeichen. Aspekte einer nichtvorhandenen musikalischen Semiotik. *Musica, 27(1)*, 9-12.

Kramer, G. et al. (1999). *The sonification report: Status of the field and research agenda. Report prepared for the National Science Foundation by members of the International Community for Auditory Display*, Santa Fe, NM: ICAD, http://sonify.psych.gatech.edu/publications/pdfs/1999-NSF-Report.pdf. <04/08/2006>

Kroeber-Riel, W. (1990). Zukünftige Strategien und Techniken der Werbung [Future strategies and techniques of advertising]. *ZfbF, 42(6)*, 481-491.

Langer, S. K. (1942). *Philosophy in a new key. A study in the symbolism of reason, rite, and art.* Cambridge, MA: Harvard University Press.

Lannon, J. (1992). Asking the right questions: what do people do with advertising? *Admap*, March, 11-16.

Larsen, P. (2002). Mediated fiction. In K. B. Jensen (Ed.), *A handbook of media and communication research. Qualitative and quantitative methodologies* (pp. 117-137). London: Routledge.

Lehnerer, M. (1987). Music video: a uses approach. *OneTwoThreeFour: A Rock 'n' Roll Quarterly, 5,* 74-79.

Lidov, D. (1986). Music. In T. A. Sebeok (Ed.), *Encyclopedic dictionary of semiotics* (pp. 577-587). Berlin: de Gruyter.

Lindlof, T. R. (1988). Media audiences as interpretive communities. In J. Anderson (Ed.), *Communication Yearbook Vol. 11.* (pp. 81-107). Thousand Oaks, CA: Sage.

Livingstone, S. (1993). The rise and fall of audience research: an old story with a new ending. *Journal of Communication, 43(4),* 5-12.

Lull, J. (1987). Listener's communicative uses of popular music. In J. Lull (Ed.), *Popular music and communication* (pp. 140-174). Newbury Park: Sage.

MacInnis, D. J., & Park, C. (1991). The differential role of characteristics of music on high- and low-involvement consumers' processing of ads. *Journal Consumer Research, 18(2),* 161-173.

Macklin, M. C. (1988). The relationship between music in advertising and children's response: An experimental investigation. In S. Hecker, & D. W. Stewart (Eds.), *Nonverbal communication in advertising* (pp. 225-252). Lexington: Lexington

Maeß, B., Koelsch, S., Gunter, T., & Friederici, A. (2001). Musical syntax is processed in Broca's area: An MEG study. *Nature Neuroscience, 4(5),* 540-545.

Mantel, S., & J. J. Kellaris. (1996). Congruity of peripheral and central ad cues: a contingency underlying AAD to AB affect transfer? *Unpublished working paper* presented at Society for Consumer Psychology 1996 Winter Conference, Hilton Head.

McLaren, C. (1998). Licensed to sell: Why the jingle is dead and commercial pop rule. *Stay Free, 15,* 9-12.

McLaren, C., & Prelinger, R. (1998). Salesnoise. A timeline of music & advertising. *Stay Free, 15,* 14-23.

McQuarrie, E. F. (1989). Advertising resonance: a semiological perspective, In E. Hirschman (Ed.), *Interpretive consumer research* (pp. 97-114). Provo: ACR.

McQuarrie, E. F., & Mick, D. (1992). On resonance: a critical pluralistic inquiry into advertising rhetoric. *Journal of Consumer Research, 19(2),* 180-197.

Merriam, A. P. (1964). *The anthropology of music.* Evanston: Northwestern University Press.

Meyer, L. B. (1956). *Emotion and meaning in music.* Chicago: University of Chicago Press.

Mick, D., & Buhl, C. (1992). A meaning-based model of advertising experiences. *Journal of Consumer Research, 19,* 317-338.

Middleton, R. (1990). *Studying popular music.* Milton Keynes: Open University Press.

Moisala, P. (1995). Cognitive study of music as culture. Basic premises for 'cognitive ethnomusicology'. *Journal of New Music Research, 24*, 8-20.

Monelle, R. (1992). *Linguistis and semiotics in music*. Chur: Harwood Academic Publishers.

Morris, J. D., & Boone, M. A. (1998). The effects of music on emotional response, brand attitude, and purchase intent in an emotional advertising condition. *Advances in Consumer Research, 25*, 518-526.

Motte-Haber, H. (1982). Musikalische Hermeneutik und empirische Forschung [Musical hermeneutics and empirical research]. In C. Dahlhaus, & H. Motte-Haber (Eds.), *Systematische Musikwissenschaft. Neues Handbuch der Musikwissenschaft Vol. 10*. (pp. 171-244). Wiesbaden: Akad. Verl.-Ges. Athenaion.

Murray, J., & Ozanne, J. (1991). The critical imagination: Emancipatory interest in consumer research. *Journal of Consumer Research, 18*, 129-144.

Nettl, B. (1983). *The study of ethnomusicology*. Urbana: University of Illinois Press.

O'Donohoe, S. (1997). Raiding the postmodern pantry. Advertising intertextuality and the young adult audience. *European Journal of Marketing, 31(3-4)*, 234-253.

Olsen, G. D. (1995). Creating the contrast: The influence of silence and background music on recall and attribute importance. *Journal of Advertising, 24(4)*, 29-44.

Olson, J. C. (1986). Meaning analysis in advertising research. In J. C. Olson, & K. Sentis (Eds.), *Advertising and Consumer Psychology Vol. 3* (pp. 275-283). New York: Praeger Press.

Park, C., & Young, S.M. (1986). Consumer response to television commercials: The impact of involvement and background music on brand attitude formation. *Journal of Marketing Research, 23(1)*, 11-24.

Rabinow, P., & Sullivan, W. (1979). The interpretive turn: Emergence of an approach. In P. Rabinow & W. Sullivan (Eds.), *Interpretive social science. A reader*. (pp. 1-21). Berkeley: University of California Press.

Rigg, M. G. (1964). The mood effects of music: A comparison of data from four investigators. *Journal of Psychology, 58*, 427-438.

Ringe, C. (2005). *Audio Branding: Musik als Markenzeichen von Unternehmen* [Audio branding: Music as a symbol of companies]. Berlin: VDM Verlag Müller.

Ritscher, I. (1966). *Akustische Werbung: Ihre Wirkung und Anwendungsmöglichkeiten* [Audio branding: Effects and uses]. Berlin: Duncker & Humblot.

Saussure de, F. (1974). *Course in general linguistics*. London: Fontana.

Schrøder, K. (1986). Snapshot fables: The true nature of magazine advertisements. In L. M. Henny (Ed.), *The semiotics of advertisements, International Studies in Visual Sociology and anthropology Vol. 1* (pp. 78-98). Aachen: Ed. Herodot im Rader-Verl.

Scott, L. M. (1990). Understanding jingles and needledrop: A rhetorical approach to music in advertising. *Journal of Consumer Research, 17(2)*, 223-236.

Scott, L. M. (1992). Playing with pictures: Postmodernism, poststructuralism, and advertising visuals. *Advances in Consumer Research, 19*, 596-612.

Scott, L. M. (1994a). Images in advertising: the need for a theory of visual rhetoric. *Journal of Consumer Research*, *21(September)*, 252-273.

Scott, L. M. (1994b). The bridge from text to mind: adapting reader response theory to consumer research. *Journal of Consumer Research*, *21(December)*, 461-480.

Serafine, M. L. (1988). *Music as cognition. The development of thought in sound*. New York: Columbia University Press.

Sherry, J. F. (1991). Postmodern alternatives: The interpretive turn in consumer research. In T. S. Robertson, & H. H. Kassarjian (Eds.), *Handbook of consumer behavior* (pp. 548-591). Englewood Cliffs: Prentice-Hall.

Stefani, G. (1973). Sémiotique en musicologie [Semiotics in musicology]. *Versus*, *5*, 20-42.

Stefani, G. (1987). A theory of musical competence. *Semiotica*, *66(1/3)*, 7-22.

Stern, B. B. (1994). Authenticity and the textual persona: Postmodern paradoxes in advertising narrative. *International Journal of Research in Marketing*, *11(4)*, 387-400.

Stewart, D. W., Farmer, K. M., & Stannard, C. I. (1990). Music as a recognition cue in advertising-tracking studies. *Journal of Advertising Research*, *30(4)*, 39-48.

Thompson, W. F., Graham, Ph., & Russow, F. A. (2005). Seeing music performance: Visual influences on perception and experience. *Semiotica*, *156*, 203-227.

Tietz, B., & Zentes, J. (1980). *Die Werbung der Unternehmung* [Advertising of companies]. Reinbek b. Hamburg: Rowohlt.

Williamson, J. (1978). *Decoding advertisements*. London: Marion Boyars.

THE JYSK JINGLE
On the use of pre-existing music as a musical brand

Nicolai Graakjær

INTRODUCTION

A jingle can be broadly described as a short, rounded melodic motif appearing in a commercial. Its distinctiveness is conveyed by an easily remembered and recognizable musical structure and by being synchronized with logo and/or slogan. Jingles can be instrumental or sung, and usually the jingle is composed for a commercial, i.e. a piece of so-called original commercial music (see chapter 2, this volume). Moreover, jingles regularly 'speak directly' to their audience with two main purposes: firstly to *present* by way of emphasizing and attracting attention and secondly to *represent* by way of characterizing and signifying the advertised product and producer.

This characterizes only to some extent the jingle used in commercials for JYSK.[1] In these ads two extraordinary features are manifest. Firstly, the jingle appears *diegetic*, and this quite atypical audiovisual embedding of a jingle entails more varied functions of communication than ordinarily encountered in TV commercials. Secondly, the jingle in these particular ads is derived from a piece of pre-existing music. Furthermore, the pre-existing music in question has apparent regional and national references, and the fact that these commercials have been broadcasted internationally makes up for an intriguing case of musical signification. The chapter therefore sets out to examine the signifying potential of the piece of music in question; an examination which will be illustrative of the ways in which jingles function in TV commercials. For this purpose, the chapter begins by looking in closer detail into the historical preconditions.

Hi' there

"Hi' there. My name is Lars Larsen. I have a special offer for you" – in this manner, the founder and owner of JYSK, Lars Larsen, opened a series of TV commercials back in 1988. Broadcasted in the very beginning of the history of commercial TV in Denmark,[2] the commercials caused a sensation by their austere and unpretentious form. These early commercials differed radically from what the audience, critics and researchers had expected televised commercials would look and sound like. They were neither spectacular nor sophisticated, but the wording quoted above became a quotidian figure of speech, thus contributing to a kind of viral marketing. This immediate success came as a big surprise for researchers (cf. Nygaard 1989 and Stigel 1991).

Lack of music is one of the main features contributing to the unpretentious appearance of these commercials. In itself, this feature may seem insignificant, however, in this case, it seems to have importance. His Jutlandic dialect, which Lars Larsen makes no attempt to hide, might be considered *sweet music* to many an (Jutlandic) ear but what is more probable, this dialect functions as a sort of musical (or 'linguistic') brand for Lars Larsen and his company. That is, the use of dialect contributes to making the communication appear personal and authentic.

In 2004, at the time of the company's 25th anniversary, an autobiography by Lars Larsen was distributed to all Danish households as well as to employees abroad. In this biography, Larsen throws light on what is, at the time of its publication, already well-known to most Danes through countless media texts since 1987; for instance, the fact that Lars Larsen is from Thy (a north western region in Denmark), and the fact that he established and developed the company from scratch, with the opening of the first store in 1979 in Aarhus (the biggest city in Jutland). The biography opens with the words: "I – 'Quilts-Larsen' – was born thin and small, but otherwise of good cheer" (Larsen 2004: 6),[3] and the alleged conception is emblematic of the more general meek point of departure of Lars Larsen and his company, which might also be said to come through in the early TV commercials.

In reading the biography one is continuously reminded of Larsen's Jutlandic origin, and among other things it is made clear that the name of Larsen's company is of course no coincidence. In coming up with the name, Larsen explains, he wanted to convey impressions of his products being: "durable, strong and not too expensive" (Larsen 2004: 44),[4] and on the company's website, it says: "it [jysk (Jutlandic)] also signifies modesty, thoroughness and honesty"[5] – indeed corresponding to widely held stereotypes about people from Jutland (to be expanded on below). Speaking of *modesty*, distributing an autobiography to the whole population could seem somewhat atypical of precisely a Jutlander, and after all, Larsen in fact calls upon himself (the way a true Jutlander would do) to try to disarm any accusation of "delusions of grandeur" (Larsen 2004: 5).[6] Delusions of grandeur or not, today, the company has grown large, measured by Danish standards. The marketing still bears the imprint of unpretentiousness, but even when it comes to marketing, things have changed. For one thing, music has become an important or even essential ingredient in commercials, which I will try to demonstrate in the following analysis of one particular campaign launched in the anniversary year of 2004.

The campaign in question was supposedly intended to support the gradually growing international orientation of the company, and one remarkable initiative was the changing of the company's name from *Jysk Sengetøjslager* to simply *JYSK*[7] (only in German speaking countries, the old name *Dänisches Bettenlager* is preserved[8]). Another initiative was the launch of an international commercial campaign on television, and as of April 2004 a series of five commercials was broadcasted in Denmark, Poland, Finland, Sweden and Norway. A common feature of all commercials was the appearance of a particular piece of music: i.e. the first motif from the well-known Danish community song *Jyden* (*Man from Jutland*), also known as: *Jyden han æ stærk aa sej* (*The Man from Jutland is strong and tough*). From 1990 onwards, this motif had appeared in various ways in commercials for *JYSK*, but it is the international broadcast as well as the rather unusual audiovisual embedding of the motif that stimulated an interest of the campaign from 2004.

To the casual observer, it should be no great surprise that a song with apparent flattering references to Jutlanders is used in commercials for a company named JYSK and with an owner who proudly displays his

Jutlandic origin. But what are the more detailed workings of this piece of pre-existing music, and how are the consequences of its international broadcast to be understood?

The song

Jyden han æ stærk aa sej was composed with the purpose of being sung and experienced at rallies. The song is supposed to have had its premiere at a popular gathering in Hohoej in Jutland in 1846. People from the surrounding counties were invited to involve themselves in various cultural and entertaining activities and alongside speeches, conjurers, etc., community singing had been arranged.

The more general purpose of this and similar regional gatherings between approximately 1839 and 1845 was to identify, strengthen, and develop regional identity in a period where this issue was a matter of substantial political and cultural disputes throughout Europe.

Community singing can in this respect be considered to have had a privileged *utility value* both at a *formal level* (being a means to activate people at a gathering in a shared and readily accessible activity thus potentially enhancing cohesion and community spirit) and at a *material level* (presenting specific contents most obvious via the words). The raison d'être of this type of song was its function rather than its structure and 'autonomous musical value'. In other words, non-aesthetical functions have dominated the potential aesthetical functions (inspired by Middleton 1990: 256f). The musical and verbal structuring of the song bears witness to this (as it will be elaborated on below), and, as a more curious side-story circumstances concerning the originators of the song are also worth mentioning in this respect: While it is crucial to the history of the song that the *words* originate from an celebrated Jutlander (St. St. Blicher), it is very likely of no importance that the *music* is in fact composed by a native of Fynen[9] (H. Chr. Simonsen), who also happens to be rather unknown.[10] Thus the song presents itself as originating *from* a representative of the people of Jutland composed *for* the people of Jutland.

Thereby, the song has been widely disseminated prior to its occurrence in TV commercials for JYSK, which is precisely what motivates the term pre-existing music. Pre-existing music is here characterized by not being originally composed with the purpose to appear in TV commercials, the viewers not being the 'model listeners' or 'model singers' (paraphrasing Eco's term 'model reader'). This is unquestionably the case with *Jyden*, although its actual dissemination is in fact difficult to trace. The gathering, for which the song was composed, was in fact called off due to poor attendance, which makes the exact premiere of the song uncertain.

A print of the song in the regional newspaper *Aalborg Stiftstidende*, May 11th 1849 presents the first evidence of notational dissemination. The song soon became widely recognized and it started to appear in weighty, nationwide song and melody books, as for example *Folkehøjskolesangbogen* (1st ed. 1894), *Folkehøjskolens Melodibog* (1st ed. 1922), *555 Sange* (1st ed. 1972) and *Sangbogen* (1st ed. 1988). During the 20th century, the song hereby became part of a '*sangskat*'[11] as is reproduced by the long-time Danish tradition for community singing.[12]

In summary, today, the song is known to most adult Danes, even if Jutlanders for obvious reasons are perhaps the most engaged in reproducing the song. Whether younger Danes can sing the song by heart is more doubtful. In the present day, not all school children will have the opportunity of participating in reproducing the Danish 'sangskat'. From a marketing perspective, this might not be a problem, since adults are the main target group of JYSK.

THE SONG SUNG

A closer look at the musical expression reveals that the reference and usefulness of the song is to be found in both the words and the music. The structure of the text is rather simple: Trochaic foot throughout with accented openings and endings, and end rime in the form of a-a-b-b. The song is short, presenting only three stanzas each of four lines. Also the semantics of the song are uncomplicated: flattering traits of Jutlanders (men in particular, it seems) are explicated through a number of subjective compliments (i.e. strong, tough, and brave), and implied through descriptions of specific ways in which the Jutlanders take action (calm, modest, immovable, steadfast, and durable); see figure 1 for the text in translation.

Figure 1. Text of Jyden

Blicher's original text	Present-day version in English
1. *Jyden han æ stærk å sej,* *Modde båd i nøj å næj.* *Goer ed op, å goer ed nier,* *Åller do fåtawt ham sier.*	1. *Man from Jutland is strong and tough* *Brave to all times.* *Whether is goes well or bad* *You never see him lost.*
2. *Føst næ dær æ nøe pofahr,* *Komme jyden ud å dar.* *Men han goer ett ind igjen,* *Fa' de uhn han ha gjent hen.*	2. *Not until there is trouble in sight* *Will he come out his door.* *But he will not go back in* *Until evil has been overcome.*
3. *Læ wos ålti blyw ve de!* *Fåer sin båen ka kjennes ve!* *Søen et sind da hær i Noer* *Hall sæ ve, te alt fågoer.*	3. *Let us always stick to that!* *The father is known through his sons!* *A character like that in the North* *Shall last until the end of the world.*

These traits can be considered to (have) function(ed) both as descriptions and prescriptions of the Jutlander's character. Whether these subjective compliments correspond to any historical and/or present *reality*, is of minor importance, it is the fact that they have had some *effect* that is relevant: At least, they contribute to the construction of specific social identities, reproduced via specific stereotypes and social representations of Jutland and the Jutlander. This simultaneously implies the construction of a contrasting stereotype to the Jutlander, namely the Copenhagener.[13] It is such stereotypes to which Lars Larsen refers in his autobiography and on the website.

As mentioned, the song is musically well-suited for community singing, because of its relatively undemanding and easily remembered melody.[14] A simple binary structure – A-B (with repetition of B) – is articulated, and the three stanzas are set to the same music in a strophic form. The tonal centre is G-major and the harmonic progression is simple based on the first and fifth scale degree (tonic in A and dominant in B (cf. figure 2), representing 'home' and 'on the way home', respectively).

Figure 2. Music of Jyden

When hearing the song for the first time, people today might find the song somewhat difficult:[15] Its melodic range (ambitus) is rather large (an octave plus perfect fourth, from b to e''[16]) and it is relatively high-pitched. Furthermore, the motif opens by a v-shaped contour, based on a G-major chord in 1st inversion (from tonic to third and back), which seems more challenging that a v-shaped contour based on the root position (from fifth

105

to tonic and back). But to the average Danish person, the song is stroked up fairly effortlessly, and this is also caused by the musical structure and musical practices. The melody, presenting a diatonic tonal vocabulary, is structured around a melodic skeleton articulated by the accented downbeats (indicated with circles in figure 2) – step wise *ascending* in A (otherwise characterized by broken triads), and step wise *descending* in B (otherwise characterized by stepwise motions). Thereby, the melodic range of the song, when it comes to this melodic skeleton line, proofs to be narrow (a perfect fourth, from g' to c''). As to the somewhat demanding opening motif, it must be kept in mind that the melodic style was wide-spread at the time of composition, and examples of other well-known songs representing the same motif are easily found[17] indicating that the motif is not too demanding after all.

When it comes to practices, the song is usually sung in a key pitched lower than the original G-major. In most current song-books, the song is actually transposed from G-major to F-major (e.g. *Sangbogen*). Moreover, the distinctive feature of the song is not so much its melodic contour as its rhythm, and in addition melodic punctiliousness seems less important compared to rhythmical punctiliousness and hereunder pronunciation of the words. The similitude to a march explicated in the performance direction *Tempo di marcia* supports this view (cf., apart from the broken triads dominating the melody structure already mentioned, the rhythmic structuring characteristic of marches such as punctuations and a clear accentuation of time and beat; especially noticeable in the opening stress of core traits of the Jutlander, i.e. 'strong' and 'tough'). Of course, in real life situations, the song is performed with varying phrasing and articulation, but typically it is sung in a firm and lively way.

In a wider perspective, the song seems influenced by French revolutionary music from the end of the 18th century. A well-known example, also to Danes at the time, is the *Marseillaise* from 1792. Then, the musical structuring of *Jyden* is especially supportive of the extrovert traits (*strong*, *tough*, and *brave*) as they also stand out in the opening motif, in what could be coined the *hook line* of the song.[18] What is noteworthy here is the fact that while the words explicate the special traits of the Jutlander, the music is of a much more wide, culturally appealing character. This is also apparent when compared to the aforementioned *Den tapre landsoldat*. The two songs are similar in many respects (apart form the motif discussed above also via punctuations and *tempo di marcia*) and, in both cases, the words are referring to the same specific traits (e.g. brave, strong, effective). But interestingly, the object of the reference is not the same (i.e. Danes and Jutlanders respectively), and – also highlighted by the song's affinity to the *Marseillaisen* – it becomes clear that the musical expression of *Jyden* would actually be able to work effectively for anybody familiar with the musical style and genre (and perhaps with a predilection for combating as well). On top of this comes the fact that the composer of the music is actually not a Jutlander, and eventually what is left of the Jutlander dialect in the song, is Blicher's words.

This indicates the nearly self-evident fact that different listeners (and possible singers) will approach the song differently. Thus foreigners and Danes will hear the song with different experiences: The Dane will most likely find that 'something specifically Judlandic' is being expressed, whereas the foreigner will possibly find the music to be expressive of more diffuse meanings as for example something 'heroic and determined', caused by the apparent cross-cultural musical currency. This can be perceived as an example of differences in code competences (Stefani 1987), the Danes being competent on all levels while the foreigner obviously lacks competence on the levels of *Opus* and *Social Practice* (e.g. the specific history of the song, and typical settings, uses and listening modes, respectively). The possible experience of 'heroic and determined' is caused by competence on the more general levels *General Codes* and *Musical Techniques*, presupposing, that is, the foreigners' familiarity with what could be coined 'the musical mother tongue of western people' (Middleton 1990: 175).

THE 'SONG' OF THE TV COMMERCIAL

The commercials for JYSK in the April 2004 campaign do not constitute one continuous narrative sequence. Rather, each commercial presents a variation on the same model characterized by a small narrative with a voice-over presentation. Three parts can be identified: First, an opening of the narrative in which characters and setting is presented while the plot develops up to a point of some suspense by way of one character approaching another. Then, an intermezzo of a voice-over presenting specific offers is visualized. Finally, there is a closing of the narrative in which characters respond to the approach that has kept viewers waiting in suspense during the voice-over intermezzo.

Figure 3. Rough outline of internationally broadcasted TV commercials

Part	Duration	Visuals and characteristics	Sounds; typically
1	10-12 sec.	Opening of narrative	Diegetic Jingle in solo
2	15-19 sec.	Intermezzo Presentation of materials on sale	Non-diegetic Voice-over and environmental sounds
3	3-4 sec.	Closing of narrative	Diegetic Jingle in communion

Each commercial combines dramatic as well as 'hard sell' aspects.[19] It seems reasonable to infer, though, that the narrative is dominant in that the voice-over is introduced with an apparent reference to the narrative: Just as a disclosure of JYSK as being part of the narrative comes about (cf. the showing of plastic bags with logo), the voice-over joins in with the rhetorical question: "A bargain?" addressing viewers, as an incitement for them to wonder about the possible contents of the bags simultaneously shown. Apart from translations of voice-over and text seen on screen, accommodated for each specific country, the visual and musical elements are the same across the countries in which the commercials were broadcasted. Thus, the opening motif of *Jyden* (motif a in figure 2) appears in every commercial as part of the narrative.

The motif takes the form of a jingle and it shows a high degree of distinctiveness (see chapter 2, this volume). As mentioned, this motif has been part of JYSK commercials since 1990. Thereby, the motif can be considered a *musical brand*[20] that has, in a way, acted as a supplement to Larsen's 'linguistic brand'. In the international commercials, the musical brand has replaced the linguistic brand as Larsen himself does not appear on screen. The voice-over only speaks a sort of (quite exalted) standard Danish with no particular dialectical features. A musical brand being based on pre-existing music is rather unusual, because a musical brand is typically both exclusive and unique – features, which pre-existing music lacks. But the initial categorization of the music in Jyden as pre-existing is not entirely satisfactory. In fact, as highlighted in the above discussion on code competence, not all viewers will hear 'a motif from Jyden'.

This last reservation can be elaborated through an analysis of the structural reference of commercial music to pre-existing music. *Quotation* and *paraphrasis* are two main types of referencing. Quotation of pre-existing music means that the commercial reproduces the music without any apparent modification (i.e. apart from the music being shortened), and when paraphrasing pre-existing music, the commercial reproduces the music with noticeable modifications. In cases such as the present where there is no recorded 'original' but only notational directions and oral practices, the analysis of reference is difficult. It is my argument though, that when a recorded 'original' is lacking, the issue of reference concerns conventional and widespread practices for the use of the music prior to the commercial.[21]

Because the music in JYSK commercials appears in ways that can hardly be considered to be conventional, the commercial is *paraphrasing* Jyden. The motif is played instrumental (without words), unaccompanied, by various objects (not only by conventional music instruments nor sung only by human voice) and even structurally modified (cf. tempo, rhythm and melody). In the first commercial of the campaign (to be dealt with in further detail below), the paraphrase is articulated through first a clarinet in the opening section and later by a whole symphony orchestra in the closing section. While this commercial presents the most 'musical' expression of the motif, it still appears in a much surprising manner. *Jyden* is not intended for symphony orchestra and it has never (to my knowledge) featured in a symphonic concert program. Moreover, the actual structuring of the motif is modified. Demonstratively, the last note is much delayed, and this musical caricature is supported by the bodily expressions of the clarinet player. The motif cuts off the conductor just as he sets out to conduct the orchestra, and it seems improvised, perky and cheeky to the surprise of both the conductor and the fellow musicians, apparently motivated by the conductor arriving late with bags printed with the logo of JYSK (see overview of content in figure 4). The general instrumentation and setting of the motif here entails a somewhat parodic and self-ironic expression: The otherwise non-pretentious company is lending itself and its viewers a moment of fun by having the 'down-to-earth' motif paraphrased in a setting of high-culture.

Figure 4. Overview of content of TV Commercial for JYSK

Shot	Timeline in sec.	Visuals and story line	Sound
1	0	A symphony orchestra (SO) is ready to play in a concert room.	Instruments of SO are heard warming and tuning up
2	1	A musician looks at his watch	Do.
3	3	A conductor is entering late at a side door	Do.
4	5	Close up on musician, who suddenly turns his head to look at the side door	A loud door slam. Sudden silence.
5	6	The conductor moves toward the desk in front of the SO carrying white plastic bags	Footsteps.
6	7	A clarinettist follows the conductor with his eyes and cranes his neck to get a better view of the bags	Do.
7	8	The conductor takes of his outdoor coat	
8	8	All musicians are set to play and merely await the conductor's signal, when suddenly the motif is heard. Everybody turns their head toward the origin of the motif	At first silence, but then the first notes of the motif is heard.
9	9	The conductor stops and turns toward the clarinettist	Middle parts of the motif are heard.
10	10	The clarinettist is seen playing the last few notes of the motif looking directly at the conductor	The last few notes of the motif are heard.
11	12	The conductor is seen self-conscious looking down at his bags, which is printed with the logo of JYSK	As the logo is visualized, a voice-over commences[22]: "A bargain?...[pause]...
12	16	Display of garden furniture on terrace	..."Right! JYSK celebrates its 25th anniversary. For example a wooden table with four chairs for only 1500 kroner...

continued on the next page ...

| 13 | 21 | Display of garden furniture on terrace | ...*Or a plastic table with four five-position chairs – now only 950 kroner. Offers are good Monday, Tuesday and Wednesday.* |
| 14 | 26 | The conductor is conducting the orchestra on a visual background of logo, slogan and website address. | *JYSK; always a bargain*". The motif is heard played by full orchestra. |

Taking a closer look at the narrative, the motif can be considered to function as an *interpellation*.[23] The conductor is addressed as someone else than he is dressed up for (even though the interpellation is not quite unwarranted, in that he carries bags from JYSK). In a terminology inspired by Goffman, the conductor is positioned *out of character* – as someone shopping in JYSK (and as someone who is late) – and he abruptly finds himself being *out of face* (Goffman 1967: 5ff). Only after a moment of surprise, and subsequent self-conscious gestures, he realises what is happening. At this point, precisely when the conductor become conscious of the interpellation, the opening of the narrative is succeeded by an intermezzo in which offers of the week – a selection of garden furniture – are presented directly to the television audience in voice-over, pictures, text and sound effects.

As the concluding part of the narrative shows, the action has developed further. It appears as if the narrative has continued during the intermezzo, and the conductor and all musicians have now gathered for a collective musical expression. Acknowledging the interpellation, the conductor for a moment adopts the motif in his authoritative activity, and the motif is played in a flourishing fanfare-like style.[24] The characters of the narrative can be considered to produce a new and higher levelled group identification marked by the collective playing of the motif, namely 'customers of JYSK' (the previous and more specific group identification being '(waiting) musicians at work').

In bringing the commercial to an end, the grandiose playing of the motif has several functions: It emphasizes an affirmative closing of the narrative; it celebrates the offers of the week, and, gaily decorated, the motif is presented to international and new Danish viewers. The remaining commercials of the campaign are broadcasted in the following months, and the motif is heard played and sung in different ways (by car horns, a parrot, people at a bus stop, and street musicians; se more below). On a general level the campaign seems to imply that *anybody* is a possible target of interpellation and hence of becoming *somebody* (a customer in JYSK) in a process that can happen *anywhere anytime*.

With this analysis another noteworthy feature of the motif is touched upon. By appearing diegetic (heard by the characters of the narrative), the motif brings about a range of unusual communicative functions. Typically, jingles address their audience directly (and most often together with a logo presentation at the end, see chapter 2 this volume), but in the present case, the jingles are only *indirectly* addressing its audience. Thus, the jingle is embedded in the narrative as a determining element, and it positions the gallery of characters in a surprising and humorous way. The musical interpellation marks everyday situations with sounds of JYSK and to their surprise[25] people are moulded into customers in JYSK. In all situations, the interpellation is spontaneous and unpretentious: A car toots the motif out of tune, a man 'tra-la-la's the motif, a parrot stutters the motif in a melodic variation of the root position (from fifth to tonic and back, cf. analysis above). One of the consequences of these variations is the motif being musically freed from its harmonic root, thus standing out rounded, even when lacking a harmonic cadence. With this, the motif resembles the casual and non-specific whistling with which one can amuse oneself in moments of cheerfulness.

On top of the somewhat unrealistic nature of the actions depicted in the commercials, these frank and cheerful paraphrases allow the commercial use of *Jyden* to pass without audiences being too upset and angered. Normally, the re-mediating of pre-existing music in commercials would entail such hazards (e.g. English & Pennell 1994), but the use of *Jyden* seems properly balanced in a way that allows Danes (including both Jutlanders and Copenhageners) to smile at the humorous and self-ironic staging. In a marketing perspective, this re-mediation of *Jyden* thus presents a successful commercial 'colonization' of a well-known song.

Even though most Danish viewers might not have knowledge of all details of the song's history, most Danes would effortlessly (perhaps also involuntarily) identify the motif and the, in fact, non-present words. In this manner, the motif functions as a metonym for the entire song. Considering the audiovisual embedding of the motif, it can be argued that specific potentials for signification are made salient and realized (Cook 1998), and, as mentioned above, especially the *opus*-level is involved. However, it must be acknowledged that the potential for signification cannot be exhaustively codified and formularized. While it is reasonable to suggest that pre-existing music has exceptional, and to some extent, well defined potentials for signification when it comes to the level of *opus* (even if accepting difficulties of tracking down the musical original and its history, as discussed above), still it is important to have keep in mind that pre-existing music represents more than just an opus-level. Different and perhaps unanticipated (from the encoders point of view) significations are possibly depending not least on the particular context and code competences of the decoder.

FUNCTIONS OF COMMUNICATION

When elaborating the musical signification of commercials, the concept of *communication functions* proves constructive. In his theory of the communication process, Jakobson (1960) has distinguished a range of communicative functions, which has in turn been related by Middleton to popular music (Middleton 1990: 239ff). This model is helpful in taking account of the often complex and wide-ranging dimensions involved in communication, and specifically it highlights six dimensions, namely sender, text, context, message, channel, code and receiver. For the examination of the commercials in question, it is important to consider these dimensions in connection with the narrative, the intermezzo as well as with the genre. As a whole, the commercial consists of two parts presenting very different forms of communication. The intermezzo presents a traditional and factual addressing of the receiver dominated by the *conative* function: The voice-over puts forward a series of imperatives involving bits of information (e.g. "save x-amount of kroner") and reminders (e.g. "keep in mind"). In contrast, the narrative opening and closing of the commercial presents a much more nuanced spectrum of communicative functions.

The *emotive* function serves to express the 'sender's' state of mind or opinions. This function can be associated with both the gallery of characters and with JYSK as an unpretentious and decent company. In the narrative, characters are expressing themselves to each other via the motif, articulated in the beginning by a facetious interpellating individual, and, in the closing part, the unison motif symbolizing the group identity that has momentarily emerged. When it comes to the *conative* function the communicative process is in a way twofold. Internally (within the narrative), the motif functions as a call for the characters to identify and recognize themselves as customers in JYSK. Externally (addressing TV viewers), the motif functions more implicitly as an invitation for viewers to perceive themselves as included in the closing manifestation of a group identity. Also the viewer is reminded to think of and feel JYSK as an uncomplicated, 'natural', Jutlandic (as identified by Danes) company.

This last-mentioned point also has obvious relevance for the *referential* function: i.e. the message's way of representing an external context. Whereas the motif for most Danes works as a metonym for the song *Jyden*, a foreigner will most likely hear the motif without the stereotypical cultural references, previously discussed. More likely so, the foreigner will hear a light and cheerful melody, to be sung to and by anybody shopping in JYSK. The reference to the company JYSK is of course in both cases – for Danes as well as foreigners – apparent, in that the motif appears in association with an obvious visual display of the logo: firstly in connection to the showing of plastic bags with printed logo, and secondly in connection to the showing of the logo on the screen. Compared to all other aspects of the narrative, the reference to *Jyden* is far from obvious, in that there is no clear indication of the gallery of characters being for example Jutlanders in Jutland performing specifically Jutlandish actions.

Being played without being sung, what the motif brings to the commercial is actually – and somewhat ironically – a melodic fragment of Fionian origin. Sometimes, as a matter of fact, it is the absent part that has significance (cf. Stigel 1993): the non-appearance of Blicher's text renders the motif meaningful to Danish viewers, and at the same time it allows foreign viewers to decode the commercial as well. However, as already hinted at, the decoding by foreigners has different premises and consequences compared to the decoding by Danish viewers.

With relevance, it seems, to the *poetic* function of the motif, it is only viewers familiar with the song (mostly Danes), who will hear what is not there, so to speak, and these viewers are privileged – highly code competent – in being able to decode the 'creative' play with the words and history of the song. Danish viewers are well prepared to appreciate the self-ironic nature of the motif use, whereas foreigners will be restricted to the experience of an unusual and humorous use of a jingle. At any rate, the poetic function seems to contribute to the interpellation of a relatively sophisticated viewer, and, symptomatic of the genre as such, the level of sophistication is not higher than allowing most viewers to grasp the ironic and/or humorous play.

The motif being 'light and cheerful' emphasizes the *phatic* function of the message. Each member of the audience can connect to the message via the motif that is played twice in each commercial, in different successive commercials, and with a high degree of 'jingleness' (short, melodic, catchy). Finally, the *meta-lingual* function is apparent through the commercials' paraphrasing of tertiary texts. Thus the commercial dramatizes the unusual phenomenon of commercial expressions becoming part of everyday interaction among viewers (cf. the history of Larsen's early commercial success, discussed above), and the primary text in this case absorbs tertiary texts. In fact, this might also present an example of the poetic functioning of the commercial, which is apparent only to viewers familiar with the history of commercials for JYSK.

CONCLUSIONS

The case of JYSK's use of a fragment of *Jyden* presents a highly particular example of a *jingle* and a *musical brand*. Certainly, some of the phenomena and characteristics discussed can be found in other contemporary commercials and as an example it is not uncommon that jingles vary across different commercials, and that previously sung jingles later on become instrumental. However, the JYSK jingle is extraordinary in two respects. Firstly, this jingle is based on pre-existing music. Secondly, it serves a diegetic function. Moreover, the jingle's use in an international campaign refines and further complicates the musical signification of the commercial.

This aspect could be summed up in the following way: Some viewers will hear something specific, which is, in a way, absent. For most Danes the reference to *Jyden* will come to mind even if it is only represented in paraphrased and metonymic terms. Other viewers will hear something else than what in fact is present: Viewers not familiar with the song will hear what they might think is an original jingle, a rounded opus of commercial music.

In a functional perspective, it is interesting how a regional symbol of identity intended to *exclude* all those not belonging to a constructed in-group, can come to function as an international symbol of a company intended to *include* everybody as 'JYSK customers'. From originally expressing general ideas of 'someone in particular', the music of the commercials helps pointing out an exemplified 'anybody'. Central to this process is the musical interpellation. While interpellation might be a defining feature of all commercial music, calling upon individual viewers to identify themselves as potential consumers, the motif in commercials for JYSK functions more indirectly and subtle than usually. Thus, the motif is both dramatically filtered and musically varied.

Notes

1. JYSK is a Danish based, worldwide supplier of bedding materials, articles for the bathroom and living room, etc. The company has approximately 1350 stores in about 30 countries (2008).
2. Being some of the first on nationally produced TV, these commercials were broadcasted in the autumn of 1987 on the regional channel *TV-Syd*. Later on, from the autumn 1988, they were broadcasted on national Danish commercial TV as well (i.e. on TV 2).
3. Translated by the author from: "Jeg – Dyne Larsen – kommer til verden – lille og spinkel, men ellers ved godt mod". Soon after the broadcast of the early commercials, Quilts-Larsen grew into his nickname.
4. Translated by the author from: "*troværdigt og solidt og ikke for dyrt*".
5. Cf. www.jysk.com.
6. Translated by the author from: "*storhedsvanvid*".
7. '*Jysk Sengetøjslager*' translates approximately to '*Jutlandic stock of bed linens*'. '*Jysk*' functions both as an adjective (a designator of geographical origin and affiliation implying certain traits), and as a substantivized adjective (referring to the dialect often spoken by Jutlanders).
8. Possibly also due to the historically somewhat strained relationship between indeed Jutlanders and Germans, the reference 'Danish' seems more appropriate for Germans; see more below.
9. Fynen or Fionia, a big island in Denmark between Jutland and Zealand.

10 When it comes to the art lied, the composer is the main attraction, as implied.

11 This concept translates approximately to 'treasured songs'. It is a relatively unspecific and informal concept referring to appreciated community songs for and about Danes and their (imagined) culture and nature.

12 Community singing refers to a tradition of having secular, not musically motivated affairs (e.g. societies, clubs, schools, private anniversaries) include the singing of commonly known and appreciated songs in unison by all participants.

13 Blicher's words are aimed as a tribute to the Jutlander presenting a safeguard against Germany (why an appearance of the song in German commercials would have been quite ironic). Even though more outspoken since, already at the time the Copenhagener had been identified as a contrasting character, who would then be defined antonymic as inconstant, not accountable for his actions, etc. The process of stereotyping that takes place in relations like these can be considered from a social psychological point of view as the construction of group prototypes involving both an in-group (Jutlanders) and an out-group (Copenhageners). According to *self-categorization theory*, the process can be described as a minimizing of intra-group differences and a simultaneous maximizing of inter-group differences – coined as the *meta-contrast principle* (Turner 1987: 44ff). Moreover, formations of in- and out-groups can be identified on different levels, allowing the Jutlanders to be part of higher levelled categories (e.g. Danes vs. Germans) and to be differentiated in subcategories (e.g. Jutlanders from the North vs. Jutlanders from the West).

14 The song is composed with an accompaniment (cf. figure 2) but following the relative low importance of the accompaniment to the song's quality and dissemination, the accompaniment shall not be examined in any detail.

15 Not to discourage the reader, who at this point is invited to sight-read the song (cf. figure 2).

16 On figure 2 marked as 'Bundtone' and 'Toptone', respectively.

17 An illustrative example is the song *Den tapre landsoldat* from 1848. The song has been described as an "overwhelming hit" of the time (Bak 2005: 108) and it opens with a motif very similar to the opening motif of Jyden (only difference is the motif of Jyden not presenting an upbeat).

18 Part B's comparatively subdued and rounded expression might be considered to be illustrative of the more introvert traits (calm, modest).

19 See typology in Stigel 2001. The TV commercials for JYSK have elements of both *drama* and *voice-over*.

20 A musical brand is defined here as a piece of music appearing consistently across different media and throughout each media (for more see chapter 2, this volume).

21 The specific boundaries between quotation and paraphrasis are sometimes somewhat blurred. This has to do with the music's 'main mode of storage and distribution', which, according to Tagg, can be one of three: 'oral transmission', 'musical notation', or 'recorded sound' (Tagg 1979: 34ff). To what extent these might in fact be comparable to specific genres (e.g. folk music, art music and popular music, respectively) shall not be dealt with here (see Talbot 2000 for more on possible specifications of musical originals and 'works'), but obviously, compared to 'recorded sound', 'oral' and 'notational' transmitted music are harder to specify as quotation.

22 Translated by the author from: "Et godt tilbud? Ja, JYSK fejrer 25 års jubilæum. For eksempel med foldebord i AVC hårdttræ med fire foldestole nu kun femtenhundrede kroner.

Eller et bord i plast med fire fempositionsstole nu kun 950 kroner. Tilbuddene gælder kun mandag, tirsdag og onsdag".

23 To name the process by which individuals are subjected and positioned by being addressed or 'hailed' (Althusser 1971).

24 The analyzed TV commercial are not available for inspection on YouTube, but see the following address for a Swedish TV commercial for JYSK in which the orchestrated jingle is heard at the end (cf: www.youtube.com/watch?v=Yfs_Col0m6g&feature=related). See also this rather ironic (and somewhat amusing) 'instruction' for guitar-amateurs: www.youtube.com/watch?v=Es2Ks3MxlHw.

25 Apparently none of the people involved are able to ignore or refuse the interpellation (in line with Althusser's somewhat criticisable description of the general imperative workings of interpellations; cf. that viewers and consumers might be understood as more *reflexive* and *knowledgeable* beings, as for example argued in Giddens 1991). In another commercial this is pushed to an extreme: When passing a pet shop, a woman is hailed by an appreciating whistling parrot. While almost ignoring this first interpellation (only a small smile on her face unveils that she heard the parrot) – that seeks to position her as an attractive, sexual being – the parrot's second interpellation (the motif from Jyden) provokes her immediate attention: She stops and wonders, and then she realizes – together with the audience – that she is carrying bags from JYSK.

REFERENCES

Althusser, L. (1971). Ideology and ideological state apparatuses. In L. Althusser (Ed.), *Lenin and philosophy and other essays* (pp. 123-173). London: New Left Books.

Bak, K. S. (2005). Fællessang og danskhed [Community singing and Danishness]. In J. H. Koudal (Ed.). *Musik og danskhed*. København: C.A. Reitzels Forlag.

Cook, N. (1998). *Analysing musical multimedia*. Oxford: Oxford University Press.

Englis, B., & Pennell, G. (1994). "This note's for you": Negative effects of the commercial use of popular music. *Advances in Consumer Research, 21*, 97.

Giddens, A (1991). *Modernity and self-identity – Self and society in the late modern age*. Cambridge: Polity Press.

Goffman, E. (1967). *Interaction ritual – Essays on face-to-face behavior*. New York: Pantheon Books.

Jakobson, R. (1960). Closing statement: Linguistics and poetics. In Th. Sebeok (Ed.), *Style and Language* (pp. 350-377). Cambridge: MIT Press.

Larsen, L. (2004). *Go'daw jeg hedder Lars Larsen – jeg har et godt tilbud* [Hi' there, my name is Lars Larsen – I have a special offer for you]. Århus: Hansen Mejlgade.

Middleton, R. (1990). *Studying popular music*. Milton Keynes: Open University Press.

Nygaard, B. (1989). Lars Larsen – en bombe i underbevidstheden [Lars Larsen – A subconscious bomb]. *MedieKultur, 10*, 92-102.

Stefani, G. (1987). A theory of musical competence. *Semiotica, 66*, 7-22.

Stigel, J. (1991). Ten seconds of advertising make a long story. Genre as an important part of meaning in advertising. In Ch. Alsted et al. (Ed.), *Marketing and Semiotics: The Copenhagen Symposium* (pp. 196-210). København: Nyt Nordisk Forlag.

Stigel, J. (1993). Det vigtigste er som regel det, der ikke er der: Om kulturproduktion, reklame og propaganda [Sometimes the most important thing is the thing not present: On production of culture, commercials and propaganda]. In J.F. Jensen, T. Rasmussen, & J. Stigel (Eds.), *Reklame – kultur* (pp. 17-54). Aalborg: Aalborg Universitetsforlag.

Stigel, J. (2001). The aesthetics of Danish tv-spot-commercials. A study of Danish TV-commercials in the 1990'ies. In F. Hansen & L. Y. Hansen (Eds.), *Advertising Research in the Nordic Countries* (pp 327-350). København: Samfundslitteratur.

Tagg, Ph. (1979). *Kojak – 50 seconds of television music*. Göteborg. Musikvetenskapliga Institutionen.

Talbot, M. (2000). *The musical work: Reality or invention*. Liverpool: Liverpool University Press.

Turner, J. C. (1987). *Rediscovering the social group – a self-categorization theory*. Oxford: Blackwell.

MUSIC VIDEOS AND TV COMMERCIALS
Similarities and differences

Erkki Pekkilä

In 1981, the American media corporation Warner-Amex launched MTV, a TV channel whose programming was based on a 24-hour format. The programmes consisted of music videos, TV commercials, channel identifications, and DJ announcements. Already then, a number of scholars observed that the music videos on the channel were related to TV commercials. Aufderheide (1986: 111) claimed that music videos removed the difference between a commercial and a programme. Kaplan (1985: 5) noted that the music videos were adopting the stylistic elements of TV commercials. Kinder (1987: 6) said that MTV's programming is an unbroken series of events in which one cannot distinguish between a TV program and a TV commercial. Advertisers soon realized the new channel's potential. One of the first attempts to merge music videos and TV commercials was a remake of Robert Palmer's music video "Simply irresistible" in 1989. The Pepsi company hired Palmer to advertise their products, reshot the video as a 30-second commercial and changed the lyrics into the Pepsi slogan "It's irresistible".[1]

The American brewery Anheuser-Busch took the exploitation of music videos even further. In 1985-1987, the company ran an advertising campaign based on a night theme, and the campaign slogan was "The Night Belongs to Michelob". The campaign was planned by DDB Needham Worldwide Inc., an advertising company managed by James H. Harris. As spokesmen for the product, some of the most famous rock stars of the time were engaged, including Phil Collins, Eric Clapton, and Steve

Winwood. The stars, all of British origin and representing mainstream rock, wrote the songs used in the campaign. Eric Clapton, for instance, wrote *After Midnight*, which also appeared on Clapton's recording.[2] Even though it was originally written for a commercial, *After Midnight* won a Grammy in the United States in 1988. (Anonymous 2006).

In my chapter, I will examine a song composed by Steve Winwood for the Michelob beer campaign.[3] Entitled *Don't you know what the night can do?*, the song was used both in a TV commercial and in a "real" song, later released on the album *Roll with it* (1988). Even though it may not be unusual for an existing rock song to be used as a TV jingle, what is exceptional here is that Winwood's song was in fact intended for a commercial. When Winwood went on tour in 1988 to advertise the album in the United States, he was granted a sponsorship contract with Michelob and Anheuser-Busch. As a result, Michelob beer ads appeared on Winwood's tour posters.

Winwood's song had some measure of success, since *Don't you know what the night can do?* was, at one point, fourth on the British charts and sixth on the U.S. charts. However, fans did not seem to like the campaign. Because the commercial came out before the album *Roll with It*, Winwood had a lot of explaining to do. His sponsorship deal with Michelob prompted cries of "Sell out!", and Winwood had to justify why he composed music for a beer commercial (Anonymous 2007, Stillwell 2007b). At the same time, the campaign did not seem to be very successful from the advertiser's point of view either. One company employee, Jim Schumacker, said afterwards: "I have to admit disappointment in the response to our 'The Night Belongs to Michelob' campaign back in the '80s. It had all the elements [of a hit]: top production values, big music names like Frank Sinatra and Phil Collins, a great slogan. In the end that campaign proved to have no effect on Michelob sales at all." (Abraham 2002: 77).

Perhaps for this reason, marketing rock songs through TV commercials did not become widespread. However, Winwood's case is an interesting one for comparing the similarities and differences between music videos and TV commercials. Furthermore, even though Winwood's song is already relatively old, both the music video and the TV commercial (at least one of its many versions) have had a new lease on YouTube.

WINWOOD

For those who are not familiar with Steve Winwood (b. 1948), he is a British-born rhythm-and-blues artist, a singer-song writer who plays keyboard and the guitar. Winwood came to prominence in the 1960s as a member of the Spencer Davis Group, the Traffic and Blind Faith. Winwood is also a songwriter and the author of such well-known songs as *Gimme Some Lovin'* and *I'm a Man*. Many of Winwood's songs and especially *Gimme some lovin'* have been used in a number of films, including John Landis's *Blues Brothers* (1980), Lawrence Kasdan's *The Big Chill* (1983) or Ron Howard's *EdTv* (1999). (See Covach 2007).

The music of "Don't you know what the night can do?" was composed by Steve Winwood, and its lyrics written by Will Jennings. As mentioned, it was included on the album *Roll with it* released in 1988 by Virgin Records. Even though it is difficult to verify, it seems reasonable to suggest that Winwood and Jennings first wrote the song (with subsequent recording), and after this, the music video based on the song was filmed. However, neither the song nor the music video was released at this point. That the TV commercial was made last is quite obvious because it features some footage taken from the music video. At this point, the song was cut into a 30 second jingle with a number of omissions that I am going to discuss later. It does not seem plausible that Winwood and Jennings had consciously written a jingle nor that the advertising agency had influenced the lyrics. However, it is possible that the advertising agency may have had some influence on the nightly theme of the song that so nicely fits in the slogan of their advertising campaign, "The night belongs to Michelob". Due to a marketing strategy, the TV commercial was introduced first, well before Winwood's song was released.

The song, in A-minor and 4/4 time played in medium tempo, contains an introduction, two verses, a chorus and a coda. The form can be reduced to the scheme Intro + AABC + AABC + repetition of Intro + Coda. It begins with an eight bar introduction on the chords A minor and E minor, with A in the bass, but without any melodic material. The first verse (A), in C major, based on a two-bar motif repeated three times and concluded on the fourth. The whole verse is then repeated from the beginning to the end, with minor variations.

Ex. 1. Fragment of the first verse.

[Musical notation: C and F chords with lyrics "Feel the night music play - ing"]

The second verse (B) is also in A minor. It is based on a four-bar, question-and-answer motif, twice repeated. The purpose of the verse seems to be to guide the listener to the chorus, which is the most exciting part of the song, because it turns into the climax. The chorus starts with a two-bar, pre-hook motif, carried out by chord changes. After the pre-hook, a two-bar motif starts during which the hook line of the song, with the words "Don't you know what the night can do?" is being sung. The line is repeated three times.

Ex. 2. Fragment of the chorus.

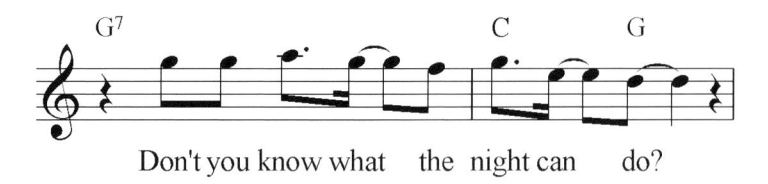

[Musical notation: G^7, C, and G chords with lyrics "Don't you know what the night can do?"]

In the coda, a women's choral group repeats the key-phrase "Don't you know what the night can do" over and over again, Winwood improvising with nonsense syllables and vowels.

THE LYRICS

The lyrics of the song are typical rock song lyrics. The place is undefined, whereas the time is obviously night-time. Verse A contains a number of suggestions that the imaginary "I" or the singer makes to the imaginary "you" or the listener. The singer tells the other person to listen to the music and to what is being said, to feel the music and the beat within.

In verse B, the singer expresses what happens if the other person agrees: dreams come true, there is only you and I, it feels so good, and it feels like flying. Even though the lyrics are somewhat vague, it is obvious that they carry sexual connotations. On a website, relating to Winwood, some female fans have noted that one of the lines is "naughty" as it says "Feel the music inside you, I'll be there too". (See Anonymous 2007).

At this point, we might introduce the term "hook" which is a known and commonly used concept in popular music. A hook is usually defined as a musical idea that stands out in a pop song and is regarded as appealing by the listeners. Burns (1987: 1) who worked out a taxonomy of musical hooks, has also consulted a number of books written by professional song writers to learn what they have to say about hooks. According to them, a hook in a pop song is "what you are selling" and it may consist of a series of notes, a lyric phrase, full lines or even an entire verse. Danceable rhythm, melody that is easily remembered and lyrics containing some dramatic action or denoting that a person or place are important. Actually, as Burns shows in his article, almost any musical element in a pop song can be used as a hook. However, in this case it clearly seems that the hook in Winwood's and Jenning's song lies in the lyrics and especially in the chorus.

The chorus consists of the song's so-called hook line, and the phrase "Don't you know what the night can do?", is repeated three times. One might speculate that Winwood wanted to ensure that the listener would remember the name of the song since the line is sung some fourteen times. The name of the song also appears in written form both in the beginning and at the end of the music video. Finally, the phrase has a connection to the "night" theme that Michelob was using in the advertising campaign, the slogan of which was "The night belongs to Michelob".

The lyrics are the starting point of the song and they represent the primary level of meaning. The visuals of the music video represent the second level, the visuals presenting an interpretation of what is being said in the song. However, because popular music is based on stardom, the representation of the star is important. In as much as the video is a commentary to the song, it is also a commentary to the image of the star.

The video

The video consists of 161 brief shots, approximately two seconds each. Steve Winwood appears in a number of the shots, many of them emphasizing that Winwood is a star and a singer-song writer. Also, Winwood's name appears in the credits in the beginning of the video, and he is seen throughout the video walking outdoors, sitting on a bed and singing or writing notes on a sheet of music paper. The outfit he is wearing – a leather jacket and a white T-shirt – is identical to what is seen on his record cover and also on the tour posters. Thus, it is quite obvious that he is not only singing but also advertising himself, his record and his tour.

The setting in the video suits the Winwood rock star image very well. Winwood is known as a wonder child who started his career at the age of sixteen. He is a British musician singing blues in the same style as Afro-Americans. The Indian reservation showing elderly Indians, dogs, hens and old cartwheels fits the blues image, as all of these symbols represent authenticity.

The same visual motifs are repeated a number of times. For instance, the shot of the singer's fingers on a keyboard is shown approximately ten to fifteen times, and the same applies to the other central shots. Some of the shots are very short, only half a second in length, and the cuts become faster towards the end of the video. Many of the shots are out of focus, making it difficult to understand what they mean. The visual elements are often commentaries to the song, especially to its lyrics. For instance, during the instrumental introduction, fingers on a keyboard are shown. When the song lyrics say "Hear the night music playing", there is a shot of a hand writing musical notes on a sheet of music paper.

Even though the visuals often seem to be a commentary to the song lyrics, it is very difficult to say what the song or the video is about. It takes several seconds for a vocalist to sing one line of text, whereas many of the shots are very short, only half a second, and unfocused. Sometimes, there are a number of different shots on screen. For instance, while the vocalist sings "Don't you know what it's saying", we see a dancing girl, the singer sitting on a bed, a man and a woman close together, and an inside view of a hotel room.

These elements give rise to a number of different readings. Is the singer telling a story about himself? Have these events happened to him?

Is it Winwood, himself, who is with the woman? We are at a liberty to interpret the video as we want. Likewise, when the singer asks whether the imaginary "you" in the song knows what the night music is saying and, says that you should feel it with him, the visuals show a man and woman first dancing close together and then preparing for a kiss.

BREAKDOWN NOTES

A literary way of analyzing the video is to work out the so-called "breakdown notes", which music editors usually write as musical cues for a scene. If we distinguish between the processes of production and reception, the breakdown notes represent a level between these two. This is close to what Nattiez (1975: 54-55) has called "niveau neutre" or neutral level which does not necessarily have anything to do with the intentions of the composer ("poiesis") or those of the listener ("esthesis"). In the breakdown notes, comments are added according to what is seen on the screen. The abbreviations are as follows: Close-up (CU), medium close-up (MCU) and telephoto-shot (TS).[4]

MUSIC: INTRODUCTION (Bars 1-8)

Shot	Time	Visuals
1	0'00	Bare skin. (CU)
2	0'01	Fingers moving on a keyboard. (CU)
3	0'02	Bare skin, unfocused. (CU)
4	003	Face of an old Indian man, sitting with a Stetson in his head, eyes closed, head down. (CU)
5	0'05	Fingers on a keyboard. (CU)
6	0'06	Singer's body and side profile, unfocused, at the bottom the caption "Steve Winwood. 'Don't you know what the night can do'. Roll with it. Virgin records." (CU)
7	0'07	Blazing fire and human figures, unfocused, the caption remaining on the bottom. (MCU)
8	0'10	The torso of a dancing male figure, the caption remaining on the bottom. (MCU).

continued on the next page ...

9	0'10	A sheet of music on the table; a hand with a pen is drawing a note. The caption disappears. (CU).
10	0'14	Winwood, wearing a leather jacket and white T-shirt, is sitting on a bed; he looks down, and then turns his eyes to the left. A bed, bedside table and desk lamp are seen behind. (MCU).
11	0'14	Fingers on a keyboard. (CU).
12	0'19	Blazing fire and the wall of a building. (TS).
13	0'20	A torso of a dancing man, unfocused. (MCU).

THE STORY

On the basis of the breakdown notes, we may end up with a literary reading of the music video. This is naturally a hypothetical reading, since it is based on literary descriptions of the video's content. In a natural viewing situation, the video is obviously received differently, i.e. in a particular situation in time and space. Besides, many of the visual details that can be observed in slow motion cannot be seen when the video is shown at normal speed. In any event, a literary description of the video's contents might be as follows: "The famous singer, Steve Winwood (or possibly the character he is playing in the video), is staying overnight in a hotel in an Indian reservation. He becomes a witness to an event about which he writes a song. In the reservation, an outdoor festival takes place by the fire. A young man, who has arrived in his pick-up truck to participate in the festival, has an affair with a young girl who lives in the reservation. The following morning, the man leaves in his truck, the girl stays in the village and watches him leave. The singer leaves the village on a bus."

Seen this way, the story seems to be synchronized with the music. The song consists of an introduction, two verses, a chorus, a bridge and a coda. In the video, the narration proceeds so that the introduction and first verse form an introduction to the narrative after which the narrative unfolds.

The story – if there is one – is not told chronologically but rather with flashbacks and forward flashes. When we analyze the scenes from the breakdown notes, we can go back and forth as we like. However, as we watch the video, it takes place in a time continuum. However, this kind of analysis evokes a number of questions. For instance, we may ask whether the singer is a witness to what is being seen or whether the events are based on his imagination and the song he has written. Is this a story about the singer himself when he was younger? Is there any connection between the young man and the young woman in the video?

Music	Visuals	Time
Introduction	Visual introduction	
A	In a hotel room	Nighttime (undefined)
A	Outdoors	The previous afternoon
B	Outdoors	The following morning
C	Indoors at a party	The following night
A	Outdoors	The following morning
A	Outdoors	The following morning
B	Outdoors	The previous morning
C	Indoors at a party	The previous night
Bridge	Outdoors at a party.	The previous night
Coda	Outdoors at a party	The previous night

It is also possible that there is no story but that the video is intentionally ambiguous so that anyone can project their own meanings into it as it is often the case with song lyrics. Song lyrics are also ambiguous. In normal circumstances, the video is an audio-visual text that is consumed on a "here and now" basis. When the viewer watches the video, it is quite impossible to understand all the brief shots, flashbacks and forward flashes.

Even though the video's narrative is to some extent linked to the flow of music and musical structures, the visual narrative does not move chronologically. The narrative scenes are thus interrupted with scenes or shots representing events before or after the action seen, that is, with forward flashes and flashbacks. To understand the story, the viewer should mentally skip some scenes, keep some others in mind and then reorganize everything – which is impossible to do.

The lyrics and the visuals

There seems to be five kinds of shots in the video. Firstly, there are shots of Winwood walking outdoors, sitting in a hotel room, writing music, playing a keyboard instrument, standing in a doorway – and singing. In the scenes where Winwood sings – even though this is clearly a playback performance – the music becomes diegetic. From these shots we know that Winwood is a star and that he is a singer-song writer. Winwood is also wearing the same outfit as on the record cover. Besides singing, he is also advertising the new album.

Secondly, there are shots of elderly Indians. The video was filmed on an American Indian reservation. The visual images of Indians force a distinction between "white men and Indians". The Indians are also a symbol of authenticity. Their old age signifies wisdom and experience. In fact, Indians suit the blues image well because both blues and Indians represent authenticity. Moreover there are a number of shots of a blazing fire, people dancing by the fire and a profile of the singer with a fire burning in the background. Fire is also a natural element. One can easily imagine fire on an Indian reservation. Furthermore, fire represents passion.

Thirdly, as the video unfolds, there are shorts of a couple dancing, the male character not wearing a shirt. We can see that this character is not Winwood. However, there is also a shot of Winwood by the fire without a shirt, and viewers might thus easily confuse him with this other male character. The fourth kind of shots encompasses shots of a young girl in a bikini top, washing her hair under a water tap and looking directly into the camera. Finally, the fifth kind of shots is characterized by shots of some vehicles arriving and departing. There are shots of somebody driving a pick-up truck while another person is tossing suitcases onto the roof of a bus, obviously signifying that somebody is about to leave.

The music video has been put together from a very limited selection of visual material. It would appear that when the video was shot, there was neither manuscript nor any fixed story. Rather, the video makers have evidently filmed scenes in different locations and ultimately put the video together by montage. It is thus quite natural that the video story is unclear and shows gaps, and it seems clear that it has been purposefully left to the viewer to uncover or make up the meaning of the story.

Connotative meanings

The video also represents a connotative level of meanings with a number of symbols evoking different kinds of associations, based on cultural mythology. For instance, the singer wears jeans and a leather jacket, clothing that often denotes masculinity and a white horse symbolizes sexuality. Furthermore, there is a fire, often associated with passion, and sheets drying on a clothesline are perhaps – in the context – implying sex. Other symbols can be seen, often associated with the countryside or authenticity, such as a dog, old cartwheels, aged Indians. Thus the mythical reading that these symbols evoke may be even more important than the "logical" or literary reading that can be derived from a written description of the video.

This situation brings to mind what John Fiske has pointed at regarding meanings that consumers themselves create. Fiske (1989: 103-104) worked out the concept of "producerly texts" from what Barthes calls "readerly" and "writerly" texts. According to Barthes, a readerly text is something that is simple and easy to read. It invites a passive reader, one who accepts the meanings of the text as being established already. Opposed to this is a writerly text, which is difficult to read and which constantly challenges the reader to rewrite and make sense of it. Fiske's "producerly text" is a combination of these two. The text is not necessarily difficult, but it tempts the reader to "rewrite" it and to project one's own meaning onto the text.

It does not seem very plausible that there was any decent script when the video was filmed. It seems instead that the video makers just shot some footage outdoors, indoors and by the fire, and that the music video was then put together later on from these bits and pieces. The video is purposefully left vague so that everyone can project their own meanings into it, just as it is often the case in song lyrics, as mentioned earlier. It could be said that what is seen in the music video is not a complete story because there are too many gaps. Rather, what are being shown are building blocks that invite the viewer to build up a story of some kind. Some of the shots are, without any obvious logic, shot in black and white, which presents an additional mystery to solve. Still, the video clearly gives an impression that there is a hidden narrative. Laden with symbols, the video presents a challenge to the viewer who perhaps is intrigued and wants to understand what the video is about.

THE MICHELOB BEER ADVERTISEMENT

Even though it is based on the same music, Winwood's TV commercial differs significantly from the music video. The setting has been totally changed and the countryside landscape has been replaced by a cityscape. The commercial takes place at night time in a city – both on a street and inside a bar.

The storyline in the commercial is, if anything, even more obscure compared to the music video. The commercial consists of sketches of people having fun while drinking beer. If the commercial is viewed at normal speed, it is quite difficult to tell what it is about. However, as with the music video, we can also make breakdown notes of the TV commercial in the following manner.

Nr	Time	Visuals	Music	Commentary
1	'00	On the TV screen, Steve Winwood, dressed in a leather jacket and white T-shirt, is seen walking outdoors. At the bottom left of the screen there is a caption saying "Steve Winwood. What the night can do".	Intro. Bar 1.	The singer framed on a TV screen: intertextual link to the music video. The outfit: intertextual link to the 1998 tour ads and 'Roll with it' record cover. Caption: intertextual link to the music video.
2	'01	An unfocused close-up of the neck of a beer bottle. As the view becomes focused, water drops become visible on the neck and a legend is seen on the label: "Michelob beer". At the bottom of the screen there is a caption "Anheuser-Busch Inc., St. Louis, Mo."		The product, the brand, and the manufacturer. Winwood + Michelob = a celebrity spokesman transferring his value as a star to a product.
3	'02	An aerial shot of a city with skyscrapers in a dim light, with lights glimmering in the windows. The Anheuser-Busch text fades out.		The setting: a city.

THE STORY AND THE SHOTS

The story is as follows: The setting is a big city and the scene takes place at night on a street and in a small bar. Individuals and couples are on their way to the bar. Inside, people are drinking beer and having fun. A lonely girl sips her beer and watches TV. On the TV screen, Steve Winwood is seen performing his song, "What the night can do" and from the billboard posters visible on the street, we conclude that the rock star is in town. The girl fixes her eye on Winwood on the TV-monitor. The voice-over says "The night belongs to Michelob", leaving the ending open. However, the implication is that the girl may later find some company, perhaps even Winwood himself.

The music is carefully synchronized with the visuals so that there is a climax in the music approximately two thirds into the commercial: when Winwood sings the hook in the chorus "Don't you know what the night can do?" Right after the hook has been repeated, a spoken answer is heard: "One taste will tell you why the night belongs to Michelob".

The commercial consists of a number of different shots that are intermixed, in a manner quite similar to that of the music video, though the cuts in the commercial come faster compared to the music video. As there are some 25 shots in a half-minute commercial, the average length of a shot is approximately one second.

There is a certain kind of internal logic to the commercial. During the introduction, the setting is shown – a big city – and the product spokesman, Steve Winwood. During stanza A, the camera is outdoors in front of the bar. And during the chorus, the musical climax of the jingle, there is also a climax in the commercial, with the camera moving inside the restaurant and focusing on the faces of the girl and Winwood, finally ending with the advertising slogan read by a low-pitched male voice.

Like the music video, the commercial consists of a number of shots that are not closely related and intermixed. There are shots of the setting of the commercial: an aerial view of the city at night, shots taken from the street and in front of as well as from inside the bar and finally shots at the bar itself so that the viewer knows exactly where the commercial is taking place.

Shots of Winwood tell us that this is a famous rock star. In addition, there are a few other shots from the music video itself, in which Winwood sits in hotel rooms and is seen singing and playing on a keyboard. Curiously, there is also a shot of a Winwood tour poster. This may be why the commercial both begins and ends with a shot of Steve Winwood on the TV screen. It becomes obvious to the viewer that the celebrity personally endorses Michelob beer, and hereby value transference occurs. That everyone recognizes Winwood is guaranteed by the text in the first shot with the record's production credits.

Furthermore, there are shots of the product: a beer bottle, the brand in a neon sign in the window of the bar, some beer in a glass and finally a hand grabbing two beer bottles at once, thus conveying the message that there is a heavy demand for this product *and* implying that this product is particularly suited for social interactions. Moreover, there is an example of the effects of the brand: a mini-story of a couple staring at each other, running in the street and finally sitting in the bar with their heads together.

Finally, there is another story, at the climax of the commercial. First, Winwood's face is seen on a TV screen, and then we partially see the face of the girl, as she pours some beer into a glass. Next, a close-up of her face is shown, and it seems as if the girl is having eye-contact with someone: Steve Winwood on the TV screen, as it turns out. Finally, a shadow is presented, as if somebody were passing by the girl (it may be Winwood himself or it may be someone else). This is when a low-pitched male voice announces: "One taste will tell you why the night belongs to Michelob".

The setting resembles what Middleton (1990: 250-251) has said of the characteristic factors of popular songs. The first is a syntagmatic or narrative structure into which listeners are placed. The second is emotion, the invitation to feel. Here, the singer is the focus and is even offered as a respondent or a partner. The third factor is a character role, typically defined by gender and class and representing a personality type with which listeners can identify. And the fourth factor is bodily participation, the invitation to map and fill out the patterns of movement offered by the rhythmic structure and texture. (Middleton 1990: 250-251). The commercial contains all of these elements: it is well-structured, the singer is in focus and invites the viewer to feel; the character roles are well delineated, the singer being a masculine figure in a leather jacket and the girl a feminine character with long hair. Finally, there is an invitation to the bodily aspect, which here means drinking beer and perhaps making romantic contact with someone.

From song into commercial

It is interesting to see what happens when a rock song is changed into a jingle. The jingle into which the song has been changed seems to emphasize the verse that contains the hook of the song. If we again think about the neutral level (le niveau neutre) of the song, the three-minute song has been cut to 30 seconds by retaining a bar from the introduction, a few bars from verse A, nothing from the verse B and almost everything from the chorus.

Music	Music video	Tv commercial	Comment
Introduction	Bars 1-8	Bar 1	Shortened
Verse A	Bars 1-8	Bars 1-4	Shortened
Verse A (repetition)	Bars 1-8	-	Omitted
Verse B	Bars 1-8	-	Omitted
Verse C	Bars 1-8	Bars 7-8	Shortened
Chorus	Bars 1-7	Bars 1-6 and fade out	The line "Don't you know what the night can do?" repeated twice.

The eight-bar introduction has been cut to a single bar, this, however, being enough to give the listener a feel for the style of the song. The eight-bar verse A (and its repetition) has been cut to four bars. During these, the singer has time to sing the song's two first lines: "Hear the night music playing" and "Don't you know what it's saying?". From verse C, the commercial only uses the two last bars, which function as a prehook for the chorus. And the chorus, originally seven bars in length, has been shortened to four. The lyrics have also been changed slightly. In the original song, the lyrics are "Don't you know what the night can do? Don't you know when it's touching you?" In the commercial, the phrase "Don't you know what the night can do?" is repeated twice. Thus, the jingle has all of the song's essential elements.

However, there is a psychological side-effect. Since there is no repetition or eight bar structures as in ordinary rock songs, the jingle seems to be incomplete and imperfect in a sense. It creates a need to hear the jingle again or to hear the original song, which is probably what the advertiser wants us to feel. In a certain sense, a jingle consisting of only the best parts of a song is comparable to a film trailer, a short, filmed advertisement for a movie containing some of the highlights of the film. The music video is also what one might call a musical trailer, an advertisement for the song itself.

SIMILARITIES AND DIFFERENCES

When we compare Winwood's music video with his beer commercial, we find that there are some important similarities. Both use the same song. Steve Winwood appears in both. In the music video, he is advertising himself and his album 'Roll with it', and in the commercial, he is advertising Michelob beer by using the authority created by his stardom.

Common to both video and commercial are the visual elements based on a montage of pleasant images – people dancing or moving about or running to a bar or drinking beer. Both are also open texts in the sense that there is no clear-cut story but only successive images that invite the viewer to construct a personal reading of the situation. Nothing is completed in the shots, and many crucial aspects are left open. The result seems to be that the viewer wishes to see the video or the commercial again to find out what they were about.

Another shared feature is that both music video and commercial are selling something. The video advertises Winwood as a star, along with his song and his album. The commercial sells beer and to some extent also Winwood himself who appears on the commercial. What is furthermore common to both is that the selling point is somewhat hidden. Neither of them says outright "buy", and instead, both aim at creating a desire and evoking pleasure.

Yet there are differences. One is length: the music video is about three minutes long, whereas the duration of the TV commercial is only some 30 seconds. The commercial is more condensed, as the shots are shorter and cuts faster. In the commercial, there are no forward flashes or flashbacks, but a more straightforward narration. However, it might be an exaggeration to use the word "narration" here, since the commercial actually consists of successive images that are somehow related to the product. On the other hand, there is a narrative of some kind in the sense that the viewer is directed towards a climax that takes place at the end.

A jingle is usually defined as a memorable slogan with an engaging melody that is used in radio and sometimes in TV commercials. Actually, even though "Don't you know what the night can do?" was initially a pop song, for the Michelob commercial it was cut into a song that is very reminiscent of a jingle or could even be regarded as one. If we now generalize a bit, we may say that music videos and TV commercials based on pre-existing songs bear a number of similarities. Both are selling things. While a TV commercial is selling goods, a music video is selling an album. Both have musical as well as visual components and both are usually based on quick montage. Also, both are based on what might be called "hooks". David Huron has even argued that in the top-40 type music, a musical "hook" can be regarded as a subspecies of an advertising jingle. As Huron (1989: 571) states, the "so-called musical 'hook' is just a species of jingle, oriented toward the achievement of the same purpose: increasing memorability and product recall. Through quotation, allusion, or plagiarism, musical gestures such as riffs, instrumental timbres, rhythms, and so forth are used both to target audiences and to establish musical authority through an established network of historical connotations." (Huron 1989: 571). In our case, the line "Dont you know what the night can do?" is clearly both a hook line in a pop song and a key element in the advertising jingle. Furthermore, Winwood's authority as a song-writer and as a blues musician is used as a means to enhance the credibility of the product.

The visual elements in music videos and TV commercials often consist of images or shots that are not necessarily related. However, because a song is heard in the background, the video creates an illusion that the images somehow belong together. The visuals, even though they often follow each other in an illogical manner, create the illusion that there is a storyline. If there are any gaps in the narration (and there usually are), the viewer instinctively tries to complete them by using imagination. The viewer thereby becomes not only a consumer but also a creator of texts.

In addition to the narrative level, there is also a connotative level behind the images, each image evoking a number of connotative meanings of different kinds (see Pekkilä 2005). This makes music videos or the TV commercials that imitate music videos even more difficult to interpret – or from another point of view, psychologically more rewarding, as the viewer can project into the video all kinds of fears, wishes and mental images.

Conclusion

Anyway, it seems that music videos are dominated by the music. The song comes first, with its lyrics, and the visuals often comment on the lyrics, expand them or give them a new meaning. One might say that, in music videos, the songs and the performers themselves play a very important role. Normally, TV commercials differ from music videos because, quite as in normal length films, the commercials are filmed and edited first and the music is produced afterwards. Thus, there may already be a slogan in the advertising campaign, which is then used in the song. In the Winwood commercial case, however, it seems that first a pre-existing song has been cut down into the length of 30 seconds by omitting certain parts and the visuals have been added afterwards, similarly to what is done in music videos. It is unknown whether the slogan "What the night can do" was written to the lyrics because it already was a slogan in the advertising campaign or whether the ad people picked it up from the song because that line sounded very much as a slogan. Anyway, because Winwoods TV commercial was made and edited similarly to music videos and also because there is the strong presence of a star, Winwood himself, it seems that the Winwood commercial represents an exceptional case compared to ordinary TV commercials.

Notes

1 As Stillwell 2007 points out, an association between rock musicians and drinks companies started at that time: Coca-Cola having George Michael and Robert Plant and Pepsi having Madonna and Michael Jackson.
2 It may be a bit contradictory that Clapton was a practicing alcoholic when making the ad. In an interview, Clapton said: "Listen, man, I was a practicing alcoholic when I made

that commercial. By the time it came out, I was in treatment. This was December of '87. I was actually in treatment in Minnesota when that came on the T.V. I was in a room full of recovering alcoholics, myself being one of them, and everybody went, "is that you?" I said, "Yep." What was I going to say? It was me when I was drinking." (Fricke 1988).

3   The commercial and the music video were taped in the Spring 1989 when I was a visiting scholar at the Indiana University, Bloomington. An earlier version of this chapter, written in Finnish, is Pekkilä 1994.

4   The music video and the commercial have been analyzed in full. However, for practical reasons, only part of the analysis is shown here.

REFERENCES

Abraham, M. (2002). Still selling after all these years: Anheuser-Busch. *Boards Magazine Tribute, October 1*, 77. [http://www.boardsmag.com/articles/magazine/20021001/busch.html. Accessed May 28]

Anonymous. (2006). ThoughtStep. [http://www.thoughtstep.com/management. Accessed May 28]

Anonymous. (2007). S[teve] W[inwood]. Lyrics: Meanings & references. [http://www.winwoodfans.com/lyr-ref.htm. Accessed March 5 2007]

Aufderheide, P. (1986). The look of the sound. In T. Gitlin (Ed.), *Watching television. A pantheon guide to popular culture* (pp. 111-135). New York: Pantheon.

Burns, G. (1987). A typology of 'hooks' in popular records. *Popular music, 6(1)*, 1-20.

Covach, J. (2007). Winwood, Steve. In L. Macy (Ed.), *Grove Music Online*. [http://www.grovemusic.com. Accessed February 28.]

DeCurtis, A. (1988). Steve Winwood: From Mr. Fantasy to Mr. Entertainment. *Rolling Stone Cover Story. December 1, 540*, 46. [http://www.winwoodfans.com/articles/rs-dec-88.htm. Accessed May 28 2006]

Fricke, D. (1988). Eric Clapton – The Rolling Stone Interview. *Rolling Stone*, August 25, 533. [http://www.12bar.de/ftp/text_info/rollin_stone_interview_1988.txt. Accessed May 28 2006]

Huron, D. (1989). Music in advertising: An analytic paradigm. *Musical Quarterly, 73*, 557-574.

Kaplan, A.E. (1987). *Rocking around the clock. Music television, postmodernism, and consumer culture*. London: Routledge.

Kinder, M. (1984). Music video and the spectator: Television, ideology and dream. In H. Newcomb (Ed.), *Television. The critical view* (pp. 229-254). Oxford: Oxford University Press.

Middleton, R. (1990). *Studying popular music*. Milton Keynes: Open University Press.

Nattiez, J.-J. (1975). *Fondements d'une sémiologie de la musique* [The basics of a semiology of music]. Paris: Union Générale d'Editions.

Pekkilä, E. (1994). Musiikkivideot ja mainoksellisuus: Tapausanalyysi Steve Winwoodin videosta ´Don't you know what the night can do? [Music videos and advertising: A case study on the music video of Steve Winwood 'Don't you know what the night can do?] . *Etnomusikologian, vuosikirja*, *6*, 25-49.

Pekkilä, E. (2005). Connotative meanings in advertising music. In P. G. Michelucci, & P. G. Marteinson (Eds.), *Applied semiotics/Semiotique appliequee* (pp. 119-131). Toronto: University of Toronto.

Stillwell, R. J. (2007a). Advertising, music in. In L. Macy (Ed.), *Grove Music Online*. [http://www.grovemusic.com. Accessed February 28.]

Stillwell, R.J. (2007b). Commercial. In L. Macy (Ed.), *Grove Music Online*. [http://www.grovemusic.com. Accessed February 28.]

On the Commercialization of Shostakovich's 'Waltz No. 2'

A case study of textual, contextual and intertextual meaning of music

Anders Bonde

Introduction

People who become acquainted for the first time with the musical composition by Dmitri Shostakovich, formerly known as *Suite for Jazz Orchestra No. 2*, might perhaps be a bit surprised when they link the stylistic traits of the music to the title of the work and the time of its release. This holds particularly true in consideration of younger generations (born in the eighties and nineties) of today's Western societies that have grown up in the post-Cold War period, and who are not likely to have any particular knowledge about neither Russian art music, nor the politicization of music culture in the former Soviet Union and Eastern Europe. Although probably compiled during the fifties (Iakubov 2001: 269, Feuchtner 2006: 9), the suite offers a much closer relationship to the *ländler* tradition of Austria, Bohemia and southern Germany at the turn of the nineteenth century, and shows virtually no associations to nowadays' general definition of jazz despite its suggestive title (Wilson 1993: 4, Fay 2003: 180).[1] And yet, the distinctive orchestration of the alto and tenor saxophones among the more traditional woodwinds might perhaps suggest a certain influence from jazz, though obviously in a rather constrained sense. Bearing in mind the repressive laws of the Stalin era with its numerous political condemnations of jazz as a decadent 'other' (suggesting a corrupted Western capitalistic lifestyle), coupled with Shostakovich's reputation as the 'chameleon' adapting into any surrounding, one can easily comprehend the difficult walk on a knife's edge of the composer seeking an acceptable balance between folksiness (or 'social realism') claimed by the Communist Party and his own integrity as a composer.[2]

An intricate blend of Viennese waltz and 'pseudo jazz' is apparent, not least in the seventh movement, 'Waltz No. 2' – an approximately three and a half minute long orchestral piece featuring alto saxophone and trombone as the characteristic melodic (and to some extent 'jazzy') instruments in the first and third stanzas respectively.[3] As noted by Claudia Gorbman (2006), the waltz "is more folksy than the »Blue Danube«" and "evokes the Old World" (ibid.: 7). It is indeed a strange and ambiguous piece, straightforward as it is like an everyday kind of orchestral music, but also subject to a variety of connotations, which, despite apparent divergences, have been accounted fairly consistently amongst commentators and analysts ever since the piece became known outside the USSR in the late eighties (cf. note 1). Signs of everydayness, regularity and predictability in combination with nostalgia, melancholy and *fin-de-siècle* (connoting a threatening mixture of hedonism, decadent sophistication, self-indulgence and a carefree living, coupled with the presentiment of an imminent radical change), as well as irony, humour, variety shows (as suggested by the suite's correct title), cabaret, flying horses, circus and buffoonery, or even Eastern Europe and Stalinism, are all recurring communicative meanings to be reported (cf. Wilson 1995: 4, Lombardi 2004: 211, Dolan 2005: 31, Riethmüller 2005: 90, Gorbman 2006: 7, Have 2006: 41). As maintained by Philip Tagg (2006), "it should be clear that music – even without words or accompanying visuals – is capable of creating and communicating semantic fields of considerable ideological potential" (ibid.: 177-178).[4] However, one ought to take into account that the distinct meanings mentioned above are all interpretations, which are rarely (or never) based on musical criteria only, but on *multimodal* interactions; i.e. shaped in a number of audio-visual 'texts',[5] through which the waltz has been popularized. In other words, such meanings are likely to be inferred from the *perceived* interactions between various verbal and non-verbal semiotic resources (cf. Leeuwen 1999: 4f). Secondly, the meanings are not to be found *in* the music, but emerge on the interpretative, connotative level,[6] and therefore we should perhaps not speak of meaning but rather *meaning potential*, "which will be narrowed down and coloured in the given context" (Leeuwen 1999: 10).[7]

Furthermore, one is generally supposed to take the issue of *intertextuality* into consideration, as the attribute meaning of the waltz in one specific text could easily influence, or even be a determining factor in another text featuring the same music. I shall return to that issue twice, second time in the conclusion. One major problem, though, is that intertextual meaning is difficult to measure whether it is premeditated by sender (e.g. the film director) or identified by recipients; that is, pointing out exactly how much and what kind of meaning is transferred from one text to another. A thorough investigation would certainly rely on interviews of the directors as well as questionnaires among a chosen population segment, but this is not the aim in the present chapter. Rather, I contend that Shostakovich's 'Waltz No. 2' incorporates certain intrinsic attributes (i.e. structural elements, stylistic indicators, etc.), and therefore represents a series of *potential* meanings, which are modified and negotiated in three different audio-visual texts.

The texts are: 1) the movie *Eyes Wide Shut* (Kubrick 1999), featuring the celebrities Tom Cruise and Nicole Kidman; 2) a TV commercial for *SkandiaBanken* (2001), which is a Swedish owned Internet bank providing services in Sweden as well as other countries; and 3) the documentary *Fogh bag facaden* (Guldbrandsen 2003), about the Danish Prime Minister Anders Fogh Rasmussen as the president of the European Union and his negotiation with ten accessing countries.[8] Consistent with the subject of *advertising* in this volume, I will concentrate principally on the commercial, for what purpose the analyses of the movie and the documentary are briefer. The analytical framework of the commercial is inspired by the principles of 'media pairing' described by Cook (1998: 135f),[9] and, most notably, the concept of *inversion* turning upside down the usual perspective of music as a mere means of underscoring scenic action, to questioning how scenic action might also express the music. Cook describes the inverse relationship as "a useful heuristic procedure" (ibid.: 135); a *safeguard* "against the kind of oversight that all too easily results from unconscious a priori assumptions" (ibid.: 140) of, say, visual primacy in a movie and musical primacy in a music video. First of all, though, it might seem instructive to specify the components of the waltz chosen for the three audio-visual texts, given the fact that the waltz is not represented in its entirety in any of the texts. Actually, the musical materials are taken from the stanza parts almost exclusively.[10] The primary components are charted in Example 1.

Example 1. Waltz No. 2: The first stanza (reduced score)

MUSICAL STRUCTURE AND MEANING POTENTIAL

In accordance with the regular 'oom-pah-pah' accompaniment, the compositional elements of the melody are rather homogeneous with four similar instantiations of unit x at the smallest structural level and three similar instantiations of the larger unit A – the latter constituting more than two thirds of the melody. The classification of x is determined by the rhythm and a descending melodic contour, while the similarity of the three instantiations of A is solely based on the shared presence of x, notwithstanding the y units that distinguish A_1 and A_2 from A_3. The final twelve bars of the melody (B), comprising the z units, are made up of contrasting materials, primary due to the rhythm characterized by the quavers, and secondary (as in the case of z_1) the cheerful hemiolas with the articulation of the third beat suggesting a sensation of 1 2, 1 2, 1 2 rather than 1 2 3, 1 2 3 (bars 31-32 and 35-36). As will be clear below in the brief inspection of the documentary, the contrast between A and B is noteworthy since the latter is used independently on more than one occasion, having its own meaning potential. Apart from the rhythmical and metrical features, as well as the descending contour, we may focus on tonality, or, to be slightly more precise, the total collection of pitch classes. There are particularly two incidents, which contribute extensively to the distinctive shaping of the melody and therefore may be the centre for attention; namely the phrase endings of y_1 (bars 10-12) and y_2 (bars 18-20), featuring the accented passing tone (G) and the extended appoggiatura (F#) respectively.[11] Especially the diminished-third interval (A♭- F#) in bars 18-19 seems to hold a potential for expressing melancholy or nostalgia, and it can possibly be viewed as a *genre synecdoche*, to use Tagg's terminology (1992: 375-376), since it might be considered as referring to a 'foreign' melodic style derived from folk music in the Balkan and some Mediterranean regions, both with strong influences from Arabic and Gypsian cultures.[12] The usage of such exotic style elements, representing an emblem of sophisticated 'orientalism' and a decadent 'otherness', has a long history in Western art music with Mozart's 'Alla turca' finale (K. 331) as a well-known example.

Of course, by stressing the importance of such details mentioned above, one could easily be accused of *over-interpretation*. On the other hand, the very same details seem crucial to the musical character. After all, a *hypothetical substitution* of the two formulas (i.e. a replacement of the non-chordal tones with the principal ones) would certainly expose the music as fundamentally changed.[13] Moreover, because of their structural weights as phrase endings, they represent a kind of 'nodal points' in the musical structure, from which all the other elements obtain discursive meaning – a situation that is reflected most obviously in the TV commercial, to which I shall return later. Another meaning, though connected with the one reported above, need also to be taken into account; that is the circus-like ambience mentioned earlier, which I believe is caused particularly by the snare drum on the second and third beat, in combination with the choice of melody instruments (saxophones and trombones) and the 'exotic' chromatism. Considering the popular style characterizing many former turn-of-the-century band leaders (e.g. Julius Fučik, 1872-1916) and circus orchestras, in which the musicians were usually travelling Gypsies who 'coloured' the music with typical phrases and licks from their own musical traditions, it is not out of place to classify 'Waltz No. 2' in the same category. Most adult people living in Western societies would probably recognize the musical style, if not the piece, but they are not likely to specify why they are familiar with it. It is a kind of music 'everybody' knows without necessarily knowing its origin, so to speak, and that is why it is excellent for use in audio-visual texts. Next, I will make a few accounts and comments on the movie and the documentary respectively.

THE IRONIC PORTRAYAL OF EVERYDAY-LIFE

Due to its wide international recognition, it is probably not erroneous to identify the movie *Eyes Wide Shut* (and the director Stanley Kubrick) as a major cause, if not *the* major cause for the popularization of 'Waltz No. 2'.[14] The reason seems evident: Even though the waltz must be categorized as 'pre-existing music' functioning independently as a work of art, no previous musical recording or live performance of the waltz – nor the London premiere in 1988 (cf. note 1) or any other major classical music event – make up a significant cultural document comparable to a Hollywood movie featuring the ultimate celebrity couple at the turn of the 2nd Millennium (Cruise and Kidman). Therefore, it seems natural to assert that more than one of the connotations mentioned above are derived from the plot in that particular movie.[15] Here, the waltz symbolizes the wealthy couple in their pleasant everyday-lives (e.g. the 'ordinary week-day' montage), supplemented with regular high-society social gatherings full of decadence, such as the Christmas celebration at the Ziegler's, where the couple is about to enter (the introduction). According to Gorbman (2006), the timbre of the saxophone "conveys warmth, a sense of nostalgia or even melancholy, yielding a sardonic, even decadent tone at odds with what we see of Bill and Alice, the handsome, modern, blank Manhattanites whom the music strangely accompanies" (ibid.: 7); and "each iteration [of the waltz] suggests Bill and Alice's image of their perfect family, the image they would like to have of themselves [and] that they would like us to have of them" (ibid.: 8). The sense of daily routine is emphasized by the buoyant and popular musical style characterizing Shostakovich's 'Russian' and restricted comprehension of jazz, but also by means of the synchronization of the visuals to the musical rhythm. As noticed by Frederick Dolan (2005):

> "The film opens with changes in title and credit cards cut precisely to the elementary meter of Shostakovich's 'Waltz #2' and that meter continues to determine Alice's movements in the brief scene where she disrobes, her feet stepping over her dress and reaching the floor precisely on the beat. Similarly, Bill's first line of dialogue begins precisely on beat. From the opening credits onward, one has a sense of inevitability and automatism, the marking out of movements of those who think themselves autonomous but who are in fact dancing to a deep and ancient tune. When Bill, in the opening scene, admonishes Alice that they are »running a little late«, he could not be more wrong. He's simply dancing to a tune he cannot hear" (ibid.: 30-31).

Gorbman (2006: 8) draws similar conclusions observing the 'puppet-like' characters with Alice's unconscious 'waltzing' to the music – which a minute after turns out to be diegetic (cf. note 10) – and the dialogue between the couple as indications of predictability and regularity.[16] However, according to Riccardo Lombardi (2004), the disrobing shot also brings forth a nostalgic dimension due to the Renaissance inspired ('Botticellian') image of a delicate, graceful woman's naked body between the Greek styled pillars.

> "[T]he music poetically evokes the fleetingness of time and a sense of loss. The jazz waltz is a reminder of the Central European origins of Kubrick's parents and, at the same time, of his American essence. The connection between the ephemerality of time and a sense of beauty is emphasized by Freud (1916) in his essay »On transience«, in which a flowering meadow is taken as a prototype of all beauty, which becomes even more precious precisely because it is short-lived: its very rarity makes it more valuable" (ibid.: 211).

To summarize the readings of Gorbman, Dolan and Lombardi, the waltz is associated with decadence and nostalgia embraced in a pleasurable but uniform high-society living. At the same time, though, the waltz brings in a sense of irony or sarcasm, by which the hedonistic lifestyle of the Manhattan couple is depicted. A different connotative complex seems to imbue the documentary of the Danish Prime Minister. Here, we are introduced to a busy and very control-minded political leader working through a tight schedule of formal appointments, and who succeeds in conducting difficult negotiations with great determination and diplomacy. There are a total of eight incidents (cf. Table 1), in which varying combinations of musical elements from the stanza parts (*Intro*, A_1, A_2, A_3 and *B*) appear. Each one relates to the visuals, displaying the Prime Minister in charge following his program meticulously, whether he is holding meetings or he is jogging with his bodyguards.

Table 1

Incident no.	Time	Story line	Music
1	05.43 – 05.56	Brussels: On the basis of an agreement between the existing EU countries, the Prime Minister has received a mandate to negotiate with the ten new countries.	B (fade out)
2	06.53 – 07.43	The Prime Minister's Office: The Prime Minister is leaving his office to welcome the Polish Prime Minister who arrives at Christiansborg. An episode takes place outside the elevator, which does not arrive in time, and the Prime Minister feels obliged to use the stairs instead to receive his guest properly.	Intro $A_1 A_2$ (sax) I $A_1 A_2 A_3$ (trombone) B (concl.)
3	09.33 – 10.12	Berlin: The Prime Minister and his bodyguards are jogging in a park.	Intro $A_1 A_2 A_3$ (strings) B
4	11.21 – 11.54	The Prime Minister's Office: The Prime Minister arrives at his office for a strategy meeting with his team. Members of the team are waiting outside the office until they are called into the meeting.	Intro $A_1 A_2 A_3$ (sax) I B (conclusion)
5	32.19 – 32.53	Bella Center, Copenhagen: A short meeting with the Turkish Prime Minister.	Intro $A_1 A_2 A_3$ (sax) B (fade out)
6	51.39 – 52.37	Bella Center, Copenhagen: A series of very short final meetings with the assessing countries.	Intro (reduced) $A_1 A_2 A_3$ (strings) B I Intro $A_1 A_2$ (strings, fade out)
7	55.11 – 55.31	Bella Center, Copenhagen: The final agreement between the EU and all the assessing countries is announced on TV.	$A_1 A_2 A_3$ (strings, fade out)
8	56.09 – 57.11	Bella Center, Copenhagen: Together with all the European leaders, the Prime Minister announces the agreement for the press.	Intro I Intro $A_1 A_2 A_3$ (sax) B I B

Just like the movie, there is a linkage between the waltz on the one hand and the notion of predictability and regularity on the other, seeing that the music's easy 'oom-pah-pah' beat reflects the Prime Minister's many actions as typical 'everyday doings' – at least of a self-confident and experienced politician. In fact, keeping in mind Dolan's interpretation of the movie, the Prime Minister is moving to the rhythm of everyday-life, too, and this is particularly evident at the second incident, where he pushes in the desk chair with his left hand (synchronized with the downbeat of bar 1) and walks out of his office starting with his right foot (synchronized with the downbeat of bar 2). However, differing from the movie, all signs of decadence, hedonism or nostalgia are absent, or at least subdued, in support of an emphasized humorous undertone, where the recurrent appearances of the waltz function as ironic commentaries to the visuals and the story line. As characterized by Have (2006):

> "Generally the music in *Fogh bag facaden* does not generate emotional intimacy but ironical distance, which corresponds to the general impression of Fogh Rasmussen in this documentary. The music helps us keep a distance to the Prime Minister. It does not take us under his skin but celebrates him from the outside" (ibid.: 41).

The commentary character of the music becomes particularly apparent through the *fragmentation*; i.e. the momentary insertion of limited material (e.g. the sole choice of unit *B* in the first incident) as well as the cutting, pasting and looping of structural units (symbolized by the vertical dashes at incidents no. 2, 4, 6 and 8 in Table 1). Hence, in spite of musical sameness and, consequently, any speculative assumptions about a possible 'influence of the reception' due to intertextual implications as mentioned sketchily by Have (ibid.), the underscoring technique in the documentary is quite different from the continual passages in the movie, and therefore the musical meaning potential might be of another kind. I shall highlight two incidents (no. 2 and 4), which I believe demonstrate how musical fragmentation accentuates an ironic perspective. The 50-second long second incident is the one containing most variation because of the insertion of the trombone (third stanza), suspending the alto saxophone (first stanza).[17] Obviously, such an arrangement is not at all accidental, and since the change of soloist instrumentation is coordinated with the episode of the not-arriving elevator, it seems straightforward to interpret the low-registered tones of the 'clumsy' trombone as a witty remark to the somewhat amusing situation of the noble Prime Minister mobilizing all his patience, though clearly irritated and anxious of not being able to get down and welcome his guest.

In the fourth incident, the comical aspect relates specificly to the insertion of the z_2 unit – the final four-bar conclusion of the waltz (part of *B*), which succeeds the saxophone melody rather hastily leaving out the essential downbeat and resulting in a composite measure (cf. Ex. 2). No matter the reason behind the abrupt succession of z_2 (if there is any reason at all), the overall effect is intriguing since the denotational (or 'pure musical') meaning of the abruption seems perfectly in line with the general portrayal of an active and insistent leader, now opening a meeting with his team. Given the fact that the concluding z_2 unit begins too early and ends with bravura before all the team members have been seated around the conference table, one might once again be left with a picture of the Prime Minister's forced patience with his surroundings, conflicting with a desire to move on. Here, the musical arrangement of the waltz can therefore be understood as an ironical commentary to the controlled Prime Minister and all the busy employees running around to fulfil his expectations. And as a whole, the viewers are in effect witnessing a kind of 'political circus' (Have 2005: 7), featuring the Prime Minister, 'waltzing' through the landscape of hardliners and pragmatics, cynics and clowns.

Example 2. (reduced score)

SKANDIABANKEN

Now, having examined the meaning potential of the waltz in the movie and the documentary, I turn to the commercial for SkandiaBanken, which has been released in between the former two texts. The commercial was originally produced in Sweden but synchronized in Danish and showed for the first time on Danish TV2 in November 2001. It encompasses a single scene, which lasts 35 seconds and consists of four objective shots concluding with two text messages; the first one dissolving during the fourth shot, and the second and final text (featuring the logo) on black background. Differing from the movie and the documentary, all transitions between the shots are abrupt and no camera movements take place inside the shots. Beginning with a long-shot view of an old-fashioned social gathering among conservatively dressed people sitting or standing in a large decorated living room, the camera cuts straight into the middle of a dialogue between four guys with a shiny wet hair look – conservatively dressed, too, wearing shirts, blazers and ties or just shirts and pullovers. The guys, probably in the mid-twenties, stand aside in the corridor with a glass of cognac having a conversation about choices of private banking services. The dialogue, which appears in Table 2 (English translation in italics), takes place between the three guys in the left side of the picture (G_1, G_3 and G_4) facing the remaining guy to the right (G_2). This is the principal setting of the commercial covering the major course (approximately two thirds), only interrupted by a brief close-up of G_2 and finally succeeded by the concluding logo.

Table 2

G_1 (Carl):	"Jeg spurgte, hvilken bank du har?"	*"I was asking you, which bank you use?"*
G_2 (Christian):	"SkandiaBanken!"	*"SkandiaBanken!"*
G_3:	"Men Christian, det (er) da ik' en bank. Carl spurgte, hvilken bank du har!"	*"But Christian, this is not a bank. Carl was asking, which bank you use!"*
G_4:	"Skål Christian, skål for SkandiaBanken!"	*"Cheers Christian, a toast to SkandiaBanken!"*

As one might notice, the spoken dialogue is quite sparse with a single sentence reserved for each character in the plot. It is incomplete, too; Carl's returning and mildly contemptuous question ("I asked you...") immediately denotes that the conversation has gone off a bit before the scene is presented to the viewer. However, along with the nonverbal forms of communication (bodily gestures, including head movements, smiling, grinning, winking, etc.) as well as the cutting rhythm, the message from addresser to addressee is very eloquent and a lot of meaning is communicated in less than twenty seconds. And this is, of course, what TV advertising is all about: struggling with a genre under economical and time-bound pressure to obtain maximum output out of minimum input (Stigel 2001: 328).

Words and pictures

Obviously, the three guys do not at all take 'SkandiaBanken' for an answer ("…this is not a bank") and they make fun of Christian (G_2) as if *he* is the one who has been misguided. The point is, of course, the opposite, which the text clarifies during the fourth shot, saying: *"Most people don't know that we have the best bank prices in Denmark"*; and to verify this information, a note is placed in the bottom of the picture referring to the August issue of *Penge & Privatøkonomi* ('Money & Private Economy'), a respected Danish magazine addressing anyone interested in getting as much as possible out of his or her money. This naturally leads toward the succeeding and concluding picture, in which the text beneath the logo says: *"High rate of interest. No fees."* SkandiaBanken thus portrays itself as a 'no-nonsense company' offering an alternative service, which is economically beneficial *and* transparent to private customers.[18] In this strategic imaging, the old myth of David defeating Goliath is beneficial, appealing as it is to people who like to signify personality and individuality. The company positions itself as the small convention-breaking David figure fighting against the power of the established financial companies and the widespread acceptance of their authority; a position, which, as one might expect, costs humiliations and stultifications as illustrated by Carl's scornful grinning and the last sarcastic commentary from G_4 ("Cheers Christian, a toast to SkandiaBanken!").

The sympathy and personal identification with this humiliated underdog-figure is a core matter, in which stakeholders are assimilated into a value-based community joining other informed and cost-conscious individuals willing to go against the stream disregarding conventional bank authorities (or any authorities, for that matter). Just as an old Danish proverb declares: 'He who laughs last, laughs best', the viewer soon recognizes Christian as the bright guy; the one who seizes the future instead of sticking to the 'old way of business'. In this manner, the alignment of conventional banks with non-recognized consequences of modern ways of purchasing products and services is presented as the general disapproving state of affairs, from which SkandiaBanken courageously takes up an opposite position. As the commercial progresses, we are given a description of a 'company of tomorrow' (personalized by Christian) in the middle of an ironical portrayal of former times' banking people living in a kind of parallel high-society universe and not having the slightest idea about the changed conditions of nowadays' financial line of business. Here, we approach a principal advertising strategy used by the company around 2001: the satirical depiction of the 'old days', which, however, have become *too* old now.[19] Like two of its predecessors, the commercial for SkandiaBanken includes numerous visual and verbal signs of traditional conduct of life and blind conventionalism combined with well-consolidated prosperity, all portrayed in a nostalgic and comical framework. First of all, the *location* with the dark-wood wainscots, a glittering crystal chandelier, dark lacquered floors with oriental carpets, and a huge renaissance gobelin tapestry hanging down the wall featuring religious motifs; secondly, the *dialogue* with its clearly-articulated pronunciation (a typical high-brow Northern-Copenhagen tongue) and the polite conversational tone we would expect from cultivated people in a wealthy, upper-class milieu some 80 years ago, combined with the use of classical (royal) names, Christian and Carl; and thirdly, the *brownish monochrome tint*, in which the four shots are presented. All these matters are portrayed rather ironically, but the irony is expressed *silently*, so to speak, underlined with the close-up of Christian keeping a straight face without correcting the ignorance and 'out-of-date mentality' of the three other guys. And with the outspoken sarcasm of G_4, the irony is elaborated further as *he* (not Christian) is the one who honours SkandiaBanken without knowing that this is exactly what he does.

MUSIC AND STORY-LINE

What has Shostakovich's 'Waltz No. 2' to do with all this? Given an account of the word-picture relationship with the possible connotations and associations it might bring forth, we will now turn to the relationships between music on the one hand, and pictures, the spoken dialogue and other diegetic sounds, on the other. At this point, one question comes into mind, that is: 'how does this particular piece of music contribute to the image of an up-to-date bank characterized by rationality and transparency?' Keeping in mind the denotational characterization of the music, we might answer immediately by concluding that the meaning of the music is *circuitous*. As mentioned before, the scenic locations do *not* signalize modern efficiency, rather an old-fashioned decadence, which seems to be reflected by the music in a manner that is similar to the introductory part in *Eyes Wide Shut* featuring the wealthy Manhattan couple. However, before delving too deeply into the field of musical-connotational meaning in the commercial, it is perhaps revealing to review previous research that has considered the presence of music in bank commercials as *inconsistent* signifying integrity and competence. For instance, Hildegrund Leo notes that the absence of music suggests 'pseudo-competence' and 'pseudo-factuality' (1999: 42). This corresponds to the German aphorism, *Beim Geld hört die Gemütlichkeit auf* ('In financial matters there is no cordiality').[20] However, such a view is hardly in agreement with the situation in the present decennium (at least not on Danish commercialized TV), where ordinary financial services have been promoted ever more as lifestyle products (Bak and Nørgaard 2006).

> "The fact that this has happened in parallel with structural changes in the financial sector, together with an increasing competition, is certainly one part of the picture. Nonetheless, the banking companies – and to some extent the building societies and the insurance companies as well – try to sell their product, service, or simply money, which are nothing more than a means to the fulfilment of our needs, as if a higher philosophy of life. The way they accomplish this is to connote a series of values to money that modern people require to form their personal identity; consumption is more than ever filled with, and determined by meaning. In such a situation, the product itself, the money, ceases to be a generic product, exclusively. On the contrary, money is not just money, but money from X bank. One might say that the foremost objective of these advertising spots is to throw into the shade an old Danish saying that »money doesn't smell«. The rewriting seems to be that »money smells indeed, and our money smells better«" (ibid.: 7).[21]

The characteristic above seems perfectly in line with the general tendency of *narrativization* and *aesthetization* of the TV commercials since the nineties (Stigel 2001: 329), and nowadays it is therefore hardly out of place to recognize music as a major semiotic resource in bank commercials, too. Now then, dealing with meaning potentials of Shostakovich's waltz in the present context, we need to model the different kinds of relationships, in which the music takes a part.

Music and words

The commercial is musically underscored through all 35 seconds, though the underscoring has been modified a bit compared with the original composition (cf. Ex. 1).[22] Example 3 represents the musical arrangement of the commercial aligned with the sentences from the spoken dialogue.[23] At the outset, the music seems diegetic; although not represented visually, it can be associated with the action on the screen, where it forms a natural part of a sonic environment, suitable for an old-fashioned social gathering as mentioned before. Merged together with the noise of the people, one may perhaps imagine a dance band of the thirties outside the screen. However, the role of the music is not only 'environmental'. Looking at the alignment of music and speech in Example 3, we may pick out a few details suggesting that the music fits more efficiently than that. For instance, it appears that the repetitive wordings in the dialogue are consistent with parallelism in the musical structure (bars 6-8 and 14-16): The lines of G_1 and G_3 (second clause) are similar (with the one-syllabled subjects 'I' and 'Carl' as the only substitutional elements), and so are the phrase endings of y_1 and y_2 (cf. the previous discussion of their structural significance). Moreover, due to the repetitive wordings of the first three lines ($G_1 - G_2 - G_3$), the dialogue is *cyclical*, too, to the cadential harmonic progression of the first sixteen measures, which exemplifies functional tonality *par excellence* with the cyclical formation of the constituting parts: (i) – subdominant (ii°⁷) – dominant (V⁷) – tonic (i). Just as G_3 repeats what has earlier been said, the harmonic cycle is accomplished as well as the first two melodic phrases (A_1 and A_2). Such close correlation between dialogue and musical frame could, of course, be merely accidental, but the approximate synchronization of the music with the verbal elements

Example 3. Music and dialogue in the commercial for SkandiaBanken

nevertheless makes a substantial contribution to a consistent and amplified 'whole', in which the verbal and musical modes of signification are combined. What is particularly noteworthy in this instance, though, is the inevitable opportunity to turn upside down the relation between speech and music (cf. Cook 1998: 135f). Not only does the music fit the dialogue; the opposite perspective of viewing the spoken words as accompaniment to the music is quite considerable. Actually, given the fact that the continuous musical underscore dominates the sonic landscape of the commercial, it seems adequate also to deal with the speech inputs giving meaning to the music. Consequently, the resulting amplified meaning is as much due to the dialogic arrangement in the musical framework as the opposite.

Music and pictures

Leaving the music-word relationship for a while in favour of a comparison of the musical and visual material, there are further important details to be identified. Figure 1 shows how the musical and pictorial materials are distributed.[24] Obviously, there is a general correspondence between the periodic metrical grouping and the pictorial rhythm of the succeeding shots and text entries: The pictorial paradigm classes begin and/or end with the downbeat of a new four-bar period, except for the third shot, which has been 'pushed forward' one beat. By this follows that the music-picture relationship appears less co-ordinated within the central component of the story-line – that is, the conversation between the four guys (Shot 2-4) – compared with the outer sections featuring the initial setting (Shot 1) and the concluding text messages (Text 1-2) respectively. However, the 'irregularity' of the third shot is perhaps one of the reasons as it draws certain attention, while its position in the middle of the commercial, making up the pivotal moment in an overall symmetrical structure, would be another.[25] A third reason, which seems particularly relevant in this present context, is the absence of spoken words (Christian remaining silent with a straight face) in conjunction with the entrance of the third melodic phrase featuring the peak tone (E^b5). As a temporary musical culmination, it will, I believe, inevitably reinforce the attention to the specific moment. Given that the close-up is presented one beat before the downbeat at bar 17, the descending saxophone melody comes about as a cheerful 'singing' commentary to Christian's calm attitude despite the ignorance of the three guys – an attitude that he can maintain, knowing that he is the one who knows best.

Figure 1

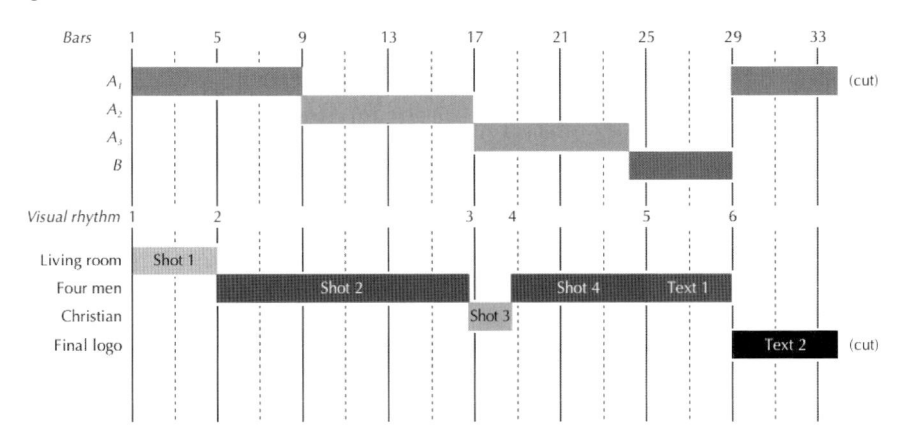

Conclusion

Up until this point, the account of connotative similarities between the movie, the documentary and the commercial has concentrated mainly on three different categories of meanings carried out through the textual and contextual aspects of 'Waltz No. 2'. The similarities can be neatly summed up in the following concepts or concept pairs: 1) irony and/or buffoonery, 2) everydayness, and 3) decadence in combination with nostalgia. While the intrinsic qualities of the music itself comprises all three categories as potential meanings besides other potential meanings, such as 'orientalism' or 'exoticism', or perhaps also 'Eastern Europeness' (Gorbman 2006: 7) and the repressive cultural climate in the Soviet during the cold war (Wilson 1993: 4, Riethmüller 2005: 90),[26] each one of the audio-visual texts covers at least *two* categories in its own distinctive way. Consequently, there is always at least one shared musical-connotational denominator between two texts, and most often there are two (cf. Fig. 2). The commercial and the movie both demonstrate signs of *decadence and nostalgia*, depicting a high-society milieu portrayed by pleasurable, old-fashioned social gatherings – or at least, as in the introductory part of the movie, a prelude to such a milieu. An impression of *everydayness* characterizes the movie as well as the documentary. In the two occasions described earlier, both encompassing the first appearance of the waltz from its opening 'oom-pah-pah' accompaniment and the succeeding saxophone theme,[27] the motions of the characters have been synchronized with the three-beat rhythm, but in a regular and unaffected way without calling any particular attention. And so, the music becomes almost 'environmental' right from the beginning, representing the 'rhythm of everyday living'. Finally, the sense of *irony and/ or buffoonery* forms the central meaning category carried out in all three texts. Each text exhibits a humorous commentary on the controlled everyday life with all its deeply rooted routines, whether taking place in high-society surroundings with people inclined to a decadent lifestyle (the movie and the commercial), or in political life (the documentary). However, the ironic feature seems particularly underlined in the latter two. In the commercial we are presented with an ironical portrayal of a decadent and hedonistic society, witnessing the hegemony of ignorance, while, in the documentary, we observe from a distance an ironical portrayal of the firmly resolved Prime Minister performing in a political circus.

Now then, dealing with the connotative similarities shown in Figure 2, it seems evident to pick up the thread of *intertextuality*. Due to the general association between 'Waltz No. 2' and the movie, as mentioned earlier, it seems fairly reasonable to assume that the latter might, at least to a certain extent, be a determining matter in the reading of the commercial and the documentary dated two and four years later respectively.[28] Without Kubrick's design, the waltz would hardly have been known, except by a few specialists, and it would probably not have been popularized further through other audio-visual texts, as for instance the commercial and the documentary included here. However, one should be cautious not to inflate this intertextual impact since neither the position of creator nor of recipients are included in the present analysis. That makes it rather problematic to postulate an influential line of reading from, say, the commercial to the documentary. Despite the fact that both have been broadcasted prime time on Danish national TV more than once, and therefore presumably have had a much larger number of (Danish) viewers than the movie, their socio-cultural legacies are certainly subordinate and moderately short-lived. This holds especially true for the 35-second commercial spot. Nevertheless, it seems reasonable to believe that the commercial and the documentary have contributed individually, through musical identicalness, to a potential re-reading of the movie, which, unlike the commercial and the documentary, will probably attain an ongoing interest.[29] Similarly, the readings, re-readings or cross-readings of all three texts might affect the reception of Shostakovich's waltz itself; it has not only been popularized, or better *commercialized*, but also given certain meanings attached to the contextual and intertextual relations. What I have done here is to infer how the waltz facilitates the shaping of certain meaning potentials, which are realized differently in three audio-visual texts, but also with some remarkable similarities, notwithstanding the disparity in respect of content as well as genre. My viewpoint has been aesthetic-hermeneutic exclusively, and a relevant issue for future research would be to extend the empirical studies to the field of reception. For the time being, though, it is worth accentuating once more that it is the intrinsic qualities of the music – the stylistic features such as rhythmic, melodic, orchestral and timbral normalities as well peculiarities, in which the germ of the 'associative power' can be found.

Figure 2. The arrows symbolize the context-bounded meanings of the waltz.

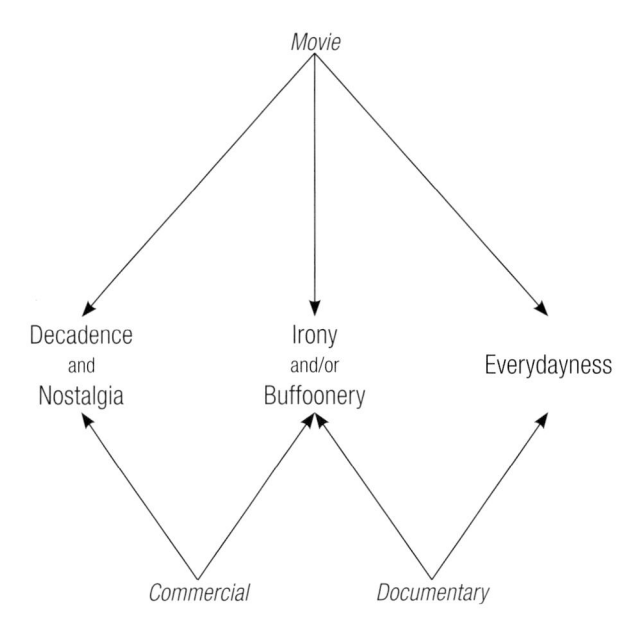

```
                        Movie
                       /  |  \
                      /   |   \
                     /    |    \
                    ↓     ↓     ↓
              Decadence  Irony
                 and    and/or    Everydayness
              Nostalgia Buffoonery
                    ↑     ↑       ↑
                     \   / \     /
                      \ /   \   /
                       ×     \ /
                      / \     ×
                     /   \   / \
                Commercial  Documentary
```

NOTES

1 The dating and cataloging of the suite is a subject matter of much confusion. Apparently, the eight-movement work has been addressed incorrectly from the time when it was given its first performance in Great Britain at Barbican Hall, London (1 December, 1988) by Mstislav Rostropovich and The London Symphony Orchestra (see the concert program, reprinted in the periodical, *Tempo* No. 166, September, 1988). The accurate title, appearing on the Russian scores, is *Suite for Variety Stage Orchestra*, which seems a lot more suitable for the character of the work: 'a suite of »pops« arrangements from film music' (Fay 1992: 586) without any particular relation to jazz, and 'possibly not even compiled by the composer himself' (ibid.). Nevertheless, the former title has survived in the latest edition of the Shostakovich catalogue by Derek Hulme (2002: 182) as a result of its general acceptance, despite the fact that the correct title appears on the first-time published score (cf. Iakubov 2001). See the review by Laurel E. Fay (2003: 180) for a further discussion about the mistake.

2 The condemnation of jazz was formulated in 1930 by the Russian Association of Proletarian Musicians in the bulletin, *Za Proletarskuyu Muzïku* ('For Proletarian Music'), but apparently the aesthetics was soon revised since jazz became 'recognized as a legitimate product of American folklore' (Slonimsky 1944: 4). As a result, various attempts were made to assimilate jazz into the doctrines of socialist realism. A state jazz commission and a state jazz orchestra were founded (in 1934 and 1938 respectively) to control the popularity of this kind of music, and Shostakovich composed two suites of jazz (or light-music) pieces to be performed by the state jazz orchestra and its conductor Victor Knushevitsky (Slonimsky 1944: 5, Feuchtner 2006: 9).

3 According to Iabukov (2001), the waltz "is an exact duplication of the waltz from the film »The First Echelon«, with another development of the main theme added on at the end" (ibid.: 270). The latter was composed in 1955-1956, which "makes it possible to date the appearance of the suite to the second half of the 1950s" (ibid.: 269).

4 The notion is due to a series of listening tests, which were conducted by Tagg in the early eighties (Tagg 2006: 172). The test persons were predominantly Swedish students below the age of thirty, and so the author cautiously limits his focus and conclusions to what he characterizes as the 'contemporary Western mass culture' (ibid.: 166) with its homogeneous audience sharing 'values and interpretations of cultural phenomena in common with others' (ibid.: 165).

5 The term 'text' is here used in its extended and generalized sense in the field of social semiotics and media studies; i.e. verbal or written as well as visual and aural textualities (Hartley 2002: 226) – or, consistent with Sonesson (1998: 83-84), anything inside a culture which can be interpreted.

6 Following Nicholas Cook (1998), the term 'music alone' does not really make sense since every musical phenomenon is constituted by interpretation and verbalized 'in the play of representations that we call musical culture' (ibid.: 23).

7 Using 'meaning *potential*' instead of 'meaning' has its advantages. While the latter implies a correlation between the intrinsic attributes of the sound structure and its meaning or semantics (Cook 1998: 23), as if musical meaning were something *fixed* – a *code* (Leeuwen 1999: 10), the former calls attention to the discursive, relational, contextual and interpretative aspects of musical meaning.

8 The title literally means 'Fogh behind the façade', though the English version is titled *The Road to Europe*. Apart from Shostakovich's 'Waltz No. 2', the documentary includes music of

Beethoven, Rossini and Tchaikovsky (Have 2006: 40-41, 46).

9   Unlike Cook's use of the term 'medium' (cf. Cook 1998: 261f), I prefer *mode* as an abstract (not physical or material) resource for semiosis. This is consistent with many researchers in the discourse analytic and social semiotics communities (cf. Kress & Leeuwen 2001: 2, Norris 2004: 11), who are inclined to view media as the physical stuff of communication, though they are not always perfectly clear about the concept. As noticed by Lars Elleström (2007), the term has lost the power of accuracy since '[m]edium' can mean both a *mediating medium*, for instance a *radio* mediating music or a weather forecast, and a *mediated medium*, for instance *music* being mediated by a radio, by an orchestra, or by both.' (ibid.: 1).

10 There is a total of four stanzas, organized two and two with a solo stanza (beginning with alto saxophone and later trombone) succeeded both times by a *tutti* stanza (strings). As the one exception, the music in *Eyes Wide Shut* moves on to its second part. However, this part is always muted in favour of the scenic action, and either interrupted, as in the introductory scene where the music is turned off by Bill Harford (Tom Cruise) pushing the button on the stereo, which suddenly depicts it as *diegetic* (Gorbman 2006: 9, Dolan 2005: 13); or it fades out, as in the later montage demonstrating an ordinary week-day in Bill and Alice's lives. Clearly, the second part of the music shows lesser importance and is therefore omitted here.

11 The two non-chordal tones, suspending the principal tones (F and G respectively), are both rather dissonant due to the half-step clashes – the former (bar 11) between G and the lowered fifth (Ab) of the subdominant (iiø7), and the latter between F# and the natural fifth of the tonic (i) (cf. Ex. 1).

12 The raised fourth and seventh in the C minor scale (F# in bar 19 and B in bars 16-17 respectively) point towards the Hungarian 'gypsy scale' with its two augmented seconds: C D E^b F# G A^b B. Besides, I suspect the diminished-third interval between A^b and F# (bars 18-19) to be one major reason why Have (2005: 7) links Shostakovich's waltz to the Godfather films of Francis Ford Coppola. Correspondingly, Nino Rota's soundtrack – notably the 'Love Theme', beginning and ending each of the films – contains a similar melodic formula in the conclusion of the B section. See Marcia J. Citron (2004: 438-442; 464) for a discussion of Rota's 'nostalgicism', 'distantness' and 'arabicness'.

13 See Tagg (1982: 50-53) for a discussion and exemplification of 'hypothetical substitution' or 'commutation', the latter being a better known term in the field of semiotics which is also used by Tagg in his later writings (e.g. Tagg 2006: 179).

14 Various notes in CD booklets and writings on the Internet confirm this (cf. Feuchtner 2006: 9, or http://en.wikipedia.org/wiki/Suite_for_Jazz_Orchestra_No._2_(Shostakovich).

15 The belief that the meaning potential of 'Waltz No. 2' is primarily associated with *Eyes Wide Shut*, rather than an opus of Shostakovich's works, is supported by the previous notion of the origin of the piece and the compiled nature of the orchestral suite (cf. note 1). The waltz has almost become 'captured' by the movie, so to speak, which, by the way, is probably the case with many lesser renowned *avant-garde works* used by Kubrick, too; e.g. György Ligeti's *Musica Ricercata* (No. 2) in the same movie, or Béla Bartók's *Music for Strings, Percussion and Celesta* (3rd movement) in *The Shining* (Kubrick 1980). This is much unlike his use of Beethoven's Ninth Symphony (transmuted through Wendy Carlos' synthetic sounding arrangement) as accompaniment to the violent images in *A Clockwork Orange* (Kubrick 1971), which naturally lean heavily on the audience's cultural baggage and its pre-understanding of the 'Ninth'. Comparing the two 'models' of using pre-existing music is interesting from a perspective of *intertextuality* vs. *autonomy*. While the second model integrates a musical artwork including all its cultural and historical weight, the first one *annexes* the musical artwork and ascribes a

certain meaning to it.

16 However, Bill's first line ('Honey, have you seen my wallet?') does actually *not* begin on the beat as stated by Dolan (see the citation above) and Gorbman (2006: 8), but rather on the second crotchet (first bar, second stanza). Therefore, Gorbman's 'musicalization' of this first line (ibid.: 9) is not fully accurate, though her idea of a 'quasi-operatic' sequence with a duet between the couple, accompanied by the large symphonic orchestra (ibid.: 8), seems compelling, considering Kubrick's reputation of assimilating pre-existing music into his own artistic purposes.

17 The sixth and eighth incidents are both longer, but parts of the music are looped – either the whole stanza as in the former case, or parts of it as in the latter.

18 The central theme of the commercial about people not recognizing SkandiaBanken as a real bank has historical implications and contributes greatly to the values, which the bank seeks to communicate to its stakeholders. SkandiaBanken – which is a subsidiary of *Skandia*, a Swedish owned concern dealing with saving solutions and financial security – was founded in 1994 as one of the first telephone banks. Later, it became an Internet bank with businesses in Norway (2000) and Denmark (2001-2007), where it was marketed as a modernized and profitable alternative to the big, well-known and conventional banks. Accordingly, the present commercial in November 2001 is the first one on Danish TV advertising for bank service; until that time (as late as September 2001) Skandia's TV advertising has had to do with pension solutions. However, the messages and values in the marketed communication are all the same: it is the small player against the big one(s).

19 The commercial for SkandiaBanken is preceded by two other Skandia commercials on Danish TV 2 (February and September, 2001) promoting a pension solution (*Skandia Bonuspension*) by re-voicing old archive films in a rather comical manner. Both of the commercials are concluded with a voice-over, saying: "Now it is probably time to grant a pension to the old pensions. Skandia Bonuspension: A new way of thinking about pension" (*Nu skal de gamle pensioner vist på pension. Skandia Bonuspension: En helt ny made at tænke pension på*). Thus, a considerable part of the communicated meaning in the commercial for SkandiaBanken is evidently intertextual as all the texts incorporate an old-days scenario with an ironic view.

20 The phrase is originally a quote from David Hansemann (1790-1864), a Prussian politician and banker.

21 This author's translation.

22 The introduction (b. 1-4) has been left out together with the two instances of z_1 (b. 28-35).

23 The transcription is based on repeated real-time hearings of the audio track. Accordingly, the notation of the spoken rhythms is only approximate as the words have been arranged proportionately to the musical rhythm.

24 The distributional chart encompasses various musical and pictorial paradigm classes all aligned with the metrical structure.

25 On condition that the first and the last shot are viewed as opposite poles as 'introduction' and 'conclusion' respectively, it is probably fair to argue for symmetry (ABCBA) since the first text message is part of the fourth shot.

26 Elizabeth Wilson (1993) characterizes the second jazz suite (*Suite for Variety Stage Orchestra*) as "rooted in the Vienna of Johann Strauss" with "a forward eye to the Red Army" (op. cit., p. 4), while Albrecht Riethmüller (2005), taking the standpoint of the specialist or professional listener, suggests a chain of associations: "jazz suite, the thirties, Soviet Union, Stalin, the authenticity of jazz, the friction between art and the state, the accusations of musicians such

as Shostakovich, critique and self critique, *Schauprozesse*, Russia vs. America, communism vs. capitalism, etc." (ibid.: 90).

27 Notice that the first incident of the stanza theme in the documentary is limited to the *B* unit.

28 As noticed by Riethmüller (2005: 87f), the presence of the waltz in *Eyes Wide Shut* has had an impression on the Taiwanese movie *Yi Yi* (Yang 2000), too. In one particular scene, featuring two girls in an apartment, preparing a special meal for their parents, one of the girls hums the melody of Shostakovich's 'Waltz No. 2'. Riethmüller concludes by imagining that the humming girl has just arrived from the cinema, or has recently been watching *Eyes Wide Shut* and kept the melody in her memory.

29 Taken into an American context, the same argument holds true, concerning a commercial spot for the telecommunications company Sprint Nextel (2007), in which 'Waltz No. 2' features too (cf. http://en.wikipedia.org/wiki/Suite_for_Variety_Stage_Orchestra_(Shostakovich).

References

Bak, A. C., & Nørgaard, J. L. (2006). Strategisk semiotik: Overvejelser om iværksættelse af kommunikation og valg af tegn i en professionel kontekst [Strategical semiotics. Considerations on the implementation of communication and the selection of signs in a professional context]. Copenhagen Business School, Working Paper 9: http://ir.lib.cbs.dk/paper/ISBN/x656517300.

Citron, M. J. (2004). Operatic style and structure in Coppola's *Godfather* trilogy. *The Musical Quarterly*, *87(3)*, 423-467.

Cook, N. (1998). *Analysing musical multimedia*. Oxford: Oxford University Press.

Dolan, F. M. (2005). Stanley Kubrick's *Eyes Wide Shut*: The metaphysics of sexual love. Paper presented at *Hawaii International Conference on Arts and Humanities*, January 13-16. Honolulu. Under submission to *The Massachusetts Review*.

Elleström, L. (2007). Mediating media and mediated media. Paper given at the conference *Imagine Media! Media Borders and Intermediality*. 1 page. Växjö University, Sweden. October.

Fay, L. E. (1992). Dmitri Shostakovich: A catalogue, bibliography, and discography. By D. C. Hulme. Forword by I. Shostakovich (2nd ed). Oxford: Clarendon Press, 1991 (review), *Notes*, *49(2)*, 585-586.

Fay, L. E. (2003). Dmitri Shostakovich: A catalogue, bibliography, and discography. By D. C. Hulme (3rd ed.). Lanham, MD: Scarecrow Press, 2002 (review), *Notes*, 49(2), 585-586.

Feuchtner, B. (2006). Shostakovich: Jazz Suites (CD notes), *Capriccio 71096*.

Gorbman, C. (2006). Eyes Wide Open: Kubrick's music. In Ph. Powrie, & R. Stilwell (Eds.) *Changing tunes: The use of pre-existing music in film* (pp. 3-18). Aldershot: Ashgate.

Guldbrandsen, Ch. (2003). Fogh bag facaden [Fogh behind the Facade]. In Ch. Guldbrandsen (Ed.), *Lykketoft finale / Fogh bag facaden*. Det Danske Filminstitut.

Hartley, J. (2002). *Communication, cultural and media studies: The key concepts* (3rd ed.). London: Routledge.

Have, I. (2005). Kognitionsteoretiske perspektiver på analysen af underlægningsmusik i audiovisuelle medier [Cognitive aspects on the analysis of background music in audiovisual media]. Paper presented at the symposium *Musikanalytiske temaer i dansk musikvidenskab* [Analytical Themes in Danish Musicology]. Aarhus University, Denmark. April.

Have, I. (2006). Danish top politicians underscored. *P.O.V.*, 22, 34-48.

Hulme, D. C. 2002. *Dmitri Shostakovich: A catalogue, bibliography, and discography* (3rd ed.) Lanham, MD: Scarecrow Press.

Iabokov, M. (2001). Dmitri Shostakovich. Suite for Variety Stage Orchestra. Score. In M. Iakubov (Ed.), *Suite for variety stage orchestra (Dmitri Shostakovich: New collected works, 2nd series. Orchestral compositions, Vol. 33)*. Moscow: DSCH Publishers.

Kress, G., & Leeuwen, Th. v. (2001). *Multimodal discourse. The modes and media of contemporary communication*. London: Arnold.

Kubrick, S. (1971). *A clockwork orange*. Warner Bros. Pictures.

Kubrick, S. (1980). *The shining*. Warner Bros. Pictures.

Kubrick, S. (1999). *Eyes wide shut*. Warner Bros. Pictures.

Leeuwen, Th. v. (1999). *Speech, music, sound*. Palgrave: Macmillan.

Leo, H. (1999). *Musik im fernsehwerbespot* [Music in TV commercials]. Frankfurt: Peter Lang.

Lombardi, R. (2004). Stanley Kubrick's swan song: "Eyes Wide Shut". *The International Journal of Psychoanalysis, 85(1)*, 209-218.

Norris, S. (2004). *Analyzing multimodal interaction. A methodological framework*. New York: Routledge.

Riethmüller, A. (2005). Kubricks letztes Wunschkonzert: Beobachtungen an der Musik zu "Eyes Wide Shut" (1999) [Kubrick's last request programme. Observations on the music in "Eyes Wide Shut"]. In A. Dorschel (Ed.), *Tonspuren, Musik in der Film: Fallstudien 1994-2001 (Studien zur Wertungsforschung 46)* (pp. 82-105). Vienna: Universal Edition.

Slonimsky, N. (1944). Soviet music and musicians. *Slavonic and East European Review. American Series, 3(4)*, 1-18.

Sonesson, G. (1998). The concept of text in cultural semiotics. *Sign Systems Studies, 26*, 83-114.

Stigel, J. (2001). The aesthetics of Danish TV-spot-commercials: A study of Danish TV-commercials in the 1990'ies. In F. Hansen & L. Y. Hansen (Eds.), *Advertising Research in the Nordic Countries* (pp. 327-350). Copenhagen: Samfundslitteratur.

Tagg, Ph. (1982). Analysing popular music: Theory, method and practice. *Popular Music, 2*, 37-67.

Tagg, Ph. (1992). Towards a sign typology of music. In R Dalmonte, & M. Baroni (Eds.), *Secondo convegno europeo di analisi musicale* (pp. 369-378). Trento: Università degli studi di Trento.

Tagg, Ph. (2006). Music, moving images, semiotics, and the democratic right to know. In S. Brown & U. Volgsten (Eds.), *Music and manipulation. On the social uses and social control of music* (pp. 163-186). New York: Berghahn Books.

Wilson, E. (1993). Dmitri Shostakovich: Jazz Suite 1 & 2 · Tahiti Trot · Concerto for piano, trumpet and strings. (CD notes), *Decca 433 902-2*.

Yang, E. (2000). *Yi Yi*. Diaphana Films, France.

http://en.wikipedia.org/wiki/Suite_for_Jazz_Orchestra_No._2_(Shostakovich). Accessed August 17 2009.

http://en.wikipedia.org/wiki/Suite_for_Variety_Stage_Orchestra_(Shostakovich). Accessed August 17 2009.

RELEVANT... BUT FOR WHOM?
On the commercial (ab)use of music on television

Nicolai Graakjær and Christian Jantzen

COMMERCE AND MUSIC IN POPULAR MEDIA

Sunday evening on June 17th 2007, Paul Potts, a shy 36 years old, Welsh, mobile phone salesman, won the first edition of the national ITV-show *Britain's Got Talent*. This programme had been aired every night since June 9th and attracted a wide audience, despite June traditionally being a low tide season in terms of audience. The overall winner was a self-made opera singer, who after spending a considerable amount on singing lessons had ended up as a salesman without much hope for a career in music. The show changed all that. Not only did Paul Potts earn a prize of £100.000 and an opportunity to sing for the queen later that year, he was also instantly offered a record contract by Sony BMG, who, in advance, had ensured an option on the winner. The CD with the telling title *One Chance* was released soon after the show, on July 16th. In the fall of 2007, the new star made his first world tour promoting the album but also indirectly the show that had brought him much deserved fame. In for example Denmark, a country of 5 million inhabitants, the CD sold the impressive amount of more than 100.000 copies. In 2007, the total sales of the album was almost 1,5 million copies earning Paul Potts a top 40 place on the *United World Chart*.

    The talent of Paul Potts contributed not only to his own success but also to making *Britain's Got Talent* a commercial success. Some 13.5 million people watched the Grand Finale live on ITV 1, a channel financed by commercials. The finals were also transmitted on ITV 2 to the American audience. After Potts' appearance, the concept has been sold to 40 countries around the world. So the production company, the Sony BMG owned Syco TV, greatly benefited from this success, having found a successor for its bestselling concepts *Pop Idol*, *American Idol* and *X Factor*. Interestingly, Simon Cowell, the founder and managing director of this company, served as one of the three expert jurors on the programme. Furthermore, the election of Potts as winner of the show was done by popular vote. Some two million people phoned in their vote, each of them paying 50 pence per call thus contributing significantly to the production costs (or to the profits generated). One may speculate how many of those phones sold by Potts himself might have been used to elect him as overall winner?

So while Potts was singing his way through Bocelli's *Con Te Partiro* and Pucini's *Nessun Dorma* to fulfil his lifelong dream, more profane dreams of both the television channel and the production company came true. By signing Potts immediately after the show, the record company also prospered from this new phenomenon that has generated extensive worldwide media interest ever since. This fascination has almost certainly been spurred by the Cinderella-theme underlying the Potts-story. But the availability of both a record and good television footage documenting the metamorphosis of this ugly duckling from the initial auditions to the Grand Finale of the show has undoubtedly increased this interest from foreign media too. (Potts' contribution in the show's audition has so far been watched over 55 million times on youtube.com). The international media exposure has propelled record sales and overnight turned Potts into a star of almost Pavarotti-like proportions. But the story has of course also promoted media sales: the selling of newspapers and magazines and the increase in viewer interest in television programmes. Telling the Potts-story has thus been a vehicle in developing audience interest in upcoming talent shows throughout the world and hence in creating a sound commercial foundation for such shows by announcing the entertaining qualities of these programmes to the audience.

The case of Paul Potts is thus an example of cross-selling, from which all parties seem to benefit. The production costs of ITV have probably been more than covered and, in addition, the channel has ensured an enormous (audience as well as commercial) interest in the 2008-version of the show. The production company has been able to sell this reality-television concept internationally. The printed media have a moving story to write about, which increases sales. Foreign television channels are able to fill news programmes with interesting 'soft news', at the same time promoting promising shows (and commercial breaks as well as sponsorship) to advertising agencies. Advertisers benefit from being associated with a popular phenomenon. The media hype serves the global interests of the record company. Paul Potts has his dream come true having the opportunity to make singing his career. And the global audience can mirror their dreams in Potts' success, while being entertained by his music.

The success of Paul Potts is an example of a perfect win-win situation. But when the relevance of music on television and in other media is assessed, it is usually its importance for the audience, for the aesthetics of the programme or for (popular) culture at large that is being debated. Hardly ever are other implications of music transmission than cultural ones discussed, despite the fact that it is an overt industry with a considerable turnover. By exposing Potts for free to the world audience, the media help to promote his records, likewise for free. The audience interest this generates serves the commercial purposes of the industry by increasing the share of viewers or readers for e.g. advertising. Music on television is thus not only relevant to viewers and channels in the cultural circuit of broadcasting but also to artists, advertisers, sponsors and record companies in the commercial circuit of broadcasting.

This second circuit is widely neglected in studies of music in the media. Even the very fact that music appears in practically every television genre is often forgotten by studies of popular music as well as of television (Negus & Street 2002: 210). As stated by Donnelly (2005: 110), "The most prominent academic texts that have looked at television programmes – such as John Ellis' *Visible Fictions* [1992] and John Fiske's *Television Culture* [1988] – always fail to deal with the music". But actually music on the screen adds up to a considerable amount, though exact figures are lacking: e.g. in one study music is reported to be present in television programmes between 37 and 70% of programming time (Tagg & Clarida 2003: 7).

This chapter intends to compensate for this double neglect by looking at the role of music in the commercial circuit of television. Ordinary commercials and music videos are obviously an easily recognizable way of promoting musical goods. But other forms are much harder to identify (or easier to neglect). We will focus on the two most frequently used ways of obscuring the promotional intent when musical goods (artists and albums) are exposed on television: product placement and 'puppet programmes'. The first category is well known from (televised) movies, whereas 'puppet programmes' denote those cases when information or entertainment programmes serve as puppets for commercial purposes, which the official presenter or channel does not control.

Music in 'puppet programmes'

Viewers watch programmes alone or in the company of others in order to feel informed on news, to have something to think or talk about, to be moved, excited or relaxed by entertainment, to engage in sport events or television drama, or simply to pass time. They stay tuned in as long as a programme or channel provides, in a relevant way, one or more of these functions. Channels on the other hand transmit programmes that they hope will be relevant to their target audience(s) so they may reach their organizational goals: e.g. to make profit or, as in the case of public service senders, to gain public acclaim or political legitimacy. When such goals are reached, the programming can be said to be relevant from the channel's point of view. 'Puppet programmes' exist: 1) because the programming is not only relevant for the viewers and the sender but also for third parties in that it serves their commercial or ideological goals; 2) when these interests are expressed without the interference of the presenter or without being interrupted or challenged by other parties; 3) when as a consequence, the message, erroneously, may be perceived as the official sender's or presenter's opinion and not as the private opinion of the third party. In such cases, the channel has become the third party's puppet.

The mixing of public and corporate interests and hence of different sets of relevance has been an issue since the early days of commercial television. In the United States, national brands overtly sponsored programmes of the national networks. Continuing the soap opera tradition of radio broadcasting, the television schedule of the 1950s thus had weekly programmes like the tremendously popular comedy *I Love Lucy*, sponsored by the Phillip Morris Tobacco Company (CBS, 1951-1957), the *Gillette Cavalcade of Sports* (NBC, 1946-1960), *Kraft Television Theatre* (NBC, 1947-

1958), and *Coke Time* (NBC, 1953-1957) starring the singer Eddie Fisher in a musical variety television show each Wednesday evening, filling the 15 minutes gap between the networked news programme and the local affiliates' programming. The ability to fill slots in the schedule with programmes produced and paid by third parties was precisely the reason why networks favoured this solution in those burgeoning days. These shows were frequently interrupted by the infamous announcement "and now a word from our sponsor" where the patron of the programme (e.g. Kraft, Gillette, Phillip Morris or Coca Cola) could explain the qualities of his product in live advertising without the interference of other competitors. The backside of this practice was inevitably that the hosting channel lost its credibility. This period therefore ended when the networks were able to regain control with the production and content of the programmes (cf. Rutherford 1994). Since then, sponsorship has been restricted to the public announcement of a corporate or brand name at the beginning and/or end of the programme. The sponsor is prohibited from controlling the content of the channel.

In 'puppet programmes', this control is once more at stake. These programmes exist for exactly the same reason as sponsored programmes existed in the early years of television. The increase in channels and the extension of the programme schedules since the coming of satellite television in the 1980s, has created a demand for 'cheap' but popular programmes to fill the slots and for catchy images (and sounds) to fill the 'soft news' section of news programmes. News about album sales or music events is an obvious way to end a news programme in a positive vein. But such features have left the realm of journalism if it is the record company who has produced the message or when the journalist uncritically adopts the perspective of the artist.

A second reason for this practice is the competition for viewers between the different programmes and channels. Showing the most popular artists attracts the largest audiences, and that is very much what stations strive for in order to attract the most prospective advertising customers. This logic was already spelled out in those early days of television when the three largest networks ran their own shows in fierce competition with one another. The *Ed Sullivan Show* (CBS, 1948-1971), Dick Clark's *American Bandstand* (ABC, 1952-1989) and *The Tonight Show* (NBC) initially hosted by Steve Allen (1952-1957), later by Jimmy Carson (1962-1992) and until May 2009 by Jay Leno (since 1992) competed for the same nationwide audience with similar formats using the same (or similar) artists. It thus became crucial to please the much-courted artist and his or her patron, the record company, to ensure future favours. That concerns for the audience's taste (and by implication the advertisers' money) and not personal preferences prevail was amply shown as early as 1956 when Ed Sullivan had to invite Presley to his show, despite his overtly expressed disgust for this pop idol. Steve Allen had surpassed Sullivan in the ratings by hosting Elvis a few months' earlier, so drastic measures were called for (Harris 1968: 116). In a wider perspective, this jockeying for position invites the host to adopt an uncritical perspective towards the artist and/or, in the extreme case, to lend their voice to the opinion of record companies' marketing departments.

Rating is at the core of television programming. Not only do audiences and advertisers constantly rate programmes, it is also the very practice of rating that gives entertainment programmes nerve and drama by introducing elements from the sport contest. As noted by Frith (2002: 288) music on television often means "charts, awards, lists, quizzes, rituals, contests." Talent shows like *Britain's Got Talent* are emblematic for this tendency. And interestingly Paul Potts' performance was placed at the end of both the semi-finals and the Grand Finale thus being both the climax of the contest in terms of narration and the beginning of the marketing campaign, seen from the perspective of the record company who, as mentioned, owns the production company. Such interweaving of interests – of wanting to put on a good show, to sell attractive advertising breaks, to sell a programme concept, and to sell records – can make a critical viewer question the 'real' intentions of this programme: Is the show staged to provide emotionally rewarding entertainment or to produce, profile and promote an upcoming star?

The essence of 'puppet programmes' is thus that they deliberately blur the interests at stake in staging the programme thereby conveying the impression that a message serving a private interest is in the interest of the general public. 'Puppet programming' works by naturalizing a commercial purpose as sober information or innocent entertainment. In this process, the selection criteria are obscured. The question why the audience has to watch for example this particular artist and not all kinds of others is never posed. Secondly, the same goes for the narrative construction of the programme: It does not only serve the purpose of constructing a satisfying plot on immanent aesthetic premises but also to generate maximum commercial effect (desire, memory). Thirdly, the 'actual' sender of the message is obscured: Apparently, the presenter or the host is talking as an 'official' sender, but in reality he or she is a mere puppet for the 'actual' sender, who lends the authority of his marionette to make the message credible – impartial, objective, true. Allowing such parasite activity to occur can, in the long run, undermine the viewers' trust in what they are watching and hearing on television and hence backfire commercially as well as politically and ethically.

Product placement

Product placement is a practice that deliberately aims at benefiting from the promotional opportunities given by exposing a commercial product in an attractive narrative sequence. When a specific car is placed in a movie depicting a car chase, it creates the impression that this product is especially suited for fast driving. Or when a CD album is offered as a prize in a quiz show, this may promote the feeling that this music is very desirable and worth battling for. The trick done by product placement is thus that it contextualizes a mass produced commodity in a 'natural' setting (i.e. outside the realm of advertising) where it is used and valued by admirable and ordinary people alike for its seemingly special qualities.

For the company, product placement is a promotional tool, implying that it is part of the marketing mix. By consequence, the company has either offered the product for free or (most often) even paid for the placement of the product. Product placement should hence be perceived as hidden advertisement. What is obscured to the public is not the product itself, which ideally should be as visible or audible as possible, but instead, the legal agreement between the producer or transmitter of the media programme and the producer of the commodity getting exposure in the programme. The use of chairs and tables is quite common in for example interview programmes. These props become placed products when they have been delivered for free to the studio. The advertising effect is moreover boosted if the host deliberately mentions the brand name of the chair. Such placement can get sales rocketing, illustrated by the placement of the famous Wegner-chairs in the televised presidential debates between Nixon and Kennedy in 1960.

The deliberate use of a specific brand of chairs is an example of 'on set placement', where the product is typically offered for free but often remains rather unnoticed in the background. Another, commercially more interesting form of placement is 'creative placement'. In that case, the commodity plays a more active role in the narration, like in the car chase: The scene gives the impression that this specific car was necessary or indispensable for the satisfactory solution of the conflict. 'Verbal placement', where the commodity is both used and mentioned, is believed to have the best effect on the audience's memory, and is hence the most expensive form (Wasko, Phillips & Purdie 1993).

From an audience point of view, placement has many similarities with 'puppet programmes' in that: 1) the selection criteria are obscured (it is often not evident why this particular car is used or this specific album is offered and not one with similar qualities from a different mark); 2) the product is placed in the sequence in order to ensure maximum effect (e.g. when the audience is expected to be emotionally most involved in the plot); 3) the host or protagonist acts like a marionette, praising the brand's qualities. From a commercial point of view, though, these two forms of obscuring the promotional intention differ in that product placement is based on a legal contract. The producer of the commodity has paid for it, and it is hence deductible. And on the other side, the producer of the programme has received the commodity (and often also money), and can therefore improve the production budget. Product placement is thus visible in the companies' accounts. Its results are likewise visible (and audible) to the public, but the economic reasons (i.e. its commercial relevance) why precisely these commodities are receiving exposure remain hidden from the eye and ear.

While product placement has attracted much attention in the last 25 years from marketers, media researchers and consumer advocates, the issue of music placement in media products has largely been ignored. Music is not mentioned in histories of product placement in movies (e.g. Segrave 2004) nor in textbooks defining and discussing the phenomenon (e.g. Clow & Baack 2004, Fill 2002, Galician 2004, Lehu 2007).[1] Illustrative for this neglect is the analysis by Galician & Bourdeau (2004) of product placement in the 15 top grossing motion pictures of 1977, 1987, and 1997. The authors carefully identified 546 instances of product placement, but somewhat disappointingly the analysis did not involve music. The placements identified, i.e. products 'seen', 'mentioned', and 'used', obviously all refer to *visual* commodities such as cars, cigarettes and beverages. However, in most films mentioned, music plays a noteworthy role, and in some of them, like *Dirty Dancing* (1987), musical products are even of pivotal importance both for the aesthetics of the film and for the earnings. To date, the soundtrack, presenting a collection of music placed in this movie, is one of the best selling albums ever: 32 million copies sold worldwide.[2]

This blatant neglect by researchers could be caused by the delusion that music primarily belongs to the realm of (popular) culture and not to that of private enterprise. But in an age of media concentration such naivety is utterly misleading. The media industry is characterized by a high degree of vertical, horizontal and diagonal integration, uniting many branches of the industry (including record companies) under corporate ownership (Herman & McChesney 1997). When Sony BMG, for example, owns production companies like Syco TV, as seen in the Potts-case, it becomes difficult to discern whether albums are spin-offs of programmes or programmes are adverts for coming albums. Most often, both perspectives are equally relevant.

Whereas it can be discussed whether the use of music in movies like *Dirty Dancing* is actually the result of product placement or is driven by the producer's urge to use (and pay for) music uniquely suited for the plot and its ambience, the case is often more clear cut in television series. In a report on the extent of commercialization in Danish public service television (Jantzen & Stigel 1995), the authors drew attention to especially American soap operas. These programmes are characterized by a short production time and a close proximity between the time of production and that of transmission on their home market. This makes these programmes extremely suitable for promoting new and fashion-sensitive products like music. By analyzing *Beverly Hills 90210* (Fox, 1990-2000) the authors found numerous examples of *music* placement, i.e. of the newest and 'hottest' music being played and discussed in a conspicuous manner. Because the fictional time (i.e. the time in which the plot is believed to happen) and the transmission time also coincided, this moreover made *event* placement possible. This opportunity was used creatively in one of the episodes transmitted in the US in the spring of 1995, when the Rolling Stones were touring the United States. (They went on to tour Europe, coinciding with the series being transmitted on the continent). On the day of Stones' visit in the LA-area, the concert set the stage for the whole episode.

This particular case of placement has given a group of almost pensioners an adolescent or perhaps teenage appeal in the cultural circuit. For the production company, it has also been an obvious advantage to have the show and its protagonists associated with the celebrity status of the rock band in this circuit. And one could also argue that this placement gives the audience some useful information about 'what's hot and what's not'. The fact that product placement may contribute to the identity construction of the viewers should nonetheless not obscure the fact that paying for exposure implies that other and possibly even more relevant lifestyle options were banned from the series. The consequence of product placement is thus that the commercial circuit sets the agenda for what is relevant (and what not) in the cultural circuit. It does not directly dictate music taste but it indicates which preferences are socially worth pursuing and which options are culturally attractive. What used to be the goal of education has now become the business of private enterprise.

Relevant... but for whom?

Music is used in a wide variety of television programmes, and often for good reasons. Music helps to contextualize the setting of fictional programmes, to regulate the mood of participants in and viewers of the programme, to signal breaks and continuity in the programming, and so forth. Music also helps sell commodities, and one of the commodities sold is music itself: artists, albums and events. This selling takes place in commercial breaks, but it also occurs in regular programmes. This is selling in disguise: What is presented as objective information or as an essential part of a quiz show or a television drama is in reality pure promotion, verbalized, staged and perhaps even scheduled by the marketing department of some corporation and not by the production company nor by the television channel.

We have sketched two different forms of hidden advertising: 'puppet programmes' and product placement. Both forms are ethically problematic for three reasons: 1) Whose interests are actually expressed? 2) Who is the 'real' sender of the message? 3) Why is the message or the material presented in precisely this way and why is this element used or presented and not something else? The real reasons motivating the presentation are thus obscured. In 'puppet programming', the trust audiences put in the channel, the programme and/or its host is abused. In product placement, the reality effect of television fiction is misused to promote a motive that is actually without relation to the plot, or a quiz shows' prize giving is misused to praise the qualities of the product.

The core of the problem with these kinds of promotion is that they seem to suggest that the relevance of the product for the viewer can be taken for granted, because the programme, and its host (e.g. 'puppet programmes') or its protagonist (product placement) endorses this relevance. This relevance is furthermore presented as something acceptable, desirable or indispensable for the viewer's personal identity and social life. But at the same time, such messages are relevant to other parties for quite different reasons: i.e. to television channels and production companies to make the budget balance (product placement) and to producers of commodities to get these goods promoted in an attractive environment (product placement and 'puppet programmes').

A basic truth about the way in which media operate today is that media are not only financed by selling programmes, papers and other products to consumers but also, and increasingly so, by selling potential consumers (viewers, readers, users) to producers of commodities. As stated, music is one such commodity. But almost nobody seems to question this logic or to consider its consequences when it comes to music. This, nevertheless, is what is called for. Producing music has not been a cottage industry for decades. The music industry is instead fully integrated in the media industry, where power has become concentrated in a few global corporate enterprises. In order to understand how mediated music functions in its cultural circuit, it is thus highly relevant to see how the commercial circuit influences and sometimes even determines this cultural circuit. Hence, more research into the commercialization of mediated music is needed.

NOTES

1 Lehu comes close, though, in an interesting discussion on product placement (or 'brand-dropping') in song lyrics (Lehu 2007: 171ff). It seems that contemporary hip-hop music presents the most conspicuous marketing case, but the phenomenon is by no means a recent one: according to Lehu, the Eagles' *Hotel California* (1976) for example had paid placement for up market brands like Mercedes and Tiffany.

2 http://en.wikipedia.org/wiki/Dirty_Dancing_%28soundtrack%29 visited Jan. 28th, 2008. Other films discussed in Galician & Bourdeau (2004) with no reference to music are *Saturday Night Fever* (1977) and *Titanic* (1997) – both films of course in the same league as Dirty Dancing when it comes to the importance of music (cf. Smith 1998 and 1999 for discussions on placements of music in films (a.o. *Titanic*)).

REFERENCES

Clow, K., & Baack, D. (2004). *Integrated Advertising, Promotion and Marketing Communications* (2nd ed.). Harlow: Prentice Hall.

Donnelly, K. (2005). *The spectre of sound: Music in film and television*. London: BFI Publishing.

Ellis, J. (1992). *Visible fictions: Cinema, television, video*. London: Routledge.

Fill, C. (2002). *Marketing communications. Contexts, strategies and applications* (3rd ed.). Harlow: Prentice Hall.

Fiske, J. (1988). *Television culture*. London: Routledge.

Frith, S. (2002). Look! hear! The uneasy relationship of music and television. *Popular music*, *21(3)*, 277-290.

Galician, M.-L. (Ed.). (2004). *Handbook of product placement in the mass media. New strategies in marketing theory, practice, trends, and aesthetics*. Binghamton: Haworth Press.

Galician, M.-L., & Bourdeau, P. G. (2004). The evolution of product placements in Hollywood cinema: Embedding high-involvement 'heroic' brand images. In M.-L. Galician (Ed.), *Handbook of product placement in the mass media. New strategies in marketing theory, practice, trends, and aesthetics* (pp. 15-36). Binghamton: Haworth Press.

Harris, M. D. (1968). *Always on sunday: Ed Sullivan, an inside view*. New York: Meredith Press.

Herman, E. S., & McChesney, R. W. (1997). *Global media: The new missionaries of global capitalism*. New York: Continuum International Publishing Group.

Jantzen, Ch., & Stigel, J. (1995). *Reklamen i dansk landsdækkende fjernsyn* [Advertising in Danish nationwide television]. Copenhagen: Statsministeriet.

Lehu, J.-M. (2007). *Branded entertainment: Product placement and brand strategy in the entertainment Business*. London: Kogan Page.

Negus, K., & Street, J. (2002). Introduction to 'Music and Television'. *Popular music, 21(3)*, 245-248.

Rutherford, P. (1994). *The new icons? Art of television advertising*. Toronto: University of Toronto Press.

Segrave, K. (2004). *Product placement in Hollywood films: A history*. Jefferson, NC: McFarland & Co.

Smith, J. (1998). *The sounds of commerce – Marketing popular film music*. New York: Columbia University Press.

Smith, J. (1999). Selling my heart. Music and cross-promotion in Titanic. In K. Sandler, & G. Studlar (Eds.), *Titanic. Anatomy of a blockbuster* (pp. 46-63). New Brunswick: Rutgers University Press.

Tagg, Ph., & Clarida, B. (2003). *Ten little title tunes*. New York: MMMSP.

Wasko, J., Phillips, M., & Purdie, C. (1993). Hollywood meets Madison Avenue. The commercialization of US films. *Media, Culture & Society, 15(2)*, 271-293.

WATCH THIS! YEARN FOR THAT! STAY TUNED!
The use of channel music as a promotional tool in television programming

Nicolai Graakjær and Christian Jantzen

INTRODUCTION

> "But in an age when, in general, silence seems abhorrent and music of a sort has become increasingly inescapable everywhere, television programmes – nature programmes, travelogues and features of all kinds, even some plays – have practically incessant music foisted on them, regardless of the fact that it often obscures the narration or dialogue. Much as this relegation of music to aural wallpaper may be deplored, the practice now seems ingrained; producers could, however, set an example by reversing the trend and helping to restore to music something of its true value" (Salter 2008).

Thus ends the entry on television music in the Grove Music Online (allegedly 'the world's premier authority on all aspects on music'). Certainly, switching on the television set implies tuning in on music of some sort, and arguably all music occurring on television is in the business of selling, as also noted by Frith: "The dominant use of music on television, one might conclude, is to sell things" (Frith 2002: 281). What is being sold is at times somewhat obscure though, in that the commercial circuit of television propels at least both channels, advertisers, artists, sponsors, and record companies through for example *puppet programmes* and *product placement* (see chapter 7 this volume). Alongside original music for series, documentaries, etc. this music infuses virtually every television genre, allowing for impressions of 'practically incessant music'. This holds true both of *music programmes*, *programmes with music*, and *programmes about music* (cf. the typology in Linz 1985). However, it might prove beneficial to add yet another category to this account: i.e. the music organized by the channel itself. This music is also in the business of selling, but the commercial circuits are less obscure: The channel uses music to attract and maintain the attention of its audience, so that these viewers can be 'sold to' advertisers or be measurable in audience research, thus contributing to the political legitimacy of the channel. This category of music could be coined *channel music* and has a distinct promotional purpose by drawing attention to coming programmes or by profiling the programme or the channel. In this chapter, we aim at giving an overview of different types of channel music and to discuss the promotional functions of this music for programming. Two basic subcategories of channel music can be identified: music in non-programmes and that in scheduled programmes.

The promotional functions of music in 'non-programmes'

Television is scheduled in ever more precise time slots. In the era prior to deregulation and (predominantly commercial) satellite television, only few programmes had their fixed place on the daily, weekly or monthly schedule: e.g. the evening news or the children's programme. In countries where only public service broadcasters operated, the remainder of the schedule was very loose, making time for programmes of shifting length and even room for longer intervals without scheduled programmes during the evening hours. The commercialization of European television in the 1980s changed all that. It intensified the inter-channel competition on programmes and audiences. The programme schedule became standardized with many more fixed programmes (especially news), an earlier and later 'prime time' programming and many programmes with a standard length of 25 or 50 minutes. Between these scheduled programmes, the time slot is filled with commercial breaks and short intervals advertising upcoming events on the channel.

These short intervals could be labelled 'non-programmes'. They are not featured in newspapers, magazines and programme news. When looking at television schedules, these non-programmes appear as unimportant padding – they are anonymous (not mentioned or specified) and, apparently, they are merely there to fill in pauses between programmes.[1] From the perspective of the channel, the appreciation of the padding is of course quite different. Padding is the material that enables the channel to tickle, attract and keep hold of the audience, thereby contributing to the channel's commercial goal of delivering a sufficient amount of viewers to its advertisers. So, the aim of these 'non-programmes' is not merely to 'waste time' in a not too unpleasant way while nothing of real importance to the viewers happens. That padding is important is also indicated by the sheer amount of time actually used on 'non-programmes' during the flow.[2] This television flow has been increasingly dominated by "bits of information that make promises for more to come" (Stigel 2004: 29). Moreover, and as a possible result of stylistic rub-off effects on other types of programmes "we are dealing with more and more self-reference within the range of programs" (ibid.). Such measures are expressed in different kinds of 'promos': that is, commercials that refer internally to the channel and/or the programmes it provides to its viewers. These promos promise that even though nothing happens right now, something interesting and relevant will occur quite soon (in five minutes or one week) on the very same channel. So stay tuned, if you don't want to miss out on the action.

The most common types of promos are:

- *Bumpers*: short-lasting lead-ins and lead-outs enclosing a programme and thus smoothening breaks between the scheduled programme and e.g. commercials (e.g. as a sponsor announcement) (Bjurström & Lilliestam 1993)
- *Teasers*: a longer presentation of a programme to come in the near future, but not immediately following the teaser
- *Channel idents:* short-lasting logo presentations identifying the channel (Brownrigg & Meech 2002)
- *Listings:* still-shots, maybe animated, of the programmes to be broadcasted on a particular time of the day, often associated with *channel idents*.

In addition *fillers* can appear: a non-scheduled programme used to fill unforeseen 'gaps' in the flow. This last type is a promo in a somewhat different sense than the ones just mentioned in that it presents a profiling of the channel – as a brand – without directly corresponding to the day- or week-schedule itself or to specific programmes on the channel.

Promos have the specific aim of directing the audience's attention to the programmes listed, which in turn (and among other things) directs the viewers' attention to yet another type of unlisted programme: *commercials*. From the perspective of the flow, commercials are alien elements that each use about 10-40 seconds for advertising some product without any obvious relation to the channel and its programmes. Both commercials and promos are in the business of pointing at and promising a desirable future experience or product, but they differ by pointing at different future scenarios. Promos point to a future experience in the present world of the channel – it points to what is on or about to come – whereas commercials point to a future appropriation of products in the absent (but perhaps 'real') world of the market.

The music used in promos and commercials differ somewhat in style and function. Commercial music is quite diverse in terms of presence, distinctiveness and origin. Music in promos on the other hand, is almost always distinctive and originally composed. Inclusion of (distinctive) music has to do with the general functions of promos structuring the flow of television in both a syntagmatic and paradigmatic way: It sequences the flow in a 'horizontal' perspective by occurring regularly and repeatedly and it segments the flow in a 'vertical' perspective by signalling, calling and making possible recognition and association. The music is crucial in this respect: It smoothes breaks and in-betweens, and it highlights current and coming programmes to the service of the perhaps absent-minded or distracted 'viewers' (or more aptly 'listeners'), the idea of promos seemingly being "What is out of sight must come in the ear". As all viewers are potentially 'listening' when in fact not looking at the screen – for instance when attending to other doings while the television is still running – the music can cause viewers to pay attention to the screen again. The music hence functions as a sort of 'umbilical cord' between the viewer and the screen; it avows the viewer that (s)he does not miss out on upcoming programmes. To the regular viewer, promos can be considered as easily recognizable and differentiable even when listening is only peripheral: Distinctiveness entails differentiation and repetition entails recognition and association.

The musical interface controlled by the channel (cf. bumpers, channels idents and listings) is important in times of numerous channels each trying to maintain and provide *identity* while addressing viewers fond of zapping and, when not-zapping, perhaps being preoccupied by other doings (i.e. not looking at the screen). Compared to previous uses of fanfare-like themes, channel music (and especially channel idents) have become more "fun-fair"-like (Brownrigg & Meech 2002). The result is reportedly "more fluid and musically more sophisticated forms" with "not one monolithic version, but a series linked both in vision and sound" (ibid.: 352f). Promo music is rarely pre-existing and, as a result, the music is not likely to be or become a product, though borderline cases can be identified. In those cases, when the total (or most) of the musical interface of the channel is standardized (or styled) by one specific artist, the product placement is arguably apparent through the (style of the) *artist* (if not the exact music used) being promoted.[3] Teasers can furthermore present musical products, in that teasers typically include excerpts of complete title tunes – often becoming products themselves – to be heard in the actual programme.

The promotional functions of music in scheduled programmes

The increase in competition between channels has intensified attention paid by broadcasters towards scheduling. The urge to create a both interesting and recurrent, and hence easily recognizable and memorable structure in the flow of weekly programming has divided especially the 'prime time hours' into distinctive parcels of shorter or longer programmes (longer programmes typically being twice as long as shorter). On the public service channels, this practice has lead to a remarkable increase in news programmes, serving as daily anchors in the weekly schedule.[4] The ability to produce interesting and reliable news coverage has become an important aspect in inter-channel competition for viewers, because building a loyal news-audience propels the share of viewers who watch the commercial breaks before and after the news or who stay tuned in for the succeeding parts of the evening schedule. Selecting relevant items from the continuous flow of news, presenting them in a comprehensible, credible and interesting way, and continuously upholding distinct criteria for the selection and presentation of news are thus of seminal importance for meeting the expectations of the viewers and hence for profiling the programme as well as the channel. The use of visual and sound logos helps to emphasize this profile. In this respect, music is often utilized to create *programme idents*, distinguishing a channel's programmes from its competitors'.

Because news has become such an important type of programme both for anchoring the schedule and for profiling the identity of the channel, the use of music in creating a distinctive signature is especially noticeable in this kind of programme. An analysis of the first 23 seconds of the most popular Danish news programme (TV2's 7 o'clock *News*) showed how music functioned to combine all the visual and sonic elements during the introduction of the programme (Graakjær 2004). Music established an underlying coherence between these various aspects, thus producing not only a continuous sequence leading up to the first news item of the evening but also a new unity clearly distinguishable from the visual and sonic impressions, which the preceding programming had left (namely a short sequence of 'non-programmes' after the commercial breaks). The music thus primarily has a syntagmatic function: It tells the viewers that a *new* programme is about to start and that this programme is different from the previous programmes in the schedule. It simply sounds different. But secondly and simultaneously, this music serves a paradigmatic function: It tells the viewers that the *same* programme as the one they usually watch at this hour is about to start. It simply sounds similar and is hence easily recognizable, implying that the handling of the news will resemble that of the preceding days, weeks, months and years. Thirdly, this music is also paradigmatic by being different from the sounds that accompany other channels' news programmes. It sounds distinct, implying that the programme as such distinguishes itself from its competitors.

The way this music actually sounds is in fact remarkable (cf. Graakjær 2004 for more details). Starting with a pronounced kettledrum and quickly (after 5 seconds) developing into something resembling a *reveille*-motif, the music of *News* has many of the 'fanfare'-like qualities that charac-terized the channel idents in the earlier years of television (Brownrigg & Meech 2002).[5] Also involved is the musical-structural feature that seems to have been a defining trait of *news-music* for quite some time, namely the 'music of the telegraph'. Musically phrased through rhythmic staccato attacks in alternating rapid succession, it resembles 'morse-coding' (as well as teleprinters and, in fact stammering), and it is associated with *speed*, *excitement* and *urgency*, all seminal aspects of the news (and a few other genres such as live sport; see Tagg & Clarida 2003: 487ff, Leeuwen 1989). The purpose of this composition is of course to signal that something else and something of importance is going to happen here and now, thus creating a rupture in the flow of the channel and alerting the viewer to pay attention. This signalling emphasizes the syntagmatic function of programme music. Subsequently, this signal is transformed into a sound structure resembling the style of late-romanticism, thus indicating that the programme is serious, dramatic as well as emotionally engaging. This style-indication emphasizes the paradigmatic function of music. This evening's programme has the same qualities and standards as last evening's, but these standards are used or expressed differently (and by implication: 'better') than on the competing channel's news. The fact that particularly late-romantic music is considered both sophisticated and relatively easily digestible (i.e. not too academic) underscores the profile of the programme – and by implication of the whole channel. The news is relevant (serious, important) as well as interesting (entertaining, involving) thereby marking a distance to adversaries who allegedly either deliver relevant news in an uninteresting way (e.g. DR1) or interesting but irrelevant news (e.g. the programmes by commercial satellite channels with a focus on celebrities and (their) scandals).

Music thus serves to promote the importance of this particular programme compared to both other programmes on the same channel and similar programmes on other channels. In the case of pronounced programme music, the composition may thus have effects on the intra- as well as the inter-channel profiling. It signals to the audience that something different from the rest of the flow is going to be presented (intra-channel profiling). This is the *presentational* function of music working on the syntagm of the flow. Simultaneously, it tells the audience that this programme differs from other examples in the same genre (inter-channel profiling), and moreover that this difference is a constant one: This particular episode of the programme will represent the same distinct qualities as previous evenings' episodes. This is the *representational* function of music, framing this programme as something else than those programmes offered by competitors. Different items, other news anchors, presenters and journalists, new sources – yet the same unique blend of seriousness and wit, of ways (form) to angle and report on a perpetually shifting world (content).

In order to function in both the presentational and representational mode, structural coherence in the programme itself is indispensable. This experience of coherence is primarily instigated by music in the introductory 23 seconds of the programme. Music is that aesthetic element that links all the other elements together in what appears to be a continuous flow of images, which without linking would fall apart as disjunctive fragments. This *linking* function in a metaphorical sense symbolizes the *representational* function of news as such. Without the coherence brought about by the practice of producing news, the occurrences in the world would fall apart as sheer, meaningless incidents. News transforms occurrences to information by giving them a stable frame of interpretation. In the same way, music gives the presentation of news a stable frame for understanding this interpretation: "This is important and/but we are dealing with it and explaining it to you in our usual, competent way. You know, you can rely on that (and on us)". Music sets the content of the programme apart from the rest of the channel's flow, at the same time reintegrating it in to the flow of each viewers existence. In a wider perspective music thus not only promotes the programme and the channel, but also the ritualization of everyday life (Selberg 1993).

WATCH THIS! YEARN FOR THAT! STAY TUNED!

Television is in the business of informing and entertaining audiences, regardless whether these are national publics, local interest groups or global niches. But television is also in the business of delivering viewers to the political system and private enterprise, thus legitimizing money spent on maintaining broadcast services. In order to succeed in this field, channels have to attract viewers and make them stay tuned so they may watch scheduled programmes. This is a main purpose of channel music: it attempts to increase awareness of prospective programmes (e.g. teasers) or to get people to stick to the channel while commercial breaks are interrupting a favoured show or television drama (e.g. bumpers). Channel music points to a more or less distant future of interesting things soon to come (again): "We will be back with you in a short moment" or "You've seen nothing yet. So wait and see".

Moreover, channel music emphasizes the continuous and constant presence (the 'here-and-now') of programming itself. The music accompanying listings and channel idents promotes the distinct profile of this particular channel and sets it apart from all other stations. The identity of the channel is always the same, and it is forever different from its competitors. Recurrent music thereby stresses the invariable and perpetual qualities of the station or network. In doing this, channel music contributes to the routinization and perhaps even ritualization of watching television. It eases viewers' orientation and their decision-making – i.e. which channel to choose as the primary one to watch; or simply: "Where to feel at home".

The same goes pre-eminently for the music used in those programmes that serve as anchors in the flow of programming. Here, music announces that something important is going to occur. Viewers should avert attention from other doings and start concentrating on the screen again. At the same time, distinct programme music guarantees that what is going to occur will be of the same quality as the viewers are accustomed to. Like channel music, these sounds function to increase the interest in *and* to maintain the relevance of the programme. The promotional function of channel and programme music is hence a double one. By punctuating the flow of images, sounds and speak, it promotes the extraordinary qualities of coming features: "Watch this!". But by presenting this punctuation in a predictable way and on fixed moments in the schedule, it promotes the regularity of this flow and by consequence the stability of everyday life. It raises our awareness of special elements in the syntagm of programming and makes us yearn for future things. But it also makes us recognize the recurrent aspects of this programming and find satisfaction in staying tuned and being present.

Notes

1. Internal records reflect the actual appearances of promos, but still commercials are listed *en bloc* without specification.
2. A study of the early morning flow of children's television shows that about 29% of the time is allocated to unscheduled programmes (Johansen & Graakjær 2007; cf. also specifications in Jantzen & Stigel 1995 and Hicketier & Bleichert 1997).
3. In Danish television, an example is the use of somewhat sophisticated jazz-grooves for DR2 (by Thomas Blachman). Another Danish example was the 'calendar music' by the modern composer Per Nørgaard in 1970. This music was used during pauses, but was cancelled after a storm of protests by angry viewers.
4. Prior to deregulation, Denmark for example was a mono-channel country with only one news programme each evening (at 7.30 pm). The coming of the new public service channel TV2 (predominantly financed by commercials) in 1988 lead to a tremendous increase in news programmes. Today, the two main public service channels, DR1 and TV2 each transmit more than 1.5 hours of news programmes between 6 pm and 10.30 pm on weekdays. Moreover, both channels broadcast daily magazines with 'light news' of approximately one hour each during early 'prime time'.
5. According to Brownrigg & Meech 2002, this was inspired by the music introducing the film company in Hollywood movies (especially Twentieth Century). The authors argue that this fanfare was replaced by softer "fun-fair" music during the 1980s and identify three new dominant forms of sound in channel idents in the UK: a softer musical style, a dance-music style and the use of other sound effects than music.

References

Bjurström, E., & Lilliestam, L. (1993). *Sälj det i toner* [Sell it in tunes]. Stockholm: Konsumentverket.

Browrigg, M., & Meech, P. (2002). From fanfare to funfair: The changing sound world of UK television idents. *Popular Music, 21(3)*, 345-355.

Frith, S. (2002). Look! hear! The uneasy relationship of music and television. *Popular Music, 21(3)*, 277-290.

Graakjær, N. (2004). Nyhedernes music [The music of news]. *MedieKultur, 37*, 36-46.

Hicketier, K., & Bleichert, J. (Eds.). (1997). *Trailer, Teaser, Appetizer. Zu Ästhetik und Design der Programbindungen im Fersehen. Beiträge zur Medienästhetik und Mediengeschichte* [Trailer, teaser, appetizer. On the aesthetics and design of programme connections in television. Contributions to the aesthetics and history of media]. vol. 3. Hamburg: LIT Verlag.

Jantzen, Ch., & Stigel, J. (1995). *Reklame i dansk landsdækkende fjernsyn* [Advertising in Danish Nationwide Television]. Copenhagen: Statsministeriet.

Johansen, S., & Graakjær, N. (2007).The sound of children's television – Or why it makes sense to watch television facing away from the screen. *P.O.V., 23*, 41-65.

Leeuwen, Th. v. (1989). Changed times, changes tunes: Music and the ideology of the news. In J. Tulloch, & G. Turner (Eds.), *Australian Television: Programs, pleasures and politics* (pp. 102-119). Sydney: Allen & Unwin.

Linz, G. (1985). Musik im Programm – Musik als Programm [Music in programme – Music as programme]. In W. Hoffmann-Riem, & W. Teichert (Eds.), *Musik in den Medien. Programmgestaltung im Spannungsfeld von Dramaturgie, Industrie und Publikum* (pp. 87-98). Baden-Baden: Nomos.

Salter, L. (2008). Television – Applied music. I *Grove Music Online* [www.oxfordmusiconline.com/subscriber/article/grove/music/41850. Assessed August 19].

Selberg, T. (1993). Television and ritualization of everyday life. *The Journal of Popular Culture, 26(4)*, 3-10.

Stigel, J. (2004). Tv's egenreklame og kanalstemmen – en kvalitativ undersøgelse [Television's self-advertising and the voice of the channel – a qualitative inquiry]. *MedieKultur, 37*, 24-35.

Tagg, Ph., & Clarida, B. (2003). *Ten little title tunes*. New York: MMMSP.

Functions of Sound in Web Advertising

Iben Jessen and Nicolai Graakjær

Watch me! This message of a web banner – composed in large white letters on a red background – aims to attract the Internet user's attention to a new car model. The somewhat childlike address is emblematic of the struggle of the web ad in its effort to make the user pay attention. However, the banner is also illustrative of web advertising as predominantly visual phenomena. Apparently, this corresponds to the research interest: If it is generally the case that music in advertising represents a rather neglected research topic (see the introduction to this volume), this in particular holds true of web advertising. Thus, a very small number of studies have focused on sound and music in web advertising (for one example see Tsang 2007 with a somewhat different approach compared to the present chapter). Motivated by the sparse research interest, *auditory phenomena*, hereunder music, shall be examined, and the chapter proposes ways of understanding and analysing the occurrences, functions, and conditions of sound in web ads.

The chapter commences by an analysis of a specific commercial website, where sound and music are important elements. In connection with insights from more wide-ranging empirical initiatives – discussed in the second part of the chapter – this case analysis will provide the background for an overview of typical functions of auditory phenomena in web advertising. The overview is discussed, exemplified, and illustrated by a model, aiming to present a useful analytical framework (cf. figure 3) for the understanding of sound and its relation to modes of 'reading' on the Internet. As the use of sound on the Internet is seemingly not consolidated, and as advertising formats are not structurally homogenised (compared to the use and formats of for example TV), the chapter will introduce different types of web advertising and also discuss the conditions of auditory phenomena on the Internet. It hereby becomes clear that web ads, and their possible sound, are inspired by different media and genres, and therefore it appears relevant to include advertisement in other media as well as the use of sound in other genres.

I. Analysis of sound on the Volvo C30 Motor Show website

For our case analysis we have chosen the website for the car model Volvo C30, which was launched on the Paris Motor show in September/October 2006.[1] Apart from practical reasons (such as the case possessing the charms of novelty and availability at the time of writing), the particular case has been chosen because it presents an illustrative expression which is both varied and relatively delimited (cf. figure 1). Generally, it seems that web ads for cars very often include sound, and expectantly the case will exemplify and bring to light a range of essential issues. At the time of the case analysis (November 2006), the website appeared as a follow-up to the Motor show where the Internet user could 'visit' the Motor show again. The website is characterized by an extensive use of sound and music, and to some extent this is probably due to the importance of music at the Volvo sales pitch at the Motor show, cf. videos and female DJs as part of the exhibition. In analysing the website, we are partly interested in identifying the different auditory elements as they present themselves in the multimodal expression, and partly in mapping the role of sound in connection with the user actions offered on the website.

Auditory elements

The website for Volvo C30 has an introduction, which leads to a navigation room. From here, three other rooms are accessible: 1) An *exhibition room* featuring the presentation of C30 from the Paris Motor show (illustrated as a miniature of the Volvo sales pitch); 2) A *design room* where one can construct customized C30's ("Unwrap your C30"); and 3) A *showroom* that

Figure 1: Excerpt from sitemap for the Volvo C3 website (the sitemap is reconstructed and translated by the authors)

(omissions indicated by [...]) (♪ =music, 🗨 =speech, ♫ =sound effect)

Introduction ♪
The navigation room ♪
  Exhibition room: Paris Motor show ["SEE THE INTRODUCTION TO THE NEW VOLVO C30 AT PARIS MOTOR SHOW"] ♪
    Videos
      Video (introduction to C30) ♪
      Video (unveiling of C30) 🗨
      Video (arrangement of the exhibition)
    Webcams ♪
      Camera (steady camera; rotating C30)
      Camera (moving camera; from the exhibition)
    Sound ♪
      Camera (video of DJ)
      Camera (introduction video) ♪
      Menu with DJs (mouse-over: additional info)
    The official Paris Motor Show website (external)

Design room ["Unwrap your C30"] ♪ ♫
  C30 ♪ ♫
    [choices (step by step)--→ → → → [result: "SHOW ME"]
    Car colours (choose) Hubcaps (choose) Extras (watch)   Colour combinations (choose)   Extras (watch)   Exterior
    -                     -   Exhaust-pipe   Fabrics   Console (video) ♪   Perfect view (video) ♪ 🗨
    -                     -   Spoiler   -   Sports pedals   Functional design (video) ♪ 🗨
    -                     -   Ski/snowboard holder (video) ♪ -   Sports carpets   Collision from behind (video) ♪ 🗨
    -                     -   Windsurf holder (video) (🗨)   Seats (1-7)*   Gear-lever cover   Collision from the side (video) ♪ 🗨
    -                     -   Bike holder for the roof (video) ♪   Carpet (video) (🗨)   Collision from ahead (video) ♪ 🗨
    -                     -   Bike holder (video) (🗨)   Carpets (1-3)*   Net (video) 🗨   Driving properties (video) ♪ 🗨
    -                     -   Canoe holder (video) ♪   -   iPod/USB (video)   Dual tone (video) ♪
    -                     -   Dashboard (1-3)*   Bluetooth (video) ♪ (🗨) Clean inside and outside (video) ♪ 🗨
    -                     -   -
    -                     -   -   Send to a friend
                                                                                                                                    Choose background
                                           (* the number of choices depends on previous choices)   Change angel

                                                                                                                                    Interior
                                                                                                                                      Sports pedals
                                                                                                                                      Cover (photo series)
                                                                                                                                      Carpets
                                                                                                                                      Console (photo series)

[...]

Showroom: the carton, entry 1: "HAVE A LOOK AT COSMIC WHITE C30" ♪
  Photo ♪ 🗨
    Slideshow ♪ 🗨
    Downloads: wallpapers, slideshow, screensaver
    Photo series

[...]

offers information on several C30 models through photos, videos, and downloads (presented as a carton with holes open for inspection).

On the website, sound is generally presented in the following three categories:

- *music* (♪ on the sitemap, cf. figure 1), mainly extra-diegetic and only occasionally diegetic (in specific videos). Two of the most prevailing functions of this music is *supportive* and *mood enhancing*.
- *speech* (💬 on the sitemap, cf. figure 1), both via a (diegetic) presenter (e.g. a video of the manager unveiling the new car model) and via a (extra-diegetic) voice-over in videos presenting properties and qualities of the car.
- *sound effect* (🔊 on the sitemap, cf. figure 1), partly initiated by the users' actions, such as mouse-over, point-and-drag and clicks, and partly corresponding to objects in the picture frame making sound without direct user influence.

We will now take a closer look at the sounds of the introduction and of the three rooms. As already mentioned, the actual website is anticipated by an introduction (see figure 2 for an outline). The introduction is predetermined, and the user can only shorten the introduction by skipping parts of it, as a small icon discloses. Since the icon is placed in the periphery, it seems that a relatively experienced user is positioned. The sounds of the introduction thus appear as part of a fixed expression, which has to be followed. In other words, the sounds appear in a pre-arranged flow, not dissimilar to some types of TV flow, cf. the gradual absorption of viewers to TV programmes such as series and news in which music plays an important role as preparation and characterization (e.g. Tagg & Clarida 2003, Graakjær 2004). The user has no option of creating a so-called viewer-sub flow *in this text*, and the experience can only be modified by paying attention to something else or by changing website (inspired by the terminology of Jensen 1994 on TV reception). The sounds of the introduction position the user in a particular, almost physical relation to the shown. With increasing intimacy, the user is firstly positioned *outside* the carton in sequence 1 and secondly as *having a peak* in sequence 2. Ultimately, in sequence 6, the user is positioned in control and *inside* the imagined universe.

Figure 2: Overview of the introduction to the website for Volvo C30

Sequence	Time in sec.(ca.)	Sound	Picture	User positioning and possibilities of interaction
1. Prelude	10	A musical expression appearing distantly and without clear contour	Slow dolly-in on carton that moves (trembles)	The user must 'follow' or go to sequence 3
2. Video	16	A rounded musical expression. *Vamp*-like condensed structure with a 'busy' *shuffle*-beat. Ends with a cut followed by a short break.	A demo-video of a driving C30; it is seen from all angles in a picturesque fictional universe	
3. Presentation of carton	4	A sound effect of a car that brakes sharply.	The carton is 'arriving', sliding, almost sideways, leaving brake marks on a white floor (in an all white room)	
4. Presentation of rooms	25	A variation of the vamp-like structure from sequence 2: Harmonically and rhythmically not clearly profiled. Fades out at the end.	A cartoon character jumps up from the carton and the character presents three rooms via gesticulation and bubbles.	The user must 'follow'
5. Presentation of mouse	5	Another variation of the vamp-like structure from sequence 2: Clear harmonic and rhythmic profile in addition to a melodic motif in the high-pitched synth. Louder volume.	A meta-communicative presentation of possible interactions. Mouse, arrows, and verbal instructions on a dimmed white background.	
6. Navigation room	[user-defined]	Similar to sequence 5, though volume is reduced again. Option to change the source of sound and to activate sounds by movement of mouse.	Overview of all rooms. Movements with the mouse changes perspective.	The user can navigate

In sequence 1, the music sounds distant and without clear contour. At an explosive opening of a carton, the music attains profile by way of an increase in dynamics and the emergence of a returning structure in an upbeat tempo: Harmonically, four positions, representing three triads of an A-doric, appear in a four bar period in the following order – I–bIII–IV–I. The harmonic positions each take up one bar, and while the harmonic progression is relatively slow, the rhythm and instrumentation are condensed: A groove, constituted by drums and percussions and middle range keyboard instruments (a.o. synth and clavinet), expresses a 'busy' *shuffle* beat (12/8), in a way that every harmonic position presents a subdivision of 12 beats (grouped as 4 times 3). No tune or song is heard, and in this respect the musical expression bears resemblance to a *vamp* or a *turnaround*.

The musical expression is heard together with pictures including objects of many shapes and colours, and the visuals seem full of activity. From various, rapidly changing angles, the C30 is seen driving in a picturesque fictional universe, and the 'busy' repeated music helps construct significations such as 'durable', 'dynamic' and 'swift'. The music is also supportive in demarcating the sequence: After precisely two turnarounds, the sequence is stopped. The exact rounding off is dramatic, though, and it occurs as a sudden cut followed by a short break (less than a second). The break is dramatic – not least because it succeeds an intensive, circulating auditory expression, principally able of endless continuation, and the break most likely attracts the attention and interest of the user. Seemingly, the user is 'called to order', and the subsequent sound of car brakes, accompanying the sideways sliding entrée of a carton, intensifies this impression. Apart from appearing as an index of the car in the carton (the yet unseen car seems solid, relatively heavy, and fast; cf. cars have sound), the sound of brakes also functions as a symbol of change: Something is coming to a hold while something else is about to begin – in a syntagmatic perspective, the sound appears as an episodic marker. More concretely, it signals that one mode of orientation – a relatively passive mode of 'following' – has come to an end, while a new – a relatively active mode of 'navigating' – is about to begin. However, two additional sequences will have to 'educate' the user before the mouse is 'set free'.[2] Firstly, a presentation of options in the navigation room is shown (sequence 4), and secondly a meta-communicative demonstration of the functions of the mouse informs the user (sequence 5). In sequence 4, music is once again present, and at this point it appears as an attenuated variation compared to sequence 2: The music is softer and has a lighter groove, and moreover high pitched bells are added in synchronization to a cartoon-character presenting options in the navigation room. The music here clearly supports the visuals, and further visual information is presented through cartoon bubbles providing information on the use and control of the navigation room. The transition from sequence 4 to 5 is conveyed by a fade-out and a subsequent moment of silence. Again, the absence of sound functions as an episodic marker. Visually, the fade-out is synchronized to a change in the visual focus. The navigation room is left with increasing dim quality as a white, transparent middle-ground emerges. On this white-toned middle ground, the meta-communicative information is put in the foreground.

Sequence 5 presents yet another variation of the turnaround. Here, the music retains distinctiveness through increased volume and a few structural changes. A lighter and brighter expression is established through omissions and transpositions of some of the keyboard voices (up by one octave); an expression that appears visually supported by the emergence of the white-toned middle-ground, resulting in an imagined space between the navigation room and the user. The vamp also obtains a melodic profile: A stepwise descending contour is profiled through a high-registered synth, representing a doric-based movement from the octave to the perfect fifth. Whereas the melody has the effect of demarcating the turnaround even further, it does not provide a round off (the perfect fifth representing a sort of 'doorstop note'; inspired by Tagg & Clarida 2003: 806), which is underlined by the continuous rhythmic activity. A hitherto unheard sound is introduced and integrated: A simple whispering sound (as produced by wind in the trees) appears as a dynamically arched expression (crescendo/decrescendo) encompassing several turnarounds.

The transition from sequence 5 to 6 is not marked by break and silence, but a sudden shift in volume (back to the level encountered in sequence 4), precisely as the white middle-ground is cleared away, serves to highlight an episodic change. At this point, the 'education' of the user is completed, and the mouse is 'free' for use.

During sequence 6, the music continues until interrupted by the user. Whereas the music previously assisted in structuring the flow, it is at this point the only predetermined durational stimuli. Thus, the dominant function of the music changes from *structuring* to *mood enhancing*. In light of the preceding sequences, being on the website now seems monotonous, and the circular structure of the music appears endless and tedious, when accompanied by still-pictures. In a way, after just few moments of exposure, the user is probably prompt to navigate.[3] As mentioned, the mouse is 'free' for use, at the audio-visual expression can be modified: Visually, one can 'fly around' in the navigation room and have a look at the three rooms from a bird's eye view, and the whispering sound is supportive of the imaginative *spatiality* and *mobility* (even though the sound is pre-arranged and not a result of mouse movements). It is possible to manipulate the source of the sound by moving the mouse horizontally – if the mouse is moved to the left, the sound is heard in the right channel of the speaker(s) and visa versa. Mouse-over will activate sounds by the holes in the carton, and this feature highlights the possibility to manipulate the audio-visual expression. The sounds (e.g. cars beeping and laughter and talk as from a reception) appear synchronous to colourful eyeballs popping up, and they function as teasing attention grabbers offering foretastes of what are to be expected when clicking the cartons.

From the navigation room, three additional rooms can be frequented. In the exhibition room, a conventionalized setting, including a rotating car model, is accompanied by a repeating musical expression, and the music functions predominantly as mood enhancing. "VIDEOS", "WEBCAMS", and "SOUND" are titles of a menu that allows the user to choose between seven videos, all (but one) opening in a separate frame (e.g. in Windows Media Player). As it is the case with most of the introduction, the videos invite the user to 'follow' (to watch and listen), even though it is possible to manipulate the playback for instance by rewinding. In videos available under "VIDEOS" and "WEBCAMS", the music supports the audio-visual structure. A more distinctive use of music is to be found under "SOUND", where a video presents a DJ in action – apparently at the Paris Motor show. A list of information allows the user to learn more about the DJ, her female colleagues (they are all women), and their musical sources of inspiration.[4] The list gives the impression that several of the DJs have appeared for Volvo at the Paris Motor show, and the list both refers to the launch of C30 and to the music as a product in itself – representing a sort of co-branding of car and music. Interestingly, *women* are here staged in a manner far from the stereotypical norm prevailing at car shows. Whereas women have typically appeared mute and well-proportioned in tight-fitting clothes close to the cars, these women have their own space, from where they appear *casual* with a 'voice' of their own (the music played). Apparently, this rather unusual positioning of women in the particular context symbolises the attractiveness of the C30 to (also) cool and smart young women. At any rate, the music is here very distinctive, and it combines the launch of the new car model with specific lifestyles (also manifest in some of the other videos). Another noteworthy feature of the exhibition room, is the potential overlapping of different pieces of music. Thus, the playing of the two videos under "SOUND" does not automatically cause a mute of the mood enhancing music. The result is a simultaneous playback of both the videos' music and the mood enhancing music, and the impression left to users is a distressing cacophony.[5]

In the design room, the music heard is the same as in the exhibition room. However, apart from providing users with information to read and demonstration videos to watch, the design room offers the user opportunities to choose and construct as well. To go through the design room, the user has to perform a series of selections in a process of constructing the user's 'personal' C30 model with specific looks and equipment. The selections have to be made step by step. For example, the user has to pick hubcaps, colours, and fabrics for seats (cf. figure 1). Despite the linearity of events, this type of activity entails a different mode of orientation compared to 'following' and 'navigating', in that the selections made by the user leave obvious traces in the text (a personalized C30). Even though the options are limited, the selections made by the user nevertheless have an impact on the precise shaping of the website. An increase in the occurrences of sound effects underlines this new mode of orientation. Firstly, sound effects function as signals of the active selections made by the user – as a sort of auditory receipts – for instance when handling radio buttons or when dragging objects across the screen with the mouse (an example would be the dragging of hubcaps from a shelf onto the wheels of the car). Secondly, sound effects function as highlighting and characterizing animated objects, for example the sound of brush strokes when painting the car.

The third room is constituted by five separate and similar rooms. Primarily, the rooms consist of photos of different C30 models accompanied by different musical expressions: A rock-inspired, guitar-dominated tune full of vibrant chorus- and delay-effects corresponds to the simultaneous slideshow showing kaleidoscopic transformational pictures. A variation of this music, more soft with lesser chorus- and delay-effects and without melody, accompanies a series of videos providing data of the car. Thus, two dissimilar situations – the fascinating slideshow and the informational video, respectively – are constructed and highlighted through the use of dissimilar music. In addition to the music, the cardboard-like menu has sounds as well. An unfolding cardboard dial elicits a sound effect caused by both an initial animated entrée on the screen and by user activated mouse-over. Moreover, in one of the rooms (with the inviting text "watch the latest C30 photos, videos, and downloads") a cinema appears. In here, the activation of the menu causes the music to mute in favour of the sounds of a projector. Subsequently, it is up to the user to pick one of six music video-like presentations to be shown on the projector. As the presentation ends, the projector stops and the music plays again.

Sound and user-orientation

Inspired by the preceding analysis, we can identify three types of website user-orientation, namely 'following' (e.g. listening and watching a video or reading a written text), 'navigating' and 'constructing', corresponding to distinctions made by Finnemann (2001). Addressing digital texts in general, Finnemann distinguishes between three modes of 'reading': 1) 'Reading mode' 2) 'Link mode' (in hypertexts supported by links) and 3) 'Editing mode', "interactive behaviour changing the future behaviour/content of the system" (ibid.: 43). According to Finnemann, digital texts are characterized by *shifts* between the different modes of reading, representing "a discontinuous process, included as part of the reading process" (ibid.: 44).

If the types of user-orientation are related to the functions of sound, we are able to map the significance of sound on the Volvo C30 website. Figure 3 shows an overview of types of user-orientation in relation to the functions of sound that we have outlined in the case analysis. When in the mode of 'following', one watches, reads, and listens to the website present. In this mode, sounds are chiefly supportive and mood enhancing, exemplified by the music in the introduction and in the various rooms. The mode of 'navigating' involves an active and tactile contribution by the user, usually in the form of moving or clicking the mouse. Firstly, the music functions as an *indication of the user's position* for instance by the use of different music for different rooms, as showed in the case analysis. In other words, the music emphasizes the location of the user by connecting specific music with specific rooms or levels of the website structure, and thereby the music underlines *where* the user is or should be. Secondly, the music functions as a marker of link-option and interactivity, partly in the form of sound effects (cf. for instance the mouse-over of the carton in the navigation room), and partly in the form of circular expressions prompting the user to take action (cf. sequence 6). In the mode of 'constructing', the sound functions as a support to the user's editing (even if somewhat restricted and pre-arranged) when for instance designing a car. In contradiction to the mode of navigating, where sounds will normally function as *prompting* activity, the sounds of 'constructing' are rather *confirmatory* functioning as 'auditory receipts', highlighting the *result* of activity.

Figure 3: Mode of user-orientation in relation to the function of sound

Mode of user-orientation	Function of sound
Following	Mood enhancing Supporting
Navigating	Marking link option, shifts and position
Constructing	Confirming activity

It should be emphasized that the modes of user-orientation are overlapping and thereby not mutually exclusive. For instance, music with a predominantly mood enhancing function can form the auditory background of sounds marking options to link or of sounds confirming activities. Shifts between rooms are also typically marked by different kinds of music, and depending on shifts in modes of user-orientation, the functions of sound will change and possibly overlap.

II. General considerations on sound in web advertising

We have now discussed some of the most characteristic and interesting features of the case. In the next part of the chapter, we will take a step back and discuss the characteristics in connection with the genre of advertising on the Internet and the role of sound and music herein.

Web advertising as a genre

Users of the Internet are almost inevitably exposed to commercial messages, such as sponsored text links in search engines, animated banner ads, billboards, advertorials, pop-ups and commercial websites as the one just discussed. Web advertising includes a number of graphic formats, media and technologies, and contrary to for instance printed ads and TV commercials, which both have well-defined formats, a web ad is often more difficult to define clearly: How many links are related to the context of the ad? When is the ad no longer an ad?

Attempts to specify different types of ad formats on the Internet are numerous (e.g. Rodgers & Thorson 2000, Faber et al. 2004). Empirical studies on the effect of web ads either focus on embedded ads *on* host websites where the advertising message is competing with the surrounding content, e.g. banner ads in online newspapers,[6] or employ a broader conception of web advertising *as* commercial websites (see e.g. Hwang & McMillan 2004). Such delimitations are useful in the study of different characteristics of web ads, for example the effect of animation and interactivity. However, when it comes to structural characteristics of web ads, it is the hyperlinked composition that is most important. It is a general conception that web ads should be regarded as a relation or structural connection between an embedded web ad (e.g. a banner ad) and its linked website (the *target ad*). A general outline of this structure is worked out by Anja Janoschka (2004), who describes web ads as a succession of advertising messages: Web ads consist of an "initial advertising message" (e.g. a banner ad), which links to a "linked advertising message" (the destination of the banner ad, e.g. a web page about the product), and finally an "extended advertising message", which are the links from the destination of the banner ad (Janoschka 2004: 49f). This structural outline by Janoschka shows the complexity of the web ad: It is composed of several communicative layers, and it employs a number of different formats as well as media and technologies.

However, what are the characteristics of web advertising as a genre? A possible way to answer this question would be to describe the content and form of web ads as presenting a heterogeneous genre which refers to or borrows from many other genres and modes of expression in both the Internet medium and in other media. This reflects a general logic of remediation (Bolter & Grusin 1999), which in the realm of web ads can be identified in two ways: Firstly, the web ad borrows from ad formats in other media. For instance, static banner ads on websites resemble printed ads in newspapers or banners at stadiums and sport centres. Moreover, web ads containing film are very much similar to TV commercials and they often use the same content. Finally, sponsored text links in search engines share visual characteristics with the classified advertisement, apart from, of course, the technology behind the contextualized display of the text links. Secondly, the web ad borrows from other genres in (and outside) the Internet medium.[7] However, this parasitic characteristic is not restricted to web ads but is a common characteristic of advertising in general, as described by Guy Cook: "(…) they [ads] borrow so many features from other genres that they are in danger of having no separable identity of their own" (Cook 2001: 39). In the context of web ads, borrowed features from a broad spectrum of digital genres can be identified: At one end of the spectrum, the web ad is inspired by a functionalistic design paradigm that aims to make the interface 'user-friendly' and understandable. At the other end of the spectrum, we find web ads designed with inspiration from the immersive space of e.g. computer games, where the user is challenged and have to 'solve problems'.

The remediation of other media forms and genres can also be considered in a perspective of stages. John D. Leckenby identifies in his "Media Interaction Cycle" three phases in the development of a medium: 1) the transference of characteristics from one medium to another ("transference"), 2) focus on the capabilities specific to the medium ("exclusivity"), and 3) new media's influence on older media ("recurrence") (Leckenby 2005). To illustrate the phases, Leckenby refers to web ads: "Today's ubiquitous online banner ads are simply a product of taking known methods and ideas and transferring them to the new media from the traditional media, a common occurrence with the advent of a new medium" (ibid. 2005: 18). According to Leckenby, the first phase of web advertising is inspired by the outdoor billboard ad; the static banner ad must also communicate its message in competition with other messages in a very limited space and therefore needs to economize on the amount of information. The second phase is an exploitation of the unique features of the medium, e.g. the dynamic and interactive potential of digital media: "An ad becomes a mini-video game and requires media planners to make connections to new issues in their field such as online order fulfillment operations" (ibid. 2005: 22). And finally, in the third phase, Leckenby identifies examples of TV commercials copying features from the web ad.

Thus, Bolter & Grusin as well as Leckenby emphasize the development of genre as a result of a complex interplay between existing genres and media. In relation to web ads, we find examples of remediation of "older" forms of advertising as well as examples of new forms of advertising making use of the unique potentials of the Internet medium. Therefore, web advertising can generally be described as a simultaneous presence of Leckenby's phases 1 and 2 – or as a genre consisting of several degrees of remediation.[8] The following figure illustrates the genre related conditions of web advertising:

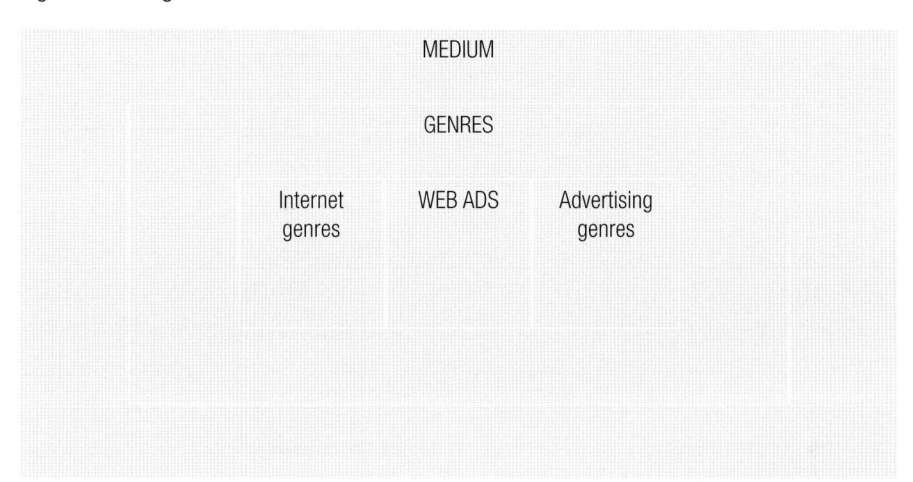

Figure 4: The genre related conditions of web ads:

	MEDIUM	
	GENRES	
Internet genres	WEB ADS	Advertising genres

ADVERTISING ON THE WEB — SOUNDS OF SILENCE

The question is now: How do auditory phenomena occur in web advertising? Inspired by the logic of remediation and the outline of web ad formats discussed above (embedded web ads versus advertising as websites), we can point to the following tendencies, while also drawing on empirical material from a Danish context:[9] A majority of the embedded web ads are without sound, and when in fact sound occurs, it is usually part of a video, a TV commercial or a film trailer, integrated into a banner or a billboard. Only a few cases have user activated sound effects.[10] As regards the destinations of the embedded web ads (hereafter referred to as commercial websites) sound is not exactly widespread, even if sound and music occur more frequently compared to the embedded web ads. The case provides an illustrative example.

Thus, the general impression is that web ads are rather silent. Probably this will change in the near future assessed by obviously impressed and optimistic commentators within the advertisement business. For instance, animated pictures with sound is considered to represent an effective and impressive means of communication (e.g. with reference to embedded web ads (cf. Gluck & Bruner 2005)), and sound is argued to have a great overall potential: "…the lack of sound on the vast majority of websites is part of its [Internet] unfulfilled potential […] we are still in the 'silent' era' of the Web but 'talkies' are not far away" (Jackson & Fulberg 2003: 7). However, foretelling is not the purpose of our discussion, as we will rather discuss the conditions of auditory phenomena on the Internet as they can be examined in ads at the time of analysis.

At first, some of the basic conditions of sound on the Internet shall be discussed. In this respect, the Internet differs considerably from more established media, such as TV. Whereas TV arguably presents sound *relatively independently* of user activity (cf. the sound is mutable but it usually emerges when the TV is switched on), the sound on the Internet is more likely to be *dependent on* (a result of) user activity in various ways. Implied are here some decisive differences between the two media: TV seems to be an audio-visual media presupposing speakers and sound (cf. TV sets have always been produced with integrated speakers), while the Internet to a greater extent has been conceptualized and used as a visual media with less focus on sound technology from both producers and users. For instance, it is no rare occurrence for the sound never to appear when opening a computer, in that opening a computer does not necessarily entail switching on speakers. Likewise, when specific web ads come into sight, it is not wholly expected for them to carry sound, indicated by the wide-spread use of imperatives in the ads such as 'turn up the sound' or 'switch me on'.

Thus, it might be concluded that the use of sound on the Internet is not characterized by neither consolidation nor familiarity, and reasons for this probably have to do with both the perspective of the sender (e.g. designers not being attentive to the potentials of sound) and the channel (e.g. the technology generally allows reproduction of sound only up to a certain degree of complexity). Also, an initial conclusion will be that sound typically appears as a result of user activity. In the following sections, we will take a closer look at specific ads on the Internet and the ways in which sound usually occurs.

Sound in embedded web ads

In embedded web ads, sounds are usually activated by the user's mouse, for instance by mouse-over – a more or less deliberate activity – or by clicking on the ad.[11] Such instances are typically formatted as embedded audio-visual videos of various periods, and often they bear resemblance to TV commercials (thus presenting a case of 'unchanged' representation of the TV commercial in another medium, cf. Bolter & Grusin 1999). However, in web ads the user is able to manipulate the playing of the video in different ways (which presents a dimension of 'improvement', cf. Bolter & Grusin 1999): If the mouse does not stay on the ad, the video will often be interrupted, only to start again when the mouse revisits the ad; a design that makes particular user activities possible (probably not intended by senders), such as *scratching* – the reactivation of a video with very short intervals.

Because it is the user's activity that causes the sound and not the reverse, this 'silent' and only potentially auditory embedded ad presents, at first sight, a peculiar audiovisual advertisement phenomenon. Thus, to *attract attention* is not the primary function of the sound – contrary to the almost archetypal function of sounds in advertising in general. Rather, the sound emphasizes and sustains attention, so as to prompt the user to leave the mouse where it is (in causes of videos) or to click. It seems that embedded ads are predominantly visual expressions (pictures, texts – and sometimes animated), attracting attention by various sorts of eye catchers (e.g. colours and movements) or verbal imperatives. Only in cases when the mouse unintentionally slides across the ad, it makes good sense to consider the sound as attention grabbing; most obvious in cases of highlighted sound right in the beginning of the video (a good example of a *scratchable* video as well).

If seen in relation to the characteristics of the medium and genre, the silent, embedded web ad might not be considered that peculiar after all. Internet users seem to experience sounds in ads as a more intrusive and negative element compared to TV viewers.[12] Probably, this can be explained by the Internet representing a *pull*-media, in which the user usually expects and experiences a high level of control over information (cf. one *search* the Internet).

Sounds of TV commercials are also often considered uninvited and disturbing (and of course empirical confirmations can be found; e.g. Schafer 1977: 268ff). However, there are mitigating circumstances: The sound of TV plays an important role in establishing both *continuity* (the unbroken and overlapping sequence of events) and *breaks* (the abrupt highlighting of present or upcoming events), useful, if not directly attractive, features of modern TV programming matching absent minded viewing/listening. A particular attribute of embedded web ads, compared to TV commercials, is the fact that they appear synchronous with non-commercial material on the website.[13] Thereby, the embedded ad with emergent sound independent of user activity would disturb the media text *simultaneous* to the user's ongoing activities. While media users of today might often use auditory phenomena to accompany demanding activities (for instance when listening to the radio while working) this is most likely a result of choice or accept. Automatically activated embedded auditory web ads would then impede on the media text as well as compromise the user's expectations of being in control.[14]

Sound on commercial websites

When it comes to commercial websites, sounds occur more often and more varied compared to the sounds in embedded web ads. As illustrated by the case analysis, a visit on a commercial website is caused by user activity (click and expectation) – they are advertising messages that users *search for* (cf. "linked advertising message"). The advertising message is no longer occurring synchronously with non-commercial materials (contrary to the case of embedded web ads), and the text is ready for 'reading' and exploration either right away – following the initial click – or succeeding an introduction like the one analysed above.

Websites without an introduction will often have sounds and music running independently of user activity (apart from the initial *getting there*). In some ways, this is similar to numerous incidents of everyday life, where music is an almost inescapable part of the activity, for instance when dining, shopping or waiting in line. Thus, the website music is enforced as a rather anonymous and mood enhancing supplement with no specific relation to any particular object or product. It is the whole situation that is being musically embraced, and the music co-constructs an ambience without drawing much attention to itself, its presence, source or history. Because the media use and the role of music do not seem to be quite habituated (as discussed above), it might be argued though that some users will react to the music with discomfort and perhaps irritation. An indication of this is the freedom of choice on most websites – the music can be switched off – much unlike in shops, where music is often inescapable (only to be avoided through private 'cover-music' in for example iPods).

On commercial websites with music appearing and remaining without user activity, it is our general impression that predominantly short-lasting, repeated (perhaps slightly varied), musical expressions are to be found. Groove and sound seem to dominate over melodic curvature and harmonic progression, and the case analysis presents an illustrative example. In a syntagmatic perspective, this type of music might be considered to be circular and elliptical rather than linear (cf. Björnberg 2000). Hereby, the supplementary website music differs from music in shops, in that the latter will normally consist of longer-lasting culminating progressions with tuneful pieces of music. Conceivably, what is reflected here is the difference between a 'stay-on-a-website' and a 'stay-in-a-shop': In shops, the stay is normally sequenced in a relatively well-defined manner (cf. a script for shopping), while a stay on a website is usually characterized by a shorter-lasting, not pre-determined exploration or visit, and the stay can be ended any time without consequence.[15] In other words, the user is *on* a website while the customer is *in* the shop, where the physical setting and spatial experience is co-constructed and modified by the music. Only rarely commercial websites provide immersive spaces to be explored, and this typically involves the user to enter into a first person perspective in which a three-dimensional space can be experienced, obviously inspired by certain computer games. Here, the music will function as a psychological and physical positioning of the user, and sounds in general will appear with varying degrees of importance to the narrative structure. Sound is not so much mood enhancing with respect to the users *in front of* the screen as it is productive of experiences, contexts, and happenings to the user projected *inside* the screen (even if the 'two users' in practice are not totally separable). Thereby, sounds will aid the user in creating the narrative structure by functioning as markers and signals of the user's choices and movements. Herein lays a substantial difference compared to an otherwise comparable audiovisual genre, namely the film. In films, the media text is pre-defined, and there is no opportunity to construct a viewer sub-flow *in* the text, the way it is possible on some websites and in certain computer games, representing a more general condition of being on the Internet (cf. the high level of user activity and control).

Compared with films, many website-menus are characterized by no or only small visual movements, except for the possible user generated movements. In cases like this, the music functions to ensure the user, that (s)he is on-line as well as counteracting potential (unwanted) boredom, which might set off on the website and the product. However, as the case study has shown, the music might additionally function as a prompt for the user to take action him/herself.

As to the history of the music, no clear tendency is shown, but one interesting occurrence must be briefly addressed. Pre-existing, often relatively unknown music (to the ordinary user) is sometimes part of the attraction of specific commercial websites. Considered as a kind of cobranding of music and product, this phenomenon has been prevalent in TV commercials for quite some time. However, the website seems to add new dimensions by providing information instantaneously and simultaneously, as the case analysis illustrates.[16]

If we take a closer look at auditory phenomena that occurs as a result of user activity, some of these are comparable to the ones already discussed in relation to embedded web ads. For instance, sound effects can be heard as a result of *mouse-over* where the sounds become indexes of the objects seen, and sound and music are part of audio-visual expressions such as the 'unchanged' (or perhaps slightly improved) remediation of TV commercials. Mouse-over activated videos have somewhat different conditions on websites compared to their status as embedded web ads: Auditory phenomena are not necessarily *up front* (loud and instantaneous) – as in many mouse-over activated embedded ads – because the users' attention can be presupposed and therefore the need for attention grabbing sounds are less. In continuation of this, remediated TV commercials do not impede on user activity (cf. the discussion on embedded ads above), and in fact they can be considered as types of promos sometimes being initiated on the website without additional user activity. Furthermore, the audio-visual expression can be embedded into the design of the website, for example as part of a collage, thus presenting a rather sophisticated refashion of TV commercials. In addition to auditory phenomena *on* the website, a range of features are typically accessible through clicks providing optional constituent elements *inside* the website (for example puzzles, games, menus, immersive scenarios, etc.).

The 'sound' of silent web ads

When web ads appear without sound, it does not mean that sounds are entirely absent. In fact, sometimes the ads *look* like having sound,[17] and 'silent sounds' appear affiliated to visual expressions in numerous ways. For example, as emphasized by Janoschka, it is typical of the usage of language in web ads to play on face-to-face communication (thereby implying sound) as a means to involve the user: "(...) web ads need more than traditional and direct advertising instruments to interact with users. Thus, web ads try to create a conversational relationship with the user, imitating interpersonal communication. This conceptual orality turns the written language communication into a more spoken-like manner (...)" (Janoschka 2004: 132). The conceptual oral character of the web ad is here to be regarded as a schema or mental model of how the user is supposed to interact. For instance, a directly addressed question needs an answer, a request must be followed by an act, etc. Thus, sound is verbally put into play in various ways, most illustrative in the examples of embedded web ads: Sound as implied and invited in the constructed communicative interaction; sound as reference in the communicated address (e.g. imperatives implying sound; e.g. "Turn up the volume", "Listen", "Hold the mouse here and hear more" and different icons indicating sound, e.g. notes and loudspeakers); sound as a (quasi) synaesthetic accompaniment (cf. Cook 1998: 24ff) – or a kind of 'muted' sound – to the often visually highlighted expression of the text of the web ad (cf. typography and graphics like capitals, bold, italics, underlining, coloured text etc.), and because they can be experienced as being 'noisy', 'invoking', or 'calling', these visual means of expressions are connected to auditory conditions.

The auditory dimension of web ads can also be expressed through animated graphics and moving pictures. In these cases, auditory associations result from our experience with other audio-visual media, primarily film and TV: We are accustomed to see moving pictures in accompaniment with sound. Therefore, moving pictures can function as an attention-grabbing device since the user might wonder whether the ad actually has a soundtrack.

In relation to animated graphics, sound can be experienced in text or visual objects looping in sequences. Visiting a website that carry many animated ads, as for instance an online newspaper, may very well entail a 'noisy' experience; partly due to the abundance of advertising messages featured simultaneously to editorial content (as mentioned earlier), and partly because of the different rhythms of the animated ads, which in an overall view of the website will probably seem to swing unsystematically. In the specific ads, the expression is not necessarily noisy, but can appear rather rhythmical and musical (to which the scratching user may contribute). However, sound associations can also arise as 'muted' sound from animated objects, which for example is seen in an ad for the rescue service company *Falck*, in which a driving car has an engine failure and bursts into fire.

In particular, sound associations are evident in those cases where animations and moving pictures present a specific audio-visual expression that is known from another context because of a distinct use of sound. This cross media strategy in market communication is most applicable to – and probably has the greatest effect – in connection with musical brands, where the musical expression is inseparable from the advertised product, allowing for the music to be rather easily associated with the visual expression. An embedded web ad for *Alm. Brand* (a Danish finance company) presents an example in which two identical men, as an illustration of the company's 'double-customer' concept, are dancing through the ad in time with non-heard music. The average TV viewer (only to be imagined) will associate the non-heard music with Bent Fabricius-Bjerre's *Alley Cat*, which for many years has been an indispensable *brand* for *Alm. Brand*. But even 'still' pictures can benefit from this type of cross media strategy in market communication. This is the case on websites where for instance *metonymical representations* of well-known audio-visual sequences in the form of still-photos can be a part of the design and thereby producing associations. An example is *Nordea*'s (an international finance company) use of still-photos of well-known scenarios from their TV commercials, where alleged customers are presenting their dreams and needs with drawings on the screen – e.g. a new boat.[18] In this case, the photo can be seen as evoking a musical supplement to which the user himself is contributing when perhaps experiencing a kind of inner music. These examples are also illustrative of a more general tendency, namely that TV commercials for financial products, to a considerable extent, are making use of music, while the corresponding commercial websites typically remain silent (this is the case for Danish or international finance companies such as *Nordea, Danske Bank, Danica Pension, Alm. Brand, BRF Kredit*). From the examples, it appears that it is not the advertised product as such that decides whether music is involved in the advertising message (cf. that music *per se* potentially compromises the advertising message for exactly finance products, Leo 1999). Rather, it seems that the characteristics of the media (e.g. the flow of TV opposite to the pull-characteristic of the Internet) and the purpose and modes of addressing of the ad (cf. TV commercials as life style oriented and commercial websites as information oriented) are decisive factors in determining the possible presence of music.

CONCLUSION

The chapter has analysed the occurrences, functions, and conditions of sound in web ads. Generally, sound and music can be considered to be rather rare phenomena, and this seems in particular to connect to conditions of sound on the Internet. Thus, technology, design, and uses do not (yet) seem to imply sound in the same (and arguably more consolidated and habituated) way that characterizes the technology, design, and use of TV. When sound in fact occurs, a wide variety of functions is involved, and, on a general level, sounds appear user activated and user defined compared to commercials in other media. In that connection, we have argued that sound is a phenomenon to be more or less deliberately 'pulled' from the ads by the users. As exemplified, this 'pulling' ranges from the unintended activation of embedded web ads to the intentional exploration of websites' use of music (e.g. pieces of music and artists) – an exploration which is possible to perform while the music plays.

The sounds of web advertising can be considered in connection with specific modes of user-orientation. In figure 3, such a connection is mapped, and even if the figure is primarily inspired by one specific commercial website, it is our clear contention that the figure encompasses most – if not all – incidents of sound on commercial websites. However, one could easily envisage alternative designs. As an example, an increase in the music's intensity on visual monotonous websites could most likely also function as an incentive to link. Moreover, one could imagine even more refined auditory indications of user positioning and shifts between rooms. However, we maintain that the figure provides an adequate map for the understanding of auditory functions on commercial websites of today.

As to the embedded web ads (e.g. banners, not involved in the case analysis), it is our impression that the figure is useful as well. In many instances though, the figure would seem 'too big' since numerous of the embedded ads do not (yet) provide users with the range of options presented in commercial websites with regard to navigation and use of sound. Therefore, one would not experience the same amount of shifts between different user-orientations, although they can occur on a reduced scale.[19]

The purpose of the figure is to demonstrate how shifts in user-orientation may be considered in connection with the functions of sound in web ads (and in different types of digital texts, for that matter). Thus, the figure offers a way to take into account the specific conditions of the digital medium when analysing auditory phenomena.

NOTES

1   The website is no longer accessible but at the time of analysis it was accessible at http://www.volvocars.dk/campaigns/MY07/C30/ParisMotorShow/default.htm (visited November 28th 2006). The website for the C30 appearing in connection with the Paris Motor show is not identical to Volvo's general campaign website for Volvo C30 (cf. http://www.volvocars.dk/modelsMY07/c30/ (visited December 12th 2006)).

2   This explicit 'education' displays that it is the *relatively* experienced users, who are positioned (cf. discussion above), and also the less consolidated use and expression of the media and genre are exemplified.

3   Monotonous experiences on the Internet seem to strongly urge users to search for meaning or, as Aarseth describes it with reference to hypertexts in general, to search for "the link out" (cf. Aarseth 1997: 91). Thus, the reading of hypertexts tends to involve the search for untried opportunities: "Instead of asking, What have I read? the critic might become preoccupied with the question, Have I read all? and come to identify the task of interpretation as a task of territorial exploration and technological mastery" (Aarseth 1999: 87). Interestingly, the music here functions opposite of the way it usually functions as for instance on-hold telephone music. The music of the telephone is normally structured around longer, melodic phrases (often representing pre-existing pieces of music), which on-hold users are invited to dwell on or even enjoy, until the waiting time comes to an end (caused by somebody else picking up the phone).

4   Cf. the following names with an outspoken female flavour: Miss Sandy, DJ Céline, DJ Lolita, DJ Missill, DJ Roussia, DJ Jennifer Cardini, DJ Joli Dragon, Lea Lisa, Lydia Jay, Miss Chrysalide, DJ Chloe and VJs Phadfinderei.

5   It is of course doubtful whether this doubling of sounds is in fact intended by the designers. Nevertheless, it highlights an interesting feature of sound in the medium, namely that different sound sources can be activated simultaneously.

6   'Banner ad' is often used as a general term for embedded web ad formats. However, embedded web ad formats include many graphic formats and bear many names: banners, skyscrapers, leaderboards, billboards, rectangles, buttons, hockeystick, wallpaper, etc.

7   As a result of the logic of remediation all Internet genres are remediations themselves, cf. Lev Manovich's description of the digital interface as a mixture of different cultural forms and traditions, primarily the printed text, film and human-computer interface components as for instance dialogue boxes, menus, windows, radio-buttons, etc. Similar to the logic of remediation, Manovich regards the cultural language of the interface as influenced by older media and supplied with (new) components, which are connected to the functions of the digital medium and give the user the possibility to interact (Manovich 2001).

8   Bolter & Grusin specify "a spectrum of different ways in which digital media remediate their predecessors" and they position digital media products on a scale consisting of representation, improvement, refashion and absorption (cf. Bolter & Grusin 1999: 45f).

9   The empirical material includes registrations made from a sample of Danish websites in 2004 and 2005 and consists of about 1100 different embedded web ads and about 600 different websites (target ads). The sample includes portals, information resources and news media, all selected because of the appeal to a broad target group, a large number of services, many visitors and a broad field of topics. Moreover, the registrations are made from predefined navigation paths on each website, and the navigation paths cover a wide range of subjects, e.g. news, health, sports, culture, business, computer, life style, and communication.

10 We use sound effects to refer to those sounds (neither speech nor music) that correspond to particular objects seen or implied on the screen. Two dissimilar categories of sound effects can be distinguished: 1) sound effects initiated by the user by way of mouse-over, point-and-drag or click and 2) sound effects not initiated by the user but appearing as an integrated part of an audiovisual expression.

11 Cf. the guidelines of the international association Interactive Advertising Bureau (IAB), where it is noted that audio should be "user initiated": http://www.iab.net/standards/richmedia.asp (visited Feb. 14th 2008).

12. Cf. Nielsen's list of the most hated advertising techniques on the Internet. Automatically activated sound is here rated very negatively (see http://www.useit.com/alertbox/20041206.html (visited Feb.14th 2008).

13. Synchronous advertising on television usually occurs through more integrated and subtle *product placements* within programmes (see chapter 7 in this volume).

14. On top of this, the sources of sounds on the screen are usually not identifiable. Automatic sounds from embedded web ads would then possibly cause a confusion of finding the exact source, and potentially sounds would mix with other sources of sound from possible concurrent embedded web ads.

15. In this respect, the stay on websites is similar to that of hyped bars and lounges, where the social interaction bears the mark of exploration and potential move. It seems that groove- and sound-dominated musical expressions are also prevalent in these settings.

16. The co-branding of music and jeans seems to provide an illustrative case ('music to wear', one might think). Cf. campaigns by Levi's, G.A.P., and Mustang. For instance, the website for Mustang plays – and provides access to – "Rock musicians with equal amount of talent and potential. Yet unknown to the majority, but rapidly this can change" (www.mustang.dk, visited Feb. 14th 2008, translated from German). Music in TV comercials is often harder to seek out, but the Internet also services databases and forums addressed to television viewers to find out what music they have been listening to on television (e.g.: www.werbesongliste.de, www.whatsthatcalled.com, and www.commercialbreaksandbeats.co.uk, visited Feb. 14th, 2008).

17. This is also the finding in a study by Mass 2002 where the presence of musical instruments in printed ads is examined.

18. Cf. http://www.nordea.dk/sitemod/default/portal.aspx?pid=10039 (visited Nov. 13th 2008).

19. Examples of auditory functions in embedded web ads could be: 1) Supportive music in video banners (often in the format of TV commercials), 2) Sound effects marking link-option or activating sound by mouse-over (e.g. in a banner ad for Opel Corsa, in which mouse-over results in a "C'mon"), 3) Sound effects functioning as receipts for having moved objects.

REFERENCES

Aarseth, E. J. (1997). *Cybertext. Perspectives on ergodic literature*. London: The Johns Hopkins University Press.

Björnberg, A. (2000). Structural Relationships of Music and Images in Music Videos. In R. Middleton (Ed.), *Reading pop – Approaches to textual analysis in popular music* (pp. 347-378). Oxford: Oxford University Press.

Bolter, J. D., & Grusin, R. (1999). *Remediation. Understanding new media*. Cambridge Mass. and London: The MIT Press.

Cook, G. (2001). *The discourse of advertising* (2nd ed.). London: Routledge.

Cook, N. (1998). *Analysing musical multimedia*. Oxford: Oxford University Press.

Faber, R. J., Lee, M., & Nan, X. (2004). Advertising and the consumer information environment online. *American Behavioral Scientist, 48(4)*, 447-466.

Finnemann, N. O. (2001). *The Internet – A new communicational infrastructure*. Papers from the Centre for Internet Research 2, http://cfi.imv.au.dk/pub/skriftserie/002_finnemann.pdf

Gluck, M., & Bruner, R. E. (2005). *The evolution of rich media advertising. Current market trends, success metrics and best practices*. Radar Research and DoubleClick, http://www.doubleclick.com/

Graakjær, N. (2004). Nyhedernes musik [The music of news]. *MedieKultur, 37*. 36-46.

Hwang, J.-S., & McMillan, S. J. (2004). How consumers think about 'interactive' aspects of web advertising. In Y. Gao (Ed.), *Web systems design and online consumer behavior* (pp. 69-89). Hershey: Idea Publishing

Jackson, D. M., & Fulberg, P. (2003). *Sonic branding*. Houndmills: Palgrave.

Janoschka, A. (2004). *Web advertising. New forms of communication on the Internet*. Philadelphia: John Benjamins Publishing Company.

Jensen, K. B. (1994). Reception as Flow: The 'new television viewer' revisited. *Cultural Studies, 8(2)*, 293-305.

Leckenby, J. D. (2005). The interaction of traditional and new media. In M. Stafford, & R. Faber (Eds.), *Advertising, promotion, and new media* (pp. 3-29). Armonk: M.E. Sharpe.

Leo, H. (1999). *Musik im Fernsehwerbespot* [Music in TV commercials]. Frankfurt: Peter Lang.

Manovich, L. (2001). *The language of new media*. Cambridge, Mass.: The MIT Press.

Mass, G. (2002). Musikalische Themen und Motive in Werbeanzeigen – ein Streifzug [Musical themes and motifs in advertising – An expedition] In G. Probst-Effah, W. Schepping, & R. Schneider (Eds.), *Musikalische Volkskunde und Musikpädagogik – Annäherungen und Schnittmengen* (pp. 251-283). Essen: Verlag Die Blauen Eule.

Motte-Haber, H. (1990). *Musikhören beim Autofahren – 8 Forschungsberichte* [Listening to music while driving – 8 research contributions]. Frankfurt am Main: Peter Lang.

Rodgers, S., & Thorson, E. (2000). The interactive advertising model: how users perceive and process online Ads. *Journal of Interactive Advertising, 1(1)*, 26-50. (http://www.jiad.org/article5)

Schafer, R. M. (1977). *The soundscape. Our sonic environment and the tuning of the world*. Rochester: Destiny Books.

Tagg, Ph., & Clarida, Bob. (2003). *Ten little title tunes*. New York: MMMSP

Tsang, L. (2007). Sound and music in website design. In J. Sexton (Ed.), *Music, sound, and multimedia* (pp. 145-171). Edinburgh: Edinburgh University Press.

THE SOUNDTRACK OF SALES
Music in Swedish radio commercials

Alf Björnberg

INTRODUCTION

Commercial radio is a fairly recent phenomenon in Sweden. Apart from the relatively short-lived (but quite consequential) radio pirates in the 1950s and 1960s, commercial radio was not established until a far-reaching broadcasting deregulation was implemented in 1993. As implied by audience ratings, commercial broadcasters have captured a considerable share of the Swedish radio audience since then, particularly in the youth and young-adult audience segments. In spite of this development, the use of music in radio commercials—as well as the programming practices of commercial music radio in general—have attracted little scholarly interest. It seems that the musical fare offered by commercial broadcasters constitutes a decidedly low-budget, low-status, inconspicuous everyday musical phenomenon, a representative example of what Kassabian (1999) has termed 'ubiquitous music'. Still, this phenomenon seems to me to warrant the attention of musicology as well as media studies, if nothing else, simply on the sole basis of the sheer size of listener figures and the amount of time these listeners spend exposed to the sounds of commercial broadcasting.

Originally, I intended the main purpose of this chapter to consist in an analysis of music use in radio commercials and the proposal of a typology of such use. An additional purpose, however, which has attracted increasing attention during the course of my work on the chapter, is a discussion of the characteristics and functions of music in commercial radio programming in general.[1] It seems to me that a detached analysis of radio commercials as isolated items of communication would tend to seriously misrepresent the conditions of real-life listening situations and modes of listening to these items in their context; on radio, commercials seem to be tightly integrated into a continuous programming flow, even more than, for instance, in the case of commercial TV.

The empirical material discussed here is taken from the broadcasts of Sweden's largest (in terms of audience figures) commercial broadcaster, *Rix FM*, a network running 36 stations across the country. The material consists of the 130 minute section broadcast from 9.00 to 11.10 AM on 23 May, 2006. It should thus be pointed out that this study is intended to be exploratory, based on a limited amount of source material and aiming at suggesting directions for further research rather than at presenting well-grounded and representative conclusions.[2]

COMMERCIAL PIONEERS/BUCCANEERS: THE RADIO PIRATES

As already stated, commercial broadcasting on Swedish airwaves originated with the radio pirates, transmitting from ships anchored outside Swedish territorial waters. The pirate era lasted from 1958 (*Radio Mercur*) to 1966 (*Radio Syd*; i.e., 'Radio South'); however, the most influential pirate broadcaster was *Radio Nord* ('Radio North'), despite its being operative for barely 16 months (from March 1961 to June 1962). Radio Nord was forced to close down due to legislation changes, but the station had, by then, had far-reaching effects on programme formats in Swedish public service radio, mainly due to the fact that its transmissions, in contrast to those of the pirates located in the Sound between southern Sweden and Denmark, covered the capital area. In May 1961, *Sveriges radio*, the public-service broadcasting organization, launched the new popular music channel *Melodiradion* ('Melody Radio') as a direct attempt at driving the commercial competition out of the market. Somewhat ironically, in its first period of existence, Melodiradion presented a format even more 'commercial' than that of the pirate stations, insofar as its broadcasts featured a 12-hours-a-day continuous flow of light music (albeit covering a stylistically wider range than in pirate radio), interspersed with amiable DJ chat. The pirates thus engendered a major breakthrough for a functional easy-listening radio format in the middle of the otherwise fairly conservative Swedish public-service mediascape, a fact underlined by the quite intensive exchange of personnel and competence between the pirates and public-service radio during and after the pirate era.

The Swedish pirate radio stations have kept attracting a persistent interest from certain aficionado groups long after the fact. Today, more than 40 years after the closing down of the last pirate, there are several websites in Sweden devoted to the subject of pirate radio history.[3] One manifestation of this 'fan culture' is a compilation CD entitled *Historien om Radio Nord* ('The Story of Radio North'), issued in 1992 and featuring jingles and commercials from the station's active period, as well as some of the hit songs popularized by Radio Nord. In the following, I will use a few sound clips from this compilation as comparison material, providing at least a glimpse of a historical perspective on the practices of music use in Swedish radio commercials.

WHY MAKE COMMERCIAL RADIO? THE SENDER'S POINT OF VIEW

Contemporary commercial radio in Sweden is organized in terms of nation-wide networks rather than independent local stations.[4] In this respect, the Swedish situation is similar to the Canadian one described by Berland (1990: 181) in terms of "a re-emergence of programme syndication" and "commercial radio's de-localization", in spite of the fact that "radio represents itself as the local medium". Today, the broadcaster most efficiently fulfilling the functions of local radio in Sweden is the public service channel P4, with 26 local stations broadcasting in daytime and combining a light music format with local news, weather forecasts and traffic reports, as well as interviews and features of local interest. In contrast, in most commercial broadcasting, local content is limited to localized jingles, weather forecasts and a few local commercials.

From the listeners' point of view, the primary incentive to listening to a commercial radio station would allegedly—at least in promotion discourse—be the music, and possibly other forms of entertainment, presented by that station. On Rix FM's website, the channel is described as 'a broad music and entertainment channel addressed to listeners between 20 and 49 years of age', presenting 'a broad music mix of current music'.

The channel's profile is summarized in the main slogan used since its inception: *Bäst musik just nu!* ('The best music right now!'; cf. www.rixfm.com). In practice, this means a format predominantly based on current Swedish and international mainstream-pop hits.

Providing the listeners with 'the best music' is of course merely the flipside of the basic economic rationale behind commercial radio, which is the same as for all commercial media: supplying the customers—i.e., the advertisers—with the commodity on sale—i.e., the attention of an audience of maximized size during (in the case of temporal media) a measured span of time. On the website of MTG Radio, part-owner of Rix FM, the following sales arguments for radio advertising time are presented:[5]

> Why is sound the most effective message carrier in mass communication? You don't see when you're not watching, but you hear when you're not listening (...) Sound is intrusive, difficult to capture and irresistible (...) Since radio communicates in real time, you as advertiser can choose when you want your target audience to hear your spot (...) Radio is also one of the media which to the greatest extent are consumed during daytime, when one is most active as a consumer and makes most purchases (...) Radio is an intrusive medium (...) You can't skim through advertisements on the radio (...) The costs of production and exposure are often lower in radio compared to other media (...) When your spot is broadcast, you are the sole advertiser (...) Only 16% avoid radio commercials, and that figure is considerably higher for most other media. The reason for this is primarily that most people do other things while listening to the radio and don't experience commercials as an annoying factor. (www.mtgradio.se)

The last sentence in this quote indicates the general view on the production side as to the listening situations and modes of listening typically applied in the context of middle-of-the-road pop radio. Here, a certain contradiction between the 'intrusive medium' rhetoric and the 'distracted listening'—doing other things while listening—argument may be noted: if listeners do not experience commercials as 'an annoying factor', could the reason be that they do not pay them any attention at all? The solution to this contradiction seems to lie in a not quite explicitly stated but clearly implied appeal to the potential of radio commercials for 'subliminal influence'. In any case, a reasonable conclusion would be that the composition of commercial radio programming, interweaving 'the best music' with 'non-annoying' commercials, most of which also feature music as a prominent communicative dimension, requires some thorough deliberation in order to attain the desired effects for listeners as well as advertisers.

TYPES AND FUNCTIONS OF MUSIC IN RADIO COMMERCIALS

As might be expected, the commercials in my sample material indicate that music is present at least to some extent in practically every radio commercial. On the basis of this material, the following preliminary typology of music use in radio commercials may be formulated. The typology is roughly arranged in decreasing order of prominence of the musical dimension in the commercial.

1. The *through-composed commercial song*. This musical type usually fills most of or the entire time span of the commercial, and the verbal dimension of the commercial thus consists of song lyrics. The commercial song regularly contains a prominent 'hook'—i.e., a short, distinctive and easily memorable vocal phrase—featuring a brand name and/or slogan.
2. The *medley or collage*, consisting of excerpts from several pieces of music assembled together. This is typically used in conjunction with advertising a musical commodity, such as a compilation album, but my sample contains one other example of this type (see below).
3. The *instrumental underscore with voice-over*. Here, the verbal dimension is restricted to spoken language, with instrumental music as a background providing additional semiotic dimensions to the total message of the commercial.
4. The *vocal jingle*. This type consists of a short and distinctive vocal phrase, with or without instrumental accompaniment, whose lyrics consist of a slogan. The jingle is thus in principle structurally similar to the melodic 'hook' (cf. no. 1 above). It is sometimes used as a conclusion to a commercial featuring instrumental underscore with voice-over.

5. The *instrumental jingle with slogan voice-over*. Here, the slogan is spoken, with an instrumental background consisting of a short and distinctive musical figure. Purely instrumental jingles, without any accompanying verbal message, seem to be rare in radio advertising, in contrast to TV commercials, where the semantic precision necessary to secure the communication of the message may be supplied by visuals substituting for verbal information.
6. *Diegetic music in dramatization*. In this case, the main body of the commercial presents a fictive situation in dramatized form, with musical performance forming an element within this situation. I've found one example of this in my material, a dog food commercial presenting a slightly absurd domestic situation. The reasons why the music in this case appears to be diegetic have to do both with the type of music (an étude-like piano piece of a kind uncommon in commercials), its acoustic ambience and its structure (the music is repeatedly interrupted by other events).

    In conjunction with this musical type, an additional type may be hypothesized:
7. *Underscore for dramatization*. Here, a fictive situation in dramatized form is accompanied by non-diegetic music, i.e., music whose source does not appear to be contained within this situation. I've found no example of this in my material; in general, dramatizations appear to be rather uncommon in radio commercials, and it might also be expected that in the absence of a visual dimension, the distinction between diegetic and non-diegetic music may often prove rather difficult to make.

The typology proposed above is primarily based on the formal relationship of the musical dimension to the verbal dimension of a commercial. From a functional perspective, music may be demonstrated to serve several kinds of functions in the radio commercial, and in most commercials several of these functions are active simultaneously or in succession. On the basis of a tentative analysis, the following functions of music appear relevant to point out in this context:

1. Music *regulates the temporal flow* within commercials, setting off different sections of a commercial from each other and emphasizing significant moments, as well as indicating transitions from one commercial to the next one and between these and other kinds of programming. In terms of the sign typology proposed by Tagg & Clarida (2003: 99ff), there is an abundance of 'episodic markers', as would appear to be necessary in a communication context composed of several short and heterogeneous segments. In experiential terms, the effect of this abundance could be characterized as one of formal (short-term) *cohesion* rather than (long-term) *coherence*.
2. Music *supplies referential extramusical signification* to the overall meaning of commercials. In Tagg's & Clarida's typology, the relevant sign types here are 'anaphones' (musical representation of extramusical sound, movement and tactile qualities) and 'genre synecdoches' (musical signification by means of reference to particular musical styles and thereby to their concomitant extramusical associations). However, in many cases, music in radio commercials seems to do its signifying work less by means of discrete sign functions of these various types than by composite sign complexes, which serve to supply more specific extramusical information while simultaneously providing a general regulation of mood.
3. On a more general level, music seems to *'fictionalize'* the often rather mundane and trivial verbal messages of commercials. Here, an obvious parallel can be drawn to Gorbman's (1987) characterization of Hollywood film music as "a signifier of emotion itself" (ibid.: 73), conveying values of 'the universal', 'the poetic' and 'the symbolic', as opposed to 'the particular', 'the prosaic' and 'the literal' (ibid.: 82). This could also be described as a production-side counterpart to the reception practices described by Bull (2000) in his discussion of the aestheticization of everyday experience by personal

stereo use, resulting in "a monumentalization of experience" (ibid.: 22). In a comparison between radio and TV commercials, it appears that this 'larger-than-life' effect of music is even more prominent in radio, due to the absence of a visual dimension, and as I will argue below this effect seems to be of considerable importance in the programming flow of commercial radio in general.

A comparison of my 2006 Rix FM sample with the commercials from the early 1960s featured on the above-mentioned compilation CD gives a clear indication of major changes in the practices of music use in radio commercials over the intervening time span of 45 years. The 1960s commercials are regularly longer and characterized by a considerably lower degree of information density; they are often composed of several distinct segments, arranged to constitute a more distinctly 'narrative' trajectory than is typical of the 2006 material. Another conspicuous difference concerns the sonic envelope, which is quite variable in the older material, in sharp contrast to the present-day practice of extremely compressed sound resulting in a constant sound level of –6 dB throughout the entire programming flow. A final, notable difference has to do with vocal timbre: in the 2006 material, the cheerful tenor and mezzo-soprano voices of the 1960s commercials have given way to the full-bodied baritones typical of modern commercial messages.

I will refrain here from attempts at a more detailed analysis of the technological, economic, social and perception-psychological factors which might explain these considerable changes over time in radio commercial music practice. It may be noted in this context, though, that these changes appear to be clear indications of major changes in the modes of perception typically applied, and the demands made on listener competence, in the context of commercial radio. The considerable increase in information density indicates that a shorter attention span, but also a considerably higher degree of decoding competence, is expected on the part of the present-day listener. The justification of such expectations would seem to rest on an increasing media saturation of everyday life, resulting in an increased competition between different media, but also in their increasing interaction and convergence.

Media convergence

As indicated by the preceding account of the characteristics of the music in my material, a comparison between radio commercials and TV commercials often seems to lie near at hand. In a mediascape characterized by the presence of several commercial TV channels in addition to commercial radio—which, as already stated, is a fairly recently emerging situation in Sweden—radio commercials could perhaps be hypothesized to generally function in reception as 'TV commercials without visuals', i.e., the modes of reception typically applied would be based on expectations of narrative design shaped by exposure to TV commercials. If this is so, then it might be expected that music in radio commercials could be demonstrated to perform compensatory functions for the absence of visuals. In comparison to TV commercials, the limitation to the auditory dimension results in a lower degree, or a more indeterminate kind, of referentiality; in radio, the communication of the referential and narrative information conveyed by the visual dimension of TV commercials is dependent on verbal messages, possibly auditory dramatization, sound effects and music.

It is doubtful, however, to what extent commercial radio may be assumed to function as a separate, self-contained medium; rather, radio is likely to be used within a wider communication context including other media, such as TV, phonogram recordings and the Internet. The implicit presence of this wider context in commercial radio programming is perceivable, for instance, in cases where the same content is used in TV and radio commercials. One example of this in my material is a commercial for a non-prescription analgesic, designed as a parody of the film musical *The Sound of Music*, where the main protagonist in the TV version (a small man disguised as a giant pill) acts out Julie Andrews' part in scenes from the film while performing a medley of pastiches of songs from the musical. This commercial was well established on Swedish commercial TV channels by the time of the collection of my sample. In the radio version, the musical medley is retained, while the written messages of the TV version are replaced by a voice-over; however, the allusion to *The Sound of Music* is considerably less obvious in the radio version, and the point of the commercial is probably rather incomprehensible without the listener's conscious reference to the TV context.

The convergence of radio and phonograms is manifested in another commercial, advertising the compilation CD *Rix FM-festival 2006*. This is a distinct example of 'coincidence' in Graakjær's (2006) sense, i.e., the music of the commercial coincides with that of the commodity advertised, in that the former consists of a musical medley of the songs featured on the CD (with an additional voice-over).[6] It deserves mentioning here that the connection of commercial radio with recordings is not a recent phenomenon in the Swedish mediascape. Already in the 1960s, Radio Nord issued the 'souvenir' LP album *Sjung med Radio Nord* ('Sing with Radio North'), albeit with the important difference that that album contained the station's own jingles and title tunes, whereas the Rix FM CD is a compilation of current hits featured on the station's playlist.

A prominent feature of the contemporary mediascape is the convergence of broadcasting media—commercial as well as public service—with the Internet. In purely quantitative terms, the Internet offers a considerably higher and more cost-efficient potential for interactivity than older forms of interactivity such as, for instance, phone-ins in live broadcasts. On the website of Rix FM, listeners may participate in polls, the results of which have influence on the station's playlists, place orders for records, such as the aforementioned compilation CD, and participate in competitions arranged by the station.

FUNCTIONAL CONVERGENCE AND THE TIME SENSE OF COMMERCIAL MUSIC RADIO

As I have already argued, from a reception perspective the use of music in radio commercials appears scarcely separable from the overall flow of sonic events in radio programming. In addition to the hit songs played by the station—the alleged *raison d'être* of commercial 'music radio'—these events include categories such as DJ chat, listener phone-ins, commercials, station jingles and sound effects. However, these categories are generally not very clearly distinguishable from each other; instead, their succession and rapid alternation appears to be designed to form a 'seamless' and continuous flow.

In his analysis of TV sports, Whannel (1992) states that there are "three principal sets of practices in television—those related to journalism, to entertainment and to drama" (ibid.: 60) and goes on to argue that TV sports can be viewed as situated at the intersection of these practices, combining all three principal programming genres. Although there are considerable differences, as to functions and programming practices, between TV sports and music radio, tendencies towards the erasure of the distinctions between these genres may be observed in the case of commercial radio as well. Music radio in general is situated closer to the 'entertainment' corner of Whannel's conceptual triangle, with the 'journalism' aspect restricted to the occasional newsflash or weather forecast, and the 'drama' aspect to the intermittent quiz or similar event.[7] In terms of structure and sonic character, however, in commercial radio programming these different practices seem to have converged to a considerable degree, and music is one important factor enabling this convergence. Another such factor is the typical vocal practices involved: the verbal tempo and vocal timbre of the typical commercial are often quite reminiscent of those of the intense but somehow inconsequential drama of sports commentary.

Insofar as 'entertainment' is associated with a focussed attention, a more appropriate term for the effects aimed at by means of these practices would perhaps be 'aestheticization': the provision of a sonic substrate suitable for a pleasurable but distracted mode of perception. This point is aptly illustrated by the practice on *Rix FM* of underscoring local weather forecasts with background music: the forecast is accompanied by an energetic but pleasant instrumental groove, over which the weatherman presents the forecast in a slightly rhythmized manner—not with the rhythmic precision of a rapper, but still with a discernible timing of verbal phrases to the metre of the groove. To me, the experiential effect is clearly one of music aestheticizing and, as it were, fictionalizing the in itself trivial and mundane information purveyed in this utilitarian message.[8]

I would like to argue that the particular kind of aestheticization taking place here is closely related to the time sense produced by commercial music radio programming. On a micro-level, the programming flow is composed of a succession of several short fragments, each potentially with its own sense of direction and closure. In terms of the typology of musical temporalities suggested by Kramer (1988), this is an instance of "non-directed linear time", where "the implied progression from one section to another is continually realized but the deeper-level implications arising from these middleground progressions fail to be fulfilled" (ibid.: 58). However, as these fragments often are too short and/or too fragmentary to make much directional sense, the time sense produced will be tending towards 'multiply-directed time', where "the implication in every section is continually frustrated by the subsequent section but is often realized elsewhere" (ibid.). The latter is a kind of temporality associated by Kramer with certain modernist avant-garde musical works of a montage type. This association may underline my suggestion above regarding the demands made on listener competence by commercial radio: if one were to listen attentively to a stretch of commercial radio programming, containing the various kinds of material enumerated above, as a 'musical work', trying to grasp the 'structure' and its implications, this would prove a challenge equal to the one posed by 'structural listening' to, say, a 'stochastic' work by Xenakis.

But of course, this is not the mode of listening expected from the listener; rather, the appropriate mode would be one of momentarily variable attention, enabling the listener to focus on single sonic items in the continuous flow without regard for (or expectations of) long-term implications. Still, structuration of the programming flow on a larger temporal level is not absent or insignificant. To elucidate the last point, it may be helpful to compare commercial radio programming to the Muzak programming practices analysed by Tagg (1984). Tagg argues that these practices produce a 'cyclicalisation' of experiential time into "affectively experienceable proportions" (ibid.: 35) by means of a regular alternation of 'batches' of music—in turn composed of pieces of roughly equal length—and silence. In contrast to this practice, however, the proportions of the experiential cycles in the programming of Rix FM often seem rather ill-defined, and their relationship to chronometric 'clock' time appears de-emphasized. One detail illustrating this last point is the fact that the station's newscasts often don't fall right on the hour, but rather a variable amount of minutes past. This stands in stark contrast to, for instance, the strict marking of the hours of the day in the programming of the public service local channel P4.

With the risk of wearing out an already somewhat worn expression, commercial music radio could thus be said to produce 'mythical time'. Commercial radio's time is mythical in a quite definite sense: it appears to stand outside of, and in a rather indeterminate relationship to, chronometric clock time, while providing a pleasurable experiential alternative to the latter. An important task for future research would be to inquire into how listeners utilize and make sense of the experiential temporal structure thus offered them in their own personal quotidian economies of time.

Notes

1. In this connection, I would like to thank the participants of the Musicology PhD seminar at Göteborg for helpful comments and suggestions.
2. The 130 minute section contains 35 commercials; since some of these are repeated within this period of time, the sample in all comprises 27 different commercials.
3. These websites may give an impression of a rather nostalgic indulgence in the past on the part of a few aging rebels for the cause of 'free radio'; however, the pirate era forms an important part of Swedish broadcasting history and one of which an exhaustive account still remains to be written.
4. The name 'Rix FM' is significant in this connection: the syllable 'rix', in that orthography meaningless in Swedish, is a homophone to the prefix 'riks-', meaning 'national' as in *riksradio* ('national radio'), which previously was part of the name of the public-service radio broadcasting organization.
5. The two main owners of Rix FM are MTG Radio and Svensk Radioutveckling ('Swedish Radio Development'), the latter being a media enterprise owned in its turn by a major Swedish newspaper group.
6. Otherwise, in comparison with TV commercials, radio commercials seem to make little use of pre-existing music, i.e., music with a preceding 'career' (Graakjær 2006), probably due to the relatively low-budget production conditions involved.
7. Whannel situates the quiz close to the 'entertainment' corner of his triangle. My reference to 'drama' in this context is motivated by the element of competition ('who will win?') or suspense ('will the contestant answer correctly?') inherent in the genre. Admittedly, this is 'drama' in a rather restricted sense.
8. This effect appears to me to be related to what Moore (1993: 85) has termed the 'fictionality' of the popular song as 'a self-contained entity'.

REFERENCES

Berland, J. (1990). Radio space and industrial time: Music formats, local narratives and technological mediation. *Popular Music*, *9(2)*, 179–92.

Bull, M. (2000). *Sounding out the city: Personal stereos and the management of everyday life.* Oxford & New York: Berg.

Gorbman, C. (1987). *Unheard melodies: Narrative film music.* Bloomington & Indianapolis: Indiana University Press.

Graakjær, N. (2006). Musical meaning in TV commercials: A case of cheesy music. *Popular Musicology Online*. Issue 5. [http://www.popular-musicology-online.com/issues/05/nicolai-01.html. Accessed 1 March, 2007].

Kassabian, A. (1999). Popular. In B. Horner, & T. Swiss (Eds.), *Key terms in popular music and culture* (pp. 113-123). Oxford: Blackwell.

Kramer, J. D. (1988). *The time of music: New meanings, new temporalities, new listening strategies.* New York: Schirmer.

Moore, A. (1993). *Rock: The primary text: Developing a musicology of rock.* Buckingham & Philadelphia: Open University Press.

MTG Radio, http://www.mtgradio.se. Accessed 23 May, 2006.

Rix FM, http://www.rixfm.se. Accessed 23 May, 2006.

Tagg, Ph. (1984). Understanding musical 'time sense'—Concepts, sketches and consequences. In *Tvärspel – trettioen artiklar om musik: Festskrift till Jan Ling* (pp. 21-43). Göteborg: Göteborg University, Department of Musicology.

Tagg, Ph., & Clarida, B. (2003). *Ten little title tunes.* New York: MMMSP.

Whannel, G. (1992). *Fields in vision: Television sport and cultural transformation.* London: Routledge.

Music for Shopping
Supplementary sounds of consumption

Nicolai Graakjær and Christian Jantzen

Music for millions

90 million daily listeners is the average audience of the Muzak Company (Lanza 2004: 5). Muzak has been producing and distributing music since 1934 and still has a leading position on the global market. The early success of the company was based on its system of music and sound transmission, patented by Muzak's founder George O. Squirer in 1922. This system made it possible to mass distribute and mass communicate phonograph recordings by wire to various settings. Technological advances soon enabled transmission by telephone cables and wireless and, today, the system is based on satellite transmission. That the company has been able to keep its position as market leader for decades despite competition from other distribution companies such as Philips, 3M, Mood Media, DMX Music or Music Choice and the emergence of numerous radio channels specializing in popular music, is probably caused by Muzak's ability to convince customers (i.e. shop managers) of its unique insight in producing and selecting music suited for shopping and work related activities.

The music initially distributed by Muzak and other providers was pre-existing music composed for quite different settings and purposes than shopping or working. This type of music had a history of its own prior to being distributed in sites of consumption and labour. After World War II, another type of music became prevalent when Muzak distributed original music composed solely for the purpose of being transmitted to commercial settings. The tremendous impact of this ambient music on the sound of the burgeoning consumer society is illustrated by the fact that artists in the 1970s started to copy and emulate it (e.g. Brian Eno's *Music for Airports* 1978). Since the 1990s, Muzak has predominantly distributed pre-existing music once more. The service offered by the company is allegedly a deep understanding of how music functions and the ability to program a precisely balanced sequence of sounds and tunes that fits almost any public setting. The fact that this kind of music is often labelled simply as "muzak" in daily speech shows how successful this company has been in producing and selecting appropriate ambient music (Jones & Schumacher 1992).

"Muzak" often simply connotes light and unspecific background music of low complexity lacking any aesthetic quality. Such an assessment is not without prejudice. The sound structure of *muzak* is certainly not less complex than many other kinds of music. It might seem easy to listen to, but as the case of Brian Eno amply illustrates, this does not make it easier or less demanding to produce. In fact, it is not easy to listen to at all: It does not attract attention to itself, and even though one might attempt to listen to it attentively, this often proves very difficult. It cannot easily be "foregrounded", implying that even the term *background music* is somewhat misleading. It is crafted for being perceived without necessarily being actively understood, interpreted or remembered. Like (other) music, it is intended to affect the mood and behaviour of the listener. But this aesthetic effect is aimed at furthering a goal external to the realm of music production and reception. In that respect, it is certainly functional: It relaxes or entices the consumer, thereby serving the interests of shop assistants, managers and owners. Precisely this very mundane functional character is probably the very reason why *muzak* is denied aesthetic value. Contrary to the ideals of Kantian aesthetics (Kant 1952), this kind of music is a purposeful structure *with* a purpose. By deliberately being crafted in a way that enhances positive moods or positive perceptions of the goods for sale, it aims at facilitating interactions in commercial settings.

Ontologically speaking, music for shopping might perhaps not qualify as music at all (see chapter 13 this volume). These sound structures are a supplementary aspect of shop design like colouring, scent, architecture, decor and other ornamental elements utilized to enhance sales. Such elements are forced on the consumer in order to increase the shopping experience, rarely being the defining aspect of this experience. They usually seem to function most efficiently, when they pass unnoticed. Nonetheless, they are artistic effects for millions, in terms of audience as well as turnover. Figures from the National Music Council (1996) suggest that, in 1995, the estimated value of royalties for music played at restaurants, bars, clubs and shops was £31 million in the United Kingdom alone. On top of this come expenses for installing reproduction technology and, not least, expenses paid to music distributors like Muzak. When such figures are capitalized for the whole Western world, the annual costs of playing music in commercial settings must be said to be staggering.

As argued by Dissanyake (1992), the evolutionary function of art in general may very well be that it adapts human beings to their social surroundings and prepares them to the tasks at hand. Like (other) music, music for shopping has these art-like qualities too by creating a proper mood for consumption. On a basic physiological level, it reduces stress and tensions, thereby minimizing the risk of conflicts between consumers or between consumers and sales assistants. But it may also serve to increase arousal, thereby optimizing interest and chances of unexpected but welcome experiences. Such mood enhancements are the affect of some basic features of music encountered but hardly listened to during shopping. We will try to explore these features in this chapter. Characterizing this music as light background music of low complexity does not explain why it is traded for millions each year and exposed to millions each day. Its efficiency should instead be understood as a result of being at once enforced on the consumer and unnoticed by the consumer, thus serving as a supplemental tool that contributes to the proper "atmospherics" for shopping: i.e. to a deliberate design that generates "specific emotional effects in the buyer that enhance his purchase probability" (Kotler 1973-74: 50). Our study is based on interviews with shop managers and costumers and on observations made in department stores, shopping malls, supermarkets and different kinds of shops in one of the larger cities in Denmark, where we are living. We start with a short survey of the existing literature on this subject.

Earlier studies of music for shopping

Systematic research in the effects of supplementary music started with Ayres (1911). By experimenting with music during a six-day indoor cycling event, Ayres was able to document that the pace increased when the band played. Music was thus seen as having "a real and considerable stimulating influence on physical effort" (Ayres 1911: 321). Whether this influence on the athletes was direct or indirect remained uncertain. The data suggested that the presence or absence of music was an independent variable causing a certain output of effort (dependent variable). But as noted by Ayres, the increase in effort might also be an effect of increased audience response (enthusiasm) caused by the band playing. Although this research aimed at documenting the effects of music on work place behaviour, it also pointed at the positive effects of music on audience participation and hence on consumption. Further independent research into this topic has been rather scattered, whereas the Muzak Company allegedly has done extensive research documenting the profound impact of music on consumers and employees (e.g. Lanza 2004: 150ff). But this privately funded research has not been published. Public research on this topic has typically been based on experimental designs similar to Ayres (Bruner 1990, North & Hargreaves 1997b, 2006 for overviews). Subjects are exposed to different musical stimuli to measure the effect of music on consumer behaviour (response). This effect can either be understood in physiological or cognitive terms.

In the first group of studies, it is presupposed that music as an independent variable affects the organism's level of arousal. This causes the organism to either speed up or slow down on its activity. Based on a psychobiological tradition in experimental aesthetics (North & Hargreaves 1997a), this line of research is hence interested in measuring customer activity. An important study by Milliman (1982) in supermarkets showed that the *tempo* of music affected the pace of shopping. Perhaps not surprisingly, customer movements were significantly slower when the tempo was slow. Interestingly, more money was spent under these slow conditions than under the faster ones. Earlier research by Smith & Curnow (1966) had shown a correspondence between the *loudness* of the music and the pace of the customers. When shopping to loud music, less time is spent instore than when exposed to soft music. In this study though, no differences in sales between the two types of music were documented.

The second group of studies is interested in measuring the impact of in-store music on the customer's perceptions and evaluations of the product or the store. It is presupposed that music can lead to either more positive or more negative evaluations. This might in turn affect purchase and/or affiliation in more positive or negative direction. These studies are based on the hypothesis that music fitting existing knowledge structures primes the selection of goods matching that knowledge. They are hence labelled *knowledge activation* studies and are founded on a sound tradition within cognitive psychology. A study showed that sad music enhanced the sales of greeting cards (Alpert & Alpert 1990). Another study by Areni & Kim (1993) showed that playing classical music enhanced the sale of expensive wine in a wine shop compared to playing Top-40 music. The number of bottles sold by the two types of music showed no difference. In both cases, there was apparently a fit between the music and the purchase decision of consumers. In an interesting study by North, Hargreaves & McKendrick (1999), the influence of music on actual decision-making was elaborated. This research was also conducted in a wine shop where customers were exposed to either French or German music. When German music was played, German wine outsold French by two bottles to one. In the reversal of this experiment, French wine outsold German by five to one. Interviews with customers, moreover, showed that, apparently, they were unaware of the music and denied being influenced by it in their choice of product. All though unnoticed, the music seemed to influence decision-making significantly.

The importance of such studies is that they show "that music can be used to differentiate otherwise similar environments" (North & Hargreaves 2006: 111). Psychobiological studies in arousal effects indicate that the type of music affects the duration of the shopping activity. They may also be helpful for future research in how music can influence actual consumer trajectories in stores and malls. Cognitive studies in knowledge activation point to the importance of a match between music, product and shop for furthering sales. They may also be helpful for future research in the fit between "sonic branding" and consumer lifestyles (Jackson & Fulberg 2003).

The shared assumption in these experimental designs is that it is possible to isolate a single parameter and to study the impact of this stimulus.

Even though this has generated interesting results these are as yet far from exhaustive in explaining the complexity of music in commercial settings. Many situational factors to which music has to relate as a supplementary device influence the impact of ambient music on the physiological behaviour of and cognitive appraisal by actual consumers. Music for shopping has to function in quite versatile environments comprising large department stores and shopping malls as well as small speciality stores, targeting both wide audiences and narrowly defined target groups at nearly all hours of the day. Shoppers of all ages and both genders and with highly different social, cultural and ethnic backgrounds are exposed to these commercialized sounds, making the possibility of a perfect fit between music, product and the mind of the individual consumer an almost sheer impossibility. In the following sections, we therefore will try to illuminate how music for shopping acts upon this complexity.

Characteristics of music for shopping

No single distinctive feature defines the basic characteristics of ambient music in commercial settings. But whether pre-existing or originally composed music, what sets this kind of sound structure apart from "ordinary music" is the fact that it is not intended for active listening, dancing or singing along. It functions most efficiently when unnoticed.

Secondly, it is a supplementary device, and its impact on mood enhancement and hence on consumer behaviour cannot be meaningfully isolated from other tools of "atmospherics". Its effects are situational, relying of course on the individual consumer's predispositions, frame of mind and actual mood, on the social and cultural specificities of the targeted audience (taste, etc.) but also on the specifics of the actual setting. Music in department stores or shopping malls will typically differ from that in clothing boutiques, and boutiques for teenagers may have a "soundscape" (Schafer 1977) quite distinct from the one in shops for middle-aged women. Such situational differences are seminal for understanding the types of mood enhancement, at which this ambient music is aiming.

Thirdly, ambient music is just like advertising in general "uninvited". Most people do not watch television to see the commercials. Likewise most shoppers do not visit a particular shop to enjoy its music, although some notable exceptions exist (e.g. *Victoria's Secret, Starbucks*). But contrary to commercial breaks, ambient music is impossible to "switch of" or even to lock out without the use of modern, personal audio-technology. Music in commercial sites is forced on the shopper, whether he or she wants it or not. That this enforced and supplementary music is only on rare occasions experienced as an obstacle is caused by the fact that the sound usually remains unnoticed.

Music for shopping is thus in the first place characterized by being *unnoticed*, *supplementary* and *enforced on* the consumer. Moreover, its being situational not only implies that it has to fit into a pre-existing spatial framework (i.e. a specific shop and its target audience). This music also helps to define the situation by creating coherences in space or by marking contrasts between sections in the department store or between boutiques in a shopping mall or on a shopping street. It functions as *sonic architecture* in that it binds elements together or establishes distinctions in space. Furthermore, this music is designed to fit into the shop's or the consumer's daily time schedule. It is *programmed* to enhance moods and thereby has to modulate situational aspects of consumption: e.g. it has to relax shoppers when they are most stressed (in the late afternoon). Being unnoticed also implies being *anonymous*. This music diverts attention from its composer or origin towards the consumption setting. On location, it is hard to escape, precisely by being *mass distributed and communicated*. The overall effect at which this music is aiming is not the creation of strong, intense but relatively short-lived emotions but a balanced mood fit for the occasion. It is driven by an urge for *mood enhancement*. A more specific or local aim of music for shopping is as a branding device. The particular music of a shop in a mall or on a shopping street sets it apart from competitors by creating a special (and sometimes noticeable) ambience. By actively establishing a mental fit between music, product, shop, brand and the consumer, the music in such cases contributes to *cognitive framing* of the brand (i.e. the product or more common the chain of stores).

The sum of these features characterizes music for shopping as something distinct from other genres and uses of music. We will now look closer into each one of them.

Mass distribution and mass communication

Music for shopping is transmitted to a relatively large and varied group of people who are in the same well-defined physical setting for other purposes than listening to the music. It can thus be said to be public and thereby distinguishes itself from privately carried music used in public places (e.g. music transmitted by iPods or MP3-players). Private music typically shields of the user from other (and the others') sounds thereby defending his or her identity and integrity when exposed to strangers in the public sphere. "Muzak" on the contrary serves to erase the irritation generated by strange and potentially distracting noises, hence making the interaction between strangers more harmonic. To achieve this aim, music for shopping has to be non-obtrusive and non-specific. Whereas private music pinpoints identity, public music in public places usually blurs identity. It does not necessarily have to match everybody's or even anybody's taste perfectly. But it must certainly not appal the broad variety of shoppers.

Supplement

Music for shopping supplements an activity that has importance in itself. This music does not cause the situation, as the situation would most often take place without the presence of music as well. Secondly, the situation is not organized in accordance with the music, as is the case when activities are synchronized to fit the musical tempo (e.g. fitness centres, chain gangs or other work place situations).

The supplementary aspect also furthers a way of listening that is typical for this music. Shopping lends itself for distractive or "peripheral listening" (Lanza 1991). This perceptual mode is quite different from the one in situations where music is the defining aspect. Those situations are characterized by structural or "deep listening" (Bull & Back 2003) where distractions, i.e. stimuli that activate the other senses, are minimized (e.g. a classical concert). This is quite contrary to the shopping situation in which visual but also olfactory and tactile stimuli compete for awareness, thus furthering "peripheral listening". These two perceptual modes are extremes on a gliding scale, and listeners have the ability to shift modes abruptly. But it can be assumed that the distractive form of listening is widespread today, in that it characterizes many other public settings than shopping (restaurants, work places, waiting rooms, etc.) just like music accompanies many other activities in the private sphere (e.g. preparing meals or doing the dishes).

Enforcement

Music for shopping is enforced. It is not the shopper's own decision that there should be music in this particular setting. The kind of music played is also out of the shopper's control. Actually, if the shopper wants to avoid this music, he or she should either leave the shop or "cover the ears" with other music: a kind of counter-music, advanced by modern technology of reproduction. As stated, music for shopping in this respect resembles other kinds of commercial "uninvited" music, even though they are more easily averted.

In some cases, the stores are able to select and promote their own distinctive blend of music in a way that appeals to their customers. A chain like *Victoria's Secret* is famous for its ability to choose music that fits its "audience". In this case, music is one of the main attractions in visiting the store and serves as a marketing tool for defining (and generating) more specific target groups. The music then has to fit somebody's taste. It becomes an important parameter in a set of lifestyle choices. Moreover, the actual choice of music actively selects which consumers fit the merchandize offered by the shop. The music played in for example shops for teenager or adolescent apparel is chosen to attract a specific audience and repel others.

The change in music supply and taste since the 1960s when popular music became portable and diversified has contributed crucially to making the choice of music an individual and lifestyle based matter. This is perhaps the main reason why the distribution of originally composed music for shopping declined. This non-specific blend is no longer a common denominator for the general consumer's taste. Shops can no longer enforce just any music on the consumer. On the other hand, commercial settings with a wide range of products targeting a non-specific audience (e.g. super or hypermarkets, department stores, malls) have to rely on music already widely known and mass communicated. Instead of originally composed "muzak" or lifestyle-specific music, they play compilations of Top-40 hits mixed with "golden oldies": i.e. the kind of music many people listen to when they are doing something else (e.g. driving, jogging, and cleaning). This music is structurally prepared for accompanying other activities. It has a metronomic rhythm, lasts for approximately three minutes and consists of verses and cantabile refrains, which also makes it suitable for more or less conscious humming. Top-40 music is thus in many respects pre-programmed to serve as supplementary music. In a way, the same could be said for the consumer: The use of broadcasted music accompanying other activities leads to a sort of pre-programming when this same music is played in shops. It is perceived as supplementary to other activities, ensuring that these doings go smoothly.

Whereas ambient music for commercial settings used to be "music for shoppers", it is now gradually turning into "the shopper's (own) music". Nonetheless, the shopper's music is still picked and mediated by the store. Since the 1990s, muzak has been offering music that is targeted explicitly to fit the customer's taste. *Music – with YOU in control*, it is called (Lanza 2004: 218). "You" being the shop manager who is expected to know best which targets to reach and who does not want the program of some random radio station to determine the store's sonic profile.

Programming

Music for shopping is programmed, constituting a precisely defined and carefully designed "flow" (Radano 1989, Sterne 1997). Based on Williams' (1997) definition of flow, three levels of programming can be identified:

1. the actual day
2. the actual sequence of pieces and the intervals between them
3. the actual syntax of each piece

Shoppers are typically exposed to levels 2 and 3. Employees are also exposed to level 1: Music played in the morning typically differs from that in the late afternoon, when people shop in a hurry at their way back from work. Music in the morning should hence aim at exiting consumers, whereas it should strive for relaxation in the afternoon.

Programming of flow on level 3 is immanent in the crafting of most music, and in many cases this flow is composed deliberately to generate some explicit affects (e.g. Viennese Classiciism or Top-40 pop). But in the case of music for shopping, some of the elements in compositions intended for live performance are absent (e.g. improvization or extended solos). The principles guiding the programming of "muzak" are moreover allegedly more scientific, although the difference with other types of popular music must be said to be marginal in that they are often based on sound knowledge of conventions.

The programming of music for shopping on level 2 (and 1) bears much resemblance to that of the radio flow. This flow is produced by putting together a sequence of pieces played without too many intervals of speech or commercials. This leaves an overall impression of coherence. The coming of DAB-radio, which permits the distribution of narrowly targeted, style-conscious music, means new competition for distribution firms like Muzak. This is perhaps one of the main reasons for the change in Muzak's selling strategy. The company no longer tries to convince customers of the advantages of their originally composed supplementary music, programmed by Muzak on all three levels. Instead, Muzak is trying to persuade customers to buy their unique, scientifically generated mix of pre-existing genre-pure music with appropriate pauses, more suitable for consumption sites than the programs construed by the "happy amateurs" of radio (Owen 2006).

SONIC ARCHITECTURE

Music for shopping functions as sonic architecture by being played in a space where consumers are moving around. Music thereby guides the experience of spatiality. Basically, two opposite effects are to be identified. Music can *erase* physical boundaries between sections, and music can *mark* boundaries where no clear physical separation is visible. In supermarkets, the first operation is typical. Music creates an impression of coherence and continuity in the movement from one section to another (e.g. from the wine section to the meat or the vegetables). It functions as a wall-to-wall-carpet, uniting many different products and many separate moments of decision-making.

In other cases, the second operation prevails. In shopping malls, the music played in each separate store signals that the consumer is about to enter a "new planet" within the mall's universe. On shopping streets some shops have placed loud speakers at the entrance. The music playing from these devices is louder than in the shop itself. The function of this is to draw attention to the shop by signalling that this store is different from the rest. In department stores, some sections have their own distinct music. This music is then played louder than that in the rest of the store. In the leading department store in our home city, the section for children's clothing plays the same music as most other sections of the store. This section is neighbouring the music section and the section for teenager apparel. Both these sections play loud and (to some people) obtrusive music. In the border zone between these three sections, three different kinds of music are audible. Music for shopping could thus be said to function as a *signal* to the consumer of where he or she is located right now, what he or she is moving towards and where he or she would like (not) to arrive.

A second function of the sonic architecture is that it enables transfers between the public sphere and the private realm. Also here, two opposite effects are identifiable. Music makes *privacy in public* possible. In supermarkets, couples can have private conversations without being intruded by the other customers, because the music seems to encapsulate their speech. On the other hand, music makes anonymity bearable. You are *alone together* because the music creates a kind of social bond, indicating that many individuals are united in the same doings.

A third function of this sonic architecture is that it generates a cocoon-like experience. Loud speakers are placed everywhere but hidden from sight. This makes it difficult if not impossible to identify the source of the music: It seems to be everywhere and emanate from nowhere. Regardless where in the shop the consumer is located, the music sounds equally loud. Every corner is sprinkled with the same intensity. This conveys the impression of being immersed in a discrete universe and having a time-out from the real world. Interestingly, this experience of being in an alternative reality is furthered by the sound transmitted by the loud speakers. Compared to the loud speakers at home, the frequency range is reduced affecting especially the bass regions, which produces a shriller and "metallic" sound making the music sound in a special "supermarket-like" way.

Anonymous and unnoticed

Unlike most music, originally composed music for shopping is "authorless". It seems irrelevant to know who wrote the score, who arranged it or who performed it. This type of ambient music is furthermore anonymous because a specific piece will be difficult to distinguish from other pieces. It appears as non-unique, and hardly worth noticing.

On level 3, music for shopping is programmed not to attract attention. And it is very successful at that. We conducted a small interview outside two of our home city's supermarkets and asked 30 customers whether there had been music in the store or not. Only two respondents were certain of having heard music. None of them was able to tell what kind of music they had been exposed to. Originally composed music has some structural features that contribute to this low level of awareness. Sudden changes (*subito*-effects) and obtrusive sounds are avoided. As far as instrumentation is concerned, brass, certain percussion instruments, and singing are avoided, whereas other instruments like strings and synthesizers, suitable for more glissandy and hyper-legato, are predominant. In addition, this music has no significant "ground" or any remarkable *groove* (Fehling 1985: 85ff).

As far as the use of pre-existing music is concerned, its structural features will be more demanding, because this music was initially composed with the intention of distinguishing itself and being bought. But the pre-existing music used in commercial sites often consists of pieces with long-lasting exposure in other media. Their ability to draw attention towards their structure has worn out, and the listener has become accustomed to the sound. The listening process has become routinized and effortless. Moreover, when such music is played in routinized situations like supermarkets, this will increase the tendency of "peripheral listening" (discussed above) leading to low attention and awareness.

As stated earlier, this pre-existing music is re-functionalized when it is played in stores. It is no longer for dancing, singing or attentive listening. By furthermore being re-mediated by the shop's loud speakers and thereby transformed into "supermarket music", the original context of production is masked and the music tends to become anonymous on the third level of programming. This transformation also contributes to anonymity on level 2. Here, this metamorphosis is promoted by the fact that Top-40 music, despite its urge to profile itself as an autonomous and worthwhile artefact, is *overcoded* as a genre but *undercoded* as an *oeuvre* (Eco 1978, Middleton 1990: 173). In the flow on level 2, it is sound as an example of a particular musical genre that counts, and not the special features of the sound as an original piece of music.

In many up-market boutiques or in shops for customers with an extensive and distinguishable use of music, these two features of ambient music must be qualified some more. Shops that utilize music to attract customers either by playing it out loudly or by using their own distinctive (and perhaps sophisticated) blend of music for branding purposes (like *Victoria's Secrets* use of classical music or *Starbucks* use of world music) are scarcely interested in "their" music remaining unnoticed and anonymous. The use of "sonic branding" may even instigate the chain to sell its "own" music. *Victoria's Secrets* as well as *Starbucks* have successfully produced and sold compilations of "their" music (Kassabian 2004). In such cases, the music is re-named, turning for example into a piece of *Victoria's Secrets* music and potentially losing its reference to its origin: in the extreme case the composer or conductor become irrelevant or anonymous to the listener.

THE EFFECTS OF MUSIC FOR SHOPPING: MOOD ENHANCEMENT

Most music is composed and performed in order to generate *emotions*: short-lasting but intense responses to a specific stimulus. Such stimuli produce awareness by distinguishing themselves from the overall structure of elements surrounding them (i.e. from the flow on level 3). Moreover, the causal relationship between one stimulus and a response supports memory and recognition. Concert music is the most obvious example, but even jingles in commercials crucially depend on this mechanism. This is not the case in music for shopping. This music is not aiming at emotions but at enhancing the right *mood* for dwelling, browsing, interacting, deciding and purchasing. Contrary to emotions, a mood is a more long-lasting, less intense and above all non-specific tone of feelings (Damasio 1994, Davies 2001, LeDoux 1996, Morris 1999), partly based on personal and hence stable predispositions (Eysenck 1967, Gray 1981, Kagan 1994). Being non-specific implies that not one single stimulus affects the actual mood positively or negatively. The effect of music is more to contribute (in combination with other props) in generating an ambience for positive consumer experiences. In that respect, music for shopping resembles most (but not all) film music, whose predominant function is to convey the "right" atmosphere to the audience of the movie.

This mood enhancement operates in two distinct directions. The first one aims at reducing tension or arousal from stress (high arousal) to a more comfortable level. By relaxing the "audience", music in commercial sites promotes conditions favourable for shopping. This is especially significant in the most routinized and (often) least pleasurable sites of consumption. The indistinct but also non-confrontational mix of carefree and harmonious music in supermarkets serves to reduce irritability and avert the possibility of conflicts. The location of loud speakers in such a way that it generates the impression of dwelling in a cocoon-like environment, separated from the constraints of "real life", advances not only the impression of being in a world of dreams, so crucial to the genesis of a consumer society (Williams 1982), but also the ability to concentrate on the tasks at hand without being diverted by other concerns. The effect of this is a kind of "time-out" allowing the consumer to re-focus and at the same time dream him or herself away to a more ideal universe. Furthermore, music contributes to stabilizing this "world of dreams". The fact that music creates coherence in space and continuity in the consumer's movements in this space enhances a sense of belonging and of being safe in a well-known place. This is especially important in malls, where each shop potentially has its own sonic signature. By being encapsulated by the mall's music when leaving one of its shops contributes to the feeling of being once more in a secure haven.

Some shops in malls or on shopping streets utilize music for a quite different purpose. When loud speakers are placed at the entrance of the shop or the in-store music is louder or faster than elsewhere, this arises attention and signals that this particular shop is offering something different and, not least, something more exciting than its neighbours. In such cases, mood enhancement takes the opposite direction. It aims at increasing arousal from an uncomfortable level of lacking tension (i.e. of boredom or drowsiness) to an accentuated state of awareness. Sudden changes in the arousal level are inherently pleasurable by generating either relief (from tension) or elation (from boredom) (Scitovksky 1991).

Increasing arousal promotes fear as well as excitement, the latter state being of course the one catered for by music for shopping. But preventing "uninvited" and unwanted visitors that might ruin the store's carefully cultivated image from entering the shop can be a potentially positive side effect of using music in this vein. This strategy seems most widespread in specialty stores, particularly in shops for teenagers and adolescents. Here, the music partakes crucially in creating an up-beat atmosphere of excitement and excess that may for example stimulate customers to stage them-selves in front of large mirrors in extraordinary garments and enticing postures like the heroes and heroines of pop culture.

Whether the music is aiming at increasing or decreasing the level of arousal, it serves to adjust the consumer's mood, so he or she might be better fit for the tasks at hand. Finding the right level of arousal is pivotal to every performance as too high a level creates nervousness and too low causes slovenliness (Yerkes & Dodson 1908). In contributing to modulate this level, music may either enhance comfort or joy. Both these moods support consumer activity. Comfort increases the ability to concentrate on the task, whereas joy promotes curiosity, spontaneity and the urge to experiment.

The effects of music for shopping: cognitive framing

Mood enhancement is very much a psychobiological phenomenon. The changing of the arousal level is to a high degree non-conscious, which explains why music may produce such effects even though it remains unnoticed. The same apparently goes for knowledge activation processes (cf. North, Hargreaves & McKendrick 1999). But the outcomes of this process are much more notable than those of psychobiological processes. The music made me (perhaps inadvertently) buy this wine instead of that one. For this to happen, three cognitive operations must be activated.

Firstly, there must be a *conceptual frame*, consisting of some (more or less elaborated) knowledge of the music (a domain). Secondly, this frame must be utilized in facilitating the decision-making process. This is done by *inferencing* (Johansen 1991). And thirdly, the outcome of such inferences must be a re-framing, where a new conceptual domain has been endowed with qualities and attributes of existing domains (e.g. the music). This is called *blending* (Fauconnier & Turner 2002). In the case of buying wine, this process could be running in the following simplified way: This is French music, French music is nice, sentimental and nostalgic, and I like it (conceptual frame); this is French wine, and this wine belongs to this music, so I'll buy this wine (inferencing); this wine is nice, sentimental and nostalgic like French music, so it suits a cosy evening with my partner (blending). In this way, emotions and moods triggered or conveyed by music can be transported to the profane world of goods – the outcome perhaps being that Pomerol is being perceived as belonging to Juliette Greco, St. Emilion to Charles Trenet or Gewurztraminer to Django Reinhardt.

From a *homo oeconomicus* point of view, this may seem like very unsound reasoning. But as a matter of fact, most consumers act most of the time with imperfect knowledge and under relatively strict constraints of time. So this process enables fast decision-making, suitable for choices of no greater (or dramatic) consequence for life. Moreover, the blending-aspect may be perceived as creative and hence exciting: A new comprehension or a new network of associations is being shaped.

From a marketer's point of view, what can upset the whole process is too much or too little knowledge of the music in the first stage of reasoning. If I can't recognize Django Reinhardt, I will not start making inferences in the intended way, so I might end up buying Argentinean wine instead. On the other hand, my extensive knowledge of Juliette Greco may make me find the connection to Pomerol presumptuous or wildly exaggerated. Using music for such strategic purposes might easily backfire.

In two cases, which both apply to specialty shops, it seems particularly promising to use music to bring about cognitive (re-)framing. The first case consists of shops targeting customers with a well-defined and distinctive musical taste, e.g. stores selling teenager and adolescents apparel. Appropriate music might generate an inference like this one

> I like this music
> <u>This music belongs to those clothes</u>
> I like those clothes

Occasionally, such boutiques not only play their customers' favourite music but also show music videos, as seen in the section for this kind of clothing in our city's largest department store. This might promote even more wild or "unreasonable" inferences:

> I like this music (video)
> I like their (i.e. the artists') style
> I want to purchase this style

and, in the next split second of reasoning:

> This video is shown in a shop for clothing
> These clothes (in the shop) belong to this style
> I will buy these clothes

This hardly qualifies as logical reasoning. But despite the elliptic character of such inferences, the ambience created by the music nonetheless seems to make such decisions sensible.

The second case consists of in-store music used for branding purposes. In this case, the mix of music has to be consistent *and* profiled in style and genre. This is what successful "sonic brands" like *Victoria's Secret, Starbucks* or *Hard Rock Café* accomplish. They capitalize on inductive inferences such as:

> I like their goods (and/or services)
> I like their music
> I like them

For this to work, "they" (the brand) have to be associated with the qualities of "their" music. This blending only works if the original domain (the music) is recognizable as something particular in its own right. The implication of this being that each piece of music is seen as yet another example of this domain (and hence of the brand), and not as an autonomous work of art, an *oeuvre*. When it works, this re-mediated music starts lending itself for cross-selling in new compilations, which both *Victoria's Secret* and *Starbucks* have illustrated. In such cases, consumers might be motivated by inferences like this one:

I love this atmosphere, and would like to come or stay here more often

The music is part of this atmosphere

The music is for sale

I'll buy this music, so I can bring a piece of the atmosphere back home

Then music for shopping has turned into shopping for music. It is no longer something non-consciously forced on the consumer but consciously chosen and preferred by the consumer. Neither is it simply supplementary but rather it is perceived as an independent aspect of the place's attraction (a *genius loci*). Nor is it unnoticed. On the contrary, it has become an active part of memory.

CONCLUDING REMARKS

Music for shopping is commercialized at several levels. Firstly, it has been bought and is re-mediated by a store. Secondly, it is used to advance selling in this store. Thirdly, it may in special cases be desired and bought by consumers as a compilation sold by the store. Fourthly, in those cases where pre-existing music is being re-mediated as ambient music, a music distributor has acquired the rights in order to sell it and re-contextualize (and perhaps re-arrange) it to be used in stores.

The mere fact that this is an industry with a huge turn over indicates that in-store music is perceived as an efficient tool in promoting sales. We have pointed at two effects that might facilitate the interactions between consumers and stores: arousal modulation or mood enhancement on the one hand and, on the other, cognitive re-framing that may connect consumers to particular goods or brands. We have tried to qualify the musical, situational and behavioural aspects by which this kind of music can be distinguished from other music. This work has also shown important differences in ambient music used in supermarkets or malls and the music designated for specialty shops. In the latter case, the unnoticed, supplementary end enforced music for shopping may tend to become a notable, independent attractor to which consumers actively relate in their choices of where and what to buy.

REFERENCES

Alpert, J. I., & Alpert M. I. (1990). Music influences on mood and purchase intentions. *Psychology and Marketing*, 7, 109-133.

Areni, C. S., & Kim, D. (1993). The influence of background music on shopping behaviour. Classical versus top-forty music in a wine store. *Advances in Consumer Research*, 20. 336-340.

Ayres, L. P. (1911). The influence of music on speed in the six day bicycle race. *American Physical Education Review*, 16, 321-325.

Bruner, G. (1990). Music, mood and marketing. *Journal of Marketing*, October, 94-104.

Bull, M., & Back, L. (Eds.). (2003). *The auditory reader*. Oxford: Berg.

Damasio, A. R. (1994). *Descartes' error: Emotion, reason and the human brain*. London: Macmillan.

Davies, S. (2001). Philosophical perspectives on music and motion. In P. N. Juslin, & J. A. Sloboda (Eds.), *Music and emotion. Theory and research* (pp. 23-44). Oxford: Oxford University Press.

Dissanyake, E. (1992). *Homo aestheticus. Where art comes from and why*. New York: The Free Press.

Eco, U. (1978). *A theory of semiotics*. Bloomington: Indiana University Press.

Eysenck, H. J. (1967). *The biological bases of personality*. Springfield, Ill.: Charles C. Thomas.

Fauconnier, G., & Turner, M. (2002). *The way we think*. New York: Basic Books.

Fehling, R. (1980). Funktionelle Musik – Manipulationsversuch im Gewanden der holden Kunst [Functional music. Attempts at manipulation in the guise of art]. In R. Brinkmann (Ed.), *Musik im Alltag* (pp. 84-95). Mainz: Schott.

Gray, J. A. (1981). A critique of Eysenck's theory of personality. In H. J. Eysenck (Ed.), *A model for personality* (pp. 246-276). New York: Springer Verlag.

Jackson, D., & Fulberg, P. (2003). *Sonic Branding*. London: Palgrave.

Johansen, J. D. (1991). Utility – identity – epiphany. Some reflections on the logical structure of TV commercials. In H. H. Larsen et al. (Eds.), Marketing and Semiotics. Selected Papers for the Copenhagen Symposium (pp. 128-141). Copenhagen: Copenhagen Business School Press.

Jones, S., & Schumacher, T. (1992). Muzak: On functional music and power. *Critical Studies in Mass Communication*, 9, 156-169.

Kagan, J. (1994). *Galen's prophecy. Temperament in human nature*. New York: Basic Books.

Kant, I. (1952). *The critique of judgement*. Oxford: Oxford University Press.

Kassabian, A. (2004). Would you like some world music with your Latte? Starbucks, Putumayo, and distributed tourism. *Twentieth-Century Music*, 2/1, 209-223.

Kotler, Ph. (1973-1974). Atmospherics as a marketing tool. *Journal of Retailing*, 49, 48-64.

Lanza, J. (1991). The sound of cottage cheese (why background music is the real world beat!). *Performing Arts Journal*, 13(3), 42-53.

Lanza, J. (2004). *Elevator music. A surreal history of muzak, easy-listening and other moodsong*. Ann Arbor: University of Michigan Press.

Middleton, R. (1990). *Studying popular music*. Milton Keynes: Open University Press.

Milliman, R. E. (1982). Using background music to affect the behavior of supermarket shoppers. *Journal of Marketing, 46(3)*, 86-91.

Morris, W. N. (1999). The mood system. In D. Kahneman, E. Diener, & N. Schwarz (Eds.), *Well-Being. The foundations of hedonic psychology* (pp. 169-189). New York: Russell Sage Foundation.

National Music Council. (1996). *The value of music*. London: National Music Council.

North, A. C., & Hargreaves, D. J. (1997a). Experimental aesthetics and everyday music listening. In A. C. North & D. J. Hargreaves (Eds.), *The Social Psychology of Music* (pp. 84-103). Oxford: Oxford University Press.

North, A. C., & Hargreaves, D. J. (1997b). Music and consumer behaviour. In A. C. North & D. J. Hargreaves (Eds.), *The Social Psychology of Music* (pp. 268-289). Oxford: Oxford University Press.

North, A. C., & Hargreaves, D. J. (2006). Music in business environments. In S. Brown & U. Volgsten (Eds.), *Music and manipulation. On the social uses and social control of music* (pp. 103-125). New York: Berghahn Books.

North, A. C., Hargreaves, D. J., & McKendrick, J. (1999). The influence of in-store music on wine selection. *Journal of Applied Psychology, 84(2)*, 271-276.

Owen, D. (2006). The soundtrack of your life. *The New Yorker*. Posted 03.04.2006, on: www.newyorker.com/printables/fact/060410fa_fact

Radano, R. M. (1989). Interpreting muzak: Speculations on musical experience in everyday life. *American Music, 7(4)*, 448-460.

Scitovsky, T. (1991). *The joyless economy. The psychology of human satisfaction*. Oxford: Oxford University Press.

Schafer, R. M. (1977). *The soundscape. Our sonic environment and the tuning of the world*. Rochester, Vermont: Destiny Books.

Smith, P., & Curnow, R. (1966). 'Arousal hypothesis' and the effects of music on purchasing behavior. *Journal of Applied Psychology, 50(3)*, 255-256.

Sterne, J. (1997). Sounds like the mall of America: Programmed music and the architectonics of commercial space. *Ethnomusicology, 41(1)*, 22-50.

Williams, R. H. (1982). *Dream worlds. Mass consumption in late nineteenth century France*. Berkeley: University of California Press.

Williams, R. (1997). *Television. Technology and cultural form*. London: Routledge.

Wilson, S. (2003). The effect of music on perceived atmosphere and purchase intentions in a restaurant. *Psychology of Music, 31(1)*, 93-112.

Yerkes, R. M., & Dodson, J. D. (1908). The relation of strength of stimulus to rapidity of habit-formation. *Journal of Comparative Neurology and Psychology, 18*, 459-482.

PRODUCING CORPORATE SOUNDS
An interview with Karsten Kjems and Søren Holme on *sonic branding®*

Nicolai Graakjær and Christian Jantzen

Sound branding is the business of producing an acoustic trademark that may reinforce brand identity and thus enhance customers' memory of the product or service. An important tool in creating such corporate sounds is the sound logo, i.e. a distinctive, short melody that serves to generate an identity in a company's various interactions with its various publics. Just like visual logos, these short sonic sequences help to distinguish the company from possible competitors in the mind of the customer. In a broader perspective, all kinds of sound design that aims at helping the customer in decision-making, at increasing the consumer-experience or at guiding the user in completing specific tasks may qualify as sound branding. The explicit use of designed sounds in e.g. computer interfaces or mobile phones points at an increasing awareness of the importance of corporate sounds.

But how do producers of corporate sounds understand and use music? From an overall perspective, this question could be coined as an interest in "the place and thoughts of cultural producers" (Frith 1992: 178), and when it comes to commercial music-making in particular, these 'places and thoughts' are still not well documented.[1] An obvious reason for this neglect might be the fact that being a composer of commercial music is not a job generally looked upon with admiration. At least this seems to be one of the lessons learned from the long time 'insider' Steve Karmen (1989, 2005). Also the work done – i.e. jingles and the like – is rarely appreciated as high valued cultural artefacts, as a composer implies in an interview: "We write beautiful music, and no one ever hears it" (Shafer interviewed in Rule 1997: 75).

The business of producing corporate sounds is notoriously busy and practical. The fact that many people working in this field lack a formal education moreover impedes research. This is documented in some of the few and rather small scaled research initiatives available on the subject (e.g. Miller 1985). The actual working process of these professionals seems to rely largely on a sort of 'tacit knowledge' or 'knowing-in-action' (Schön 1987: 23ff) or as verbalized by a composer: "I think jingle stuff is a lot more knack and feeling for a song than it is having gone to Julliard and knowing a lot about theory" (Dawes interviewed in Miller 1985: 52). Findings by Leo seem to support this statement. She asked three large German advertising agencies to what extent scientific and theoretical insights are important for the way in which they tackle music. All three agencies denied the necessity of such insights; one agency claimed that their dealings with music were "…only practical. Good music is halfway there" (Leo 1999: 21).[2]

These somewhat non-theoretical approaches of practitioners should not be conceived as denigrating or disparaging. As a matter of fact, this practice could be argued to be a pivotal part of what Schön articulates as "professional artistry" (Schön 1987) and others as "expertise" (Dreyfus and Dreyfus 1986: 30ff).[3] Approaches marked by "knowing-in-action" do highlight, though, that some methods are more appropriate than others when it comes to examining specific elements of practitioners' actions. In a way, it is not always so much the 'thoughts' (cf. the quote above) of practitioners that are relevant as it is their actual 'doings', and, in pointing to this, the limits of interviews and questionnaires are implied. Observations would then seem to be a promising supplement to interviews and questionnaires, and one interesting contribution is a case-study providing a "detailed examination of the creation of a typical small-budget musical production – designed for a state-wide television promotion" (Fitzgerald 1999: 365). One of the interesting observations in this study is that composers seem to have well-developed hunches that particular musical expressions correspond to particular categories of emotions. This appears to be an underlying feature of the way practitioners work. At one point, one of the composers remarks: "the diminished always sort of works…that's fairly typical of suspense, you know" (Dodemont interviewed in Fitzgerald 1999: 366). In the working process, composers do not necessarily have a clear idea of *how* and *why* the particular musical expression works (cf. the sort of tacit knowledge mentioned above). In addition, some of the practitioners stress the importance of being able to 'translate' emotions into musical expressions, for example: "I've always said I want to write a book, a translation book…You have to get good at taking what they're [the ad agency] saying in English and translating it into musical terms" (Pecorella interviewed in Rule 1997: 69)[4].

For the present study, we have decided to interview representatives of a production company specialized in creating corporate sounds. Although this choice of methodology has some potentially negative implications for our findings, interviewing has been chosen partly because it is in line with the majority of previous research and partly because this format often produces interesting suggestions for future studies (for instance in the form of case-study and/or observation).

One of the main issues in our interview is the role of music in the overall process of producing a commercial or creating a brand identity: i.e. at what stage does music enter into this process and how seminal is music considered to be for the process. This topic has hitherto only been subject to sporadic research. Findings by Leo (cf. the aforementioned questionnaires) suggest that music is central in the process. Hence, all three agencies in Leo's study assert that music enters the process of production at an early stage. This finding is remarkably at odds with other sources that spell out the *insignificant* role that music typically plays in the process of production. Dunbar, for example, states that "…[music] is used in a very haphazard and unplanned way. Too often, a television film is finished before anyone even asks about music" (1990: 210) and outlines the typical sequence of the production process: words first, then pictures, and in the end music (ibid.: 201). Faced with such contradictory research accounts, it seems logical to ask practitioners about their experiences from the field.

Karsten Kjems is managing director and owner of the Copenhagen based company *sonic branding*®. Like most companies specialized in sound branding, the company is relatively new. It started in 2004 and has seven employees. One of them, Søren Holme, participated in the interview. Søren has a master's degree in musicology and media science, whereas

Karsten has studied information science and worked as producer, composer and musician prior to establishing *sonic branding®*. The company is one of Denmark's largest agencies within its field and produces sound (i.e. speak as well as ambience) and music for commercial purposes. Its products cover the whole range of media: From radio commercials, TV spots, homepages, product presentations, exhibition stands, podcasting, mobile phones, telephone waiting systems (IVR) to sound (sonic/audio) logos and sound brand identities.

Question: Your company both handles client consultancy, production, and implementation of sound solutions. The working process must be quite different from case to case. Could you describe the general aspects of your services?

Answer: Each job obviously depends on the clients and their wants and needs. Nonetheless, you could distinguish between two different kinds of working process categories: short-term action oriented process and long-term strategic oriented process.

Question: What characterizes short-term action oriented processes?

Answer: The short-term action oriented process (SAOP) is mainly characterized by the focus on a forthcoming deadline and to get this particular job done in a satisfying way. The time limit varies from one day to weeks depending on the task in question. SAOP is typically dictated by the needs of our clients, that is the companies or persons who buy our product and the advertising agencies that we collaborate with.

Question: How is the collaboration with the client or agency in a short-term action process?

Answer: In most cases, the agency has designed the campaign and sketched the spots, and we receive instructions, per mail or phone, suggesting what they want the music and speak to sound like. Normally, with regards to television or radio spots, *sonic branding®* receives the desired length, speaker text, some pictures of the commercial, and requests for a particular musical genre and style.

Question: How do you then go about designing the sound?

Answer: In such cases, we start with the speak establishing a guiding frame of the commercial. During this part of the process, a representative of the advertising agency is present in order to make sure that the vocal expression sounds as intended. When the speak is satisfactory, we produce the music and sound effects within this frame of speak. In this creative production phase, we focus on how to make audible room for the speak and how to let the music and speak complement each other instead of conflicting with one another. A way to do this, is by using the gaps between the speak with the more attention demanding elements in the music such as breaks, active melodic figures, or sound effects. With this technique, it is possible to keep a clear speak message and still add some energy and emotional value to the commercial. When we have come up with a raw idea of the music and recorded it, we are in a continuous dialogue with the advertising agency until we reach a result that satisfies the client. The role of *sonic branding*® in these kinds of tasks is mainly centred on production aspects.

Question: Your influence on the overall process seems minimal. Do you influence the choice of music?

Answer: In short-term action oriented processes we are primarily focused on solving the musical task, which is given to us. We ask ourselves: how can we solve the client's wishes the best way on time? So here we rarely ask why they have chosen to use this particularly kind of music for their brand or campaign. This circumstance is partly due to the time frame in which the task has to be completed – there is simply little time to discuss whether the basic choice of music is good or not. Furthermore, it is traditionally the advertising agencies who make the strategic decisions regarding campaigns and therefore also the choice of sound and music. But we always express our opinion and share our expertise to consult and guide our clients. Often, the advertising agency is open-minded towards new suggestions and ideas.

Question: Apart from commercials – are there other types of short-term actions that you solve?

Answer: Other types of tasks within this category are primarily updating telephone speaker systems (IVR) and producing sound for different product and company presentations to customer's websites.

Question: To sum up, when does music typically enter the production process in the case of short-term actions?

Answer: As said earlier, the campaign is typically already sketched when we are introduced to it. Music is normally the last step in the general production chain, and is therefore per definition added close to the final deadline. The backside of these short-term action oriented processes is the fact that it renders difficult or even hinders more strategic use of music.

Question: This strategic use of music is the other category of tasks. Could you tell us some more about these long-termed strategic oriented processes?

Answer: Yes, in those processes, sound and music is used as a more strategic aspect of market communication. Here, we are concerned with how sounds create brand effects. Music is considered to be a strategic tool in the branding of a firm, and not something added at the very end of the production process, like in the short-term action oriented processes. In short, in long-term processes, we focus on sonic branding. The timeframe of these long-term strategic oriented processes (LSOP) is more fluent, ongoing, and involves a lot more consultancy than the SAOP.

Question: Could you describe the basic idea of a long-term strategic oriented process?

Answer: The idea of a **LSOP** is to establish music and sound strategies for companies who have a lot of audible touch points in their marketing activities i.e. television, radio, homepage, telephone waiting systems, product presentations, exhibition stands, podcasts, mobile phones, e-mails, etc. By gathering the various audible touch points, it is possible for *sonic branding*®

to create a strong audible cross-media expression, thereby developing an audio brand for the firm – or *sound identity* as we call it. This holistic way of thinking about sound is obviously important for big corporate companies, who believe in the synergy effect and want to appear as one coherent organization – one brand. Our methodology in LSOP is based on what we call *sonic branding sound profile*, a kind of counterpart to the well-known graphic manual.

Question: How do you go about creating coherence between the firm's brand strategy and its sound identity?

Answer: We start with a four-hour workshop with marketing and communication staff of the company. Here, we go through different company association exercises in order to acquire a detailed picture of the corporate value codex, personality, and brand strategies. These exercises reflect a grounded belief in *sonic branding®*, and in music sociology for that matter, that music communicates values, taste and attitudes. Therefore, it matters which sound, music, and voice is chosen for a brand. Could you imagine a luxurious hotel chain like the *Radisson Hotel* playing heavy metal music or rap music in their lobbies? Or what about *Mercedes* using German Tyrol music in their product presentations of a new high tech car? We do not claim that some objective or universal recipe for the connection between specific values and music exists, but certainly cultural codes do exist, as the two examples above show. Maybe Elvis was perceived as rebellious in the 1950s, but using his music in today's context will certainly not send a particularly provoking message – more likely the opposite. Our job in *sonic branding®* is therefore to synchronize the firms' values with the present realities of musical culture in order to send an up to date message.

Question: Could you expand on how this connection between corporate values and music is created?

Answer: After having identified the value codex, personality, and brand strategy of the company, we analyze, filtrate, and categorize their words in order to translate them into sound, music, and voice. This work is based on three main principles:

1. Which values can be expressed through association?
2. Which values can be composed as intrinsic in the music?
3. Which values can not be expressed through music?

An example could be a firm who wants to signal energy, innovative technology, and excellent service. If we start with 'energy', this value could be categorized as (2): i.e. an intrinsic musical characteristic such as high tempo, percussive instrumentation and powerful dynamics. 'Innovative technology' is subtler but could be seen as (1) association to a modern/futuristic universe by means of electronic instrumentation and spacey sound effects. Alternately, one could use a musical reference to a famous science fiction movie, and thereby creating associations with a future society in which everything is possible. Musical references should be treated with care though because they may provide the listener with unintended connotations. Maybe, this particular science fiction movie has a very dystopian morale, which would be very unfortunate for the brand to be associated with. Thirdly, 'excellent service' falls into (3) as this value, because of its concreteness, is extremely difficult to translate into music, which we will clarify for the client. After having identified the value codex, personality, and brand strategy, and having translated them into musical guidelines, we help to define a standard speaker, whom will be the general voice of the company. This voice must therefore have associative coherence with the brand personality.

Question: It seems to us that this work on long-term strategic oriented processes is fairly theoretical and very systematic. How do you ensure that the results from your analyses become guidelines for the client's corporate sound?

Answer: Simply, we establish a sound and musical foundation – an audible brand ground colour – on which further production will be based. With the *sonic branding sound profile* we try both to ensure a great coherence with the company's brand strategy and to give ourselves some valuable and effective musical guidelines when we enter the production phase. Further, the client receives the *sonic branding sound profile*, which provides an overview of the various audible touch points, along with guidelines to create a coherent musical identity/brand across media, as well as a list of preferential initiatives. After completion of the *sonic branding sound profile*, we start the actual production work with the tasks specified by the company – it could be sound logo, podcasting, product presentation, etc. If the client wants a *sound identity*, we make an overall holistic strategy for the audible touch points needed; making sure that there is strong coherence across media. This could involve integrating the sound logo in the company's theme tune, and creating variations of this theme in the product presentation, radio spot or telephone system (IVR) and so forth.

Question: Could you give an example?

Answer: Well, our work with the Danish energy company SEAS-NVE. With this client, we produced the *sonic branding sound profile* after two workshops. The overall sound identity of SEAS-NVE is still in progress but, so far, we have covered its telephone system (IVR), in-house music, and company and product presentation. A sound logo and a company theme tune are still in production. All elements are coherent and in accordance with SEAS-NVE's sound profile.

Question: What is most common today, the short- or the long-term processes?

Answer: It is our experience that the most common working processes in the music and advertising industry is the SAOP, mainly because of the leading status of advertising agencies where music is ordered on daily/weekly/monthly basis dictated by the different campaign concepts. By this we do not suggest that SAOP tasks are of lower quality or create uninspiring results, since several Danish sound production firms are capable of handling these strict time frames and still keeping a high level of creativity and quality. But, we see a huge potential in working more in the LSOP as it helps more strategic audible brand thinking in market communication and makes it possible to establish synergy across media. Fortunately, there is a tendency in Denmark these years towards big corporations taking interest in our *sonic branding sound profile* and *sound identity* concept and the many advantages they can achieve from it.

Question: But is it still not difficult to convince many potential clients of these advantages?

Answer: It certainly is. The sense of hearing is simply still not recognized as a channel for strategic marketing, even though nobody rejects the strong emotional potentials of music. In comparison, it is difficult to imagine a serious company today without a graphic logo or company colour as a means of recognition and brand signalling. Opposite, there are still remarkably few companies about whom you can say the same thing, when it comes to sound logos and audible coherence across different media such as television spots, telephone systems (IVR), product presentations, reception music, etc.

Question: Does the unpredictability of the effects of music contribute to these difficulties?

Answer: Certainly so! You can't guarantee that this particular music will arouse these specific feelings. Music is simply too complex a cultural phenomenon where the listener's personal background, social orientation, and listening context have a huge impact on the overall experience. On the other hand, as mentioned earlier, cultural codes do exist, and there is obviously some kind of convergence in the way people react to music. You rarely hear about people having melancholic or sad feelings when hearing The Pointer Sisters' *I'm So Excited*, or the other hand being excited and joyful when hearing Mozart's *Requiem in D Minor*. We can not guarantee that the music produced will affect the listener in a particular way but we can presume it by looking at the way a certain genre, style, rhythmic figure, harmonic combination, etc. have been used, perceived, and interpreted in the cultural landscape.

Question: How does this influence communication with clients and marketing people?

Answer: It is quite normal for the marketing staff to operate with more reliable facts, which can be translated into tables and graphs to demonstrate that the campaign works and that it is profitable. From this point of view, it is quite vague and unsatisfying to work with presumption. We are therefore once in a while asked questions from clients like *"what exactly are* our benefits from using music, and can you document it?", "how can we be sure that it works?", and "how much does music increase our sales?". Tough questions! Even though surveys examining the effect of sound in advertisement do exist, the subject of audio/sound branding is a rather new and unexplored area of branding, which is why examination and documentation of its effects are insufficient. Whether or not music has a strong emotional impact on the consumers is hardly ever questioned. However, as said, they call for documentation. Thus, we must honestly and regretfully make it clear to our clients early in the process that documentation is limited due to two main factors. Firstly, research within this area is, as mentioned, limited in scope. Secondly, the effects of sound and music are a rather complex and intangible parameter to measure both considering emotional effects on listeners as well as contribution to brand awareness. As most branding initiatives, it is highly difficult to predict the benefits of sound and music, and therefore sound and music should rank alongside the other branding initiatives – i.e. on a strategic rather than an operational or tactical level.

Question: What about your clients. Do they always know which communicative goals the music should contribute to?

Answer: Actually, we believe that it is important to ask the clients early in the process what they really want to communicate. Despite the simplicity of the question, it is not always clarified. Still, the answer is essential for us to know, as there seems to be two main categories: 1) focus on communicating brand awareness and values without particular messages, and 2) focus on communicating specific messages like new products, services, phone numbers, homepage address, sales, etc. These two categories are not necessary clearly separated in let's say television and radio spots, but in many cases, the client adds particular importance to one of them. This helps us, as the two categories can sometimes be conflicting, and we then know what to prioritize in the production phase.

Question: Could you give an example of such a potential conflict?

Answer: Take for example a radio commercial where the client wishes to establish a happy and energetic mood through some electronic funk music and a fast talking speaker. At the same time, this client has just published a new homepage, and it is considered very important that listeners actually notice the address and is capable of memorizing it. In such cases, the energetic music and sound can easily take focus away from the message, and there will be a risk that the listener simply will not pay attention. It can therefore prove necessary to make the success criterions explicit in order to prioritize. If the no. 1 priority is to get the message out, we can as an example advise the client to let the speaker talk slower and make the music less energetic or pacing.

Question: Does this clarification of the client's communication strategies not contribute to more precision in the measurement of 'return on invest' as well?

Answer: Yes, it is crucial for these measurements. If the audible focus of the campaign has been on a clear and well-defined message, it will be misleading to measure how effective the music has been in creating brand values. Or the other way around, to measure how well the listener has understood the specific messages, if the priority was to create brand identity. Of course, this is very categorically speaking, but it says something about the discussion of measuring musical effect in advertisements. It is not just about answering how the music and sound affects the listener, but also a matter of clarifying purpose and intentions especially in those cases where the benefits of sound and music seem to conflict at some point. Examples of such conflicts in purpose are: utilizing the attention potential of the music versus convenience; optimizing short-term memorizing of information conflicting with the musical backgrounds mood qualities; or speaker clearness versus music in general.

Question: Talking of communication, how do you face the challenge of having to talk about music to people without formal training in music?

Answer: As we are in continuous dialogue with marketing staff, advertising agencies, academic institutions, and colleagues in the field, we meet quite different approaches to and thoughts about musical experiences and effects. As we see ourselves somewhere between the academic research and the non-musical marketing staff, and customers in general, we experience a huge challenge in using music and cognitive research in our direct contact with our clients. Simply, because the two worlds have two different ways of experiencing, thinking, and talking about music.

Question: Could you elaborate on this?

Answer: The majority of the clients, agencies as well as customers, do not think analytically about music. They experience music as a whole and are not, in their daily use of music, necessarily particularly conscious of the elements which constitute the music, i.e. the melody, harmony, rhythm, orchestration, timbre, etc. On the other hand, we as composers, musicians, and producers are of course deeply aware of these elements, which is also characteristic for most academic literature on music. The challenge arises in the consultancy work with clients and agencies, as we have to find a common vocabulary platform to speak from. We do not want to speak nonsense or place ourselves in arrogant monologues. On the other hand, we are expected to be experts in the field and use our knowledge to obtain the best audible result. Bottom line is that our clients generally want tangible audible results while having difficulties in discussing the means of making them. For that reason, we developed the *sonic branding sound profile* where we work with different association exercises which give us a set of musical clues before starting the actual production phase in order to diminish any misunderstandings.

Question: So while your clients want precise measurements of the effects of music they have a rather vague vocabulary when addressing musical issues. In musicology, this relationship seems to be quite the opposite: a precise vocabulary but only vague conceptions of how music actually works. How do you bridge this gap?

Answer: There are actually two gaps. One is a musical vocabulary gap between the academic and the marketing world. The other one concerns methodology: To what degree can the effect of music be measured? In musicology it has become an obvious fact that you can't predict the listener's reactions to a piece of music in a positivistic manner. But that is very much what our clients would like. So for us, it is important to have documentation of 'return on investment' for the companies. As we point out, we can of course not predict the precise musical effect on a particular listener nor the branding interpretation in general, but by utilizing our knowledge of cultural codes and relying on insights from cognitive research we can put forward plausible presumptions of what music may affect. From our point of view, it is essential to take both the sender and recipient into consideration when doing research in music and advertisement as the intention of the communicated message most often requires some different prioritizing regarding expression, music activity, mixing, and mastering. In other words, it is important not just to do research on the musical effect but also to relate the meanings, cognitions and emotions that music elicits to the sender's intention whether it is memorizing a particular message, signalling certain brand values, or creating brand awareness in general. This could contribute to a more varied sound branding documentation in a field of research that is rather limited at present. It is our view that musicology might also benefit from participating in such research issues because it could illuminate how music is produced, used and consumed in an everyday context.

Question: Is the bottom line not that music and companies producing sound branding should play a more pivotal role in designing strategies for market communication?

Answer: Even though the benefits of thinking sound and music holistically and strategically across media seem obvious, it indeed calls for a general change of discourse in the marketing and communication departments of the companies as well as in the advertising agencies that make the campaigns. Simply because long-term strategic oriented processes require a slightly different business structure letting companies such as *sonic branding*® have the overall view of all the company's audible touch points and use this to guide the advertising agencies in their consultancy work.

Thank you for these most instructive comments.

During the last decade, the business of producing corporate sounds has become remarkably more professionalized and is rapidly turning into a specialized service within the advertising industry. Whereas producing music for commercials used to be a job for gifted but often self-taught practitioners, the agencies specializing within this field consist to a large degree of professionals with a sound theoretical foundation in musicology and related areas. To be successful, these professionals have to mediate the ideals of musicology with wants and expectations of the clients. This is certainly not without tensions or inner contradiction, and the field still lacks a consistent vocabulary shared by clients as well as specialists. Moreover, clients and agencies have to reach an agreement on how to assess the effects of music in a mutually meaningful way.

An interesting aspect of this development towards specialization is that it challenges the traditional role of music in producing commercials. On the one hand, our interview did not confirm the findings by Leo (1999) that assumed that music played a role in the planning of commercials from the very beginning of the process. Music is, on the contrary, still very much the aesthetic element that is added to the commercial in the final stages of its production. On the other hand, specialization also implies a much more profound understanding of the potential importance of music in creating a holistic brand image. It thus seems that music is gradually being acknowledged as a full-fledged, long-term strategic device in market communication: i.e. as an aesthetic element of equal importance as e.g. visual signs for generating corporate identity.

NOTES

1. Hereby is meant the 3rd person perspective taken by researchers. 1st person perspectives are to be found in greater number; for instance in the form of instructional manuals (e.g. Teixeira 1974, Lockhart & Weissman 1982, Edel 1988, Garrard 1988, Zager 2003) sometimes with an analytical perspective (Miller 1985, Wüsthoff 1999) or with an inclination towards narration (Karmen 1989, Karmen 2005). See also contributions by producers themselves, more or less explicitly promoting their own business (e.g. Fulberg 2003, Jackson & Fulberg 2003).

2. Translated by the authors from "...*nur über praktische. Gute Musik ist die halbe Miete*".

3. This also has consequences for the acquisition of skills within the business, in that processes like 'trial-and-error', 'observation' and 'imitation' are reported to be wide-spread (see interviews in Rule 1997: 61, 66).

4. 'Translation books' already exist to some extent; for rather well-known historical examples see Johann Mattheson's *Der vollkommene Kapellmeister* from 1739 (Mattheson 1980/1739) and Giuseppe Becce's *Kinobibliothek* from 1919 (cf. Prendergast 1992: 6ff), and when it comes to commercial music, see the 'Instrumentabelle der Gebrauchsmusik' in Wüsthoff 1999: 40ff. It would certainly be interesting to read Pecorella's codified suggestions for comparison.

REFERENCES

Dreyfus, H., & Dreyfus, S. (1986). *Mind over machine*. Oxford: Blackwell.

Dunbar, D. (1990). Music, and advertising. *International Journal of Avertising*, 9, 97-203.

Edel, H. (1988). The jingle business. In G. Martin (Ed.), *Making music. The essential guide to writing, performing and recording* (pp. 326-327). London: Barrie & Jenkins.

Fitzgerald, J. (1999). Music in advertising: The creation of an Australian TV commercial. In T. Mitchell & P. Doyle (Eds.), *Changing sounds. New directions and configurations in popular music* (pp. 365-368). 10th IASPM: University of Sydney.

Frith, S. (1992). The cultural study of popular music. In L. Grossberg (Ed.), *Cultural studies* (pp. 174-186). New York: Routledge.

Fulberg, P. (2003). Using sonic branding in the retail environment – An easy and effective way to create consumer brand loyalty while enhancing the in-store experience. *Journal of Consumer Behaviour, 3(2)*, 193-198.

Jackson, D., & Fulberg, P. (2003). *Sonic branding*. London: Palgrave.

Garrard, M. (1988). Creating a commercial. In G. Martin (Ed.), *Making music. The essential guide to writing, performing and recording* (pp. 328-329). London: Barrie & Jenkins.

Karmen, S. (1989). *Through the jingle jungle. The art and business of making music for commercials*. New York: Billboard Books.

Karmen, S. (2005). *Who killed the jingle? How a unique American art form disappeared*. Milwaukee: Hal Leonard.

Leo, H. (1999). *Musik im Fernsehwerbespot*. Frankfurt: Peter Lang.

Lockhart, R., & Weissman, D. (1982). *Audio in advertising. A practical guide to producing and recording music, voice-overs and sound effects*. New York: Ungar.

Mattheson, J. (1980/1739). *Der volkommene Kapellmeister* [The perfect chapelmaster]. Kassel: Bärenreiter. [Faksimile-Nachdruck herausgegeben von Margarete Reimann].

Miller, F. (1985). *Music in advertising*. New York: Amsco Publications.

Prendergast, R. (1992). *Film music, a neglected art. A critical study of music in films*. New York: W.W. Norton.

Rule, G. (1997). Jingles all the way. Making music for commercials. *Keyboard, March*, 69-75.

Schön, D. (1987). *Educating the reflective practitioner*. San Francisco: Jossey-Bass Pub.

Teixeira, A. (1974). *Music to sell by. The craft of jingle writing*. Boston: Berklee Press.

Wüsthoff, K. (1999). *Die Rolle der Musik in der Film-, Funk, und Fernsehwerbung* (2nd ed.). [The role of music in film, radio and TV commercials] Kassel: Merseburger.

Zager, M. (2003). *Writing music for television and radio commercial*. Lanham: Scarecrow Press.

The Musical Ready-Made
On the ontology of music and musical structures in film
A preliminary study

Martin Knakkergaard

Abstract

This chapter discusses to what extent it is advisable to talk of music in movies, and aims to question the relevance of applying a concept of musical understanding towards sound in movies at all.

It is the writer's understanding that the use of musical means of expression in relation to any kind of moving pictures is generally to be considered as part of the sound space of the movie and not as genuine musical expressions, no matter if the music is diegetically motivated or not. Music is present as a sort of objet trouvé or ready-made.

In most cases, music accompanying moving pictures appears as a means and not as a purpose. Even when considering movies made to picturize music, this chapter suggests that the expression of the music is forced into the background by the tendency of synaestheticism to emphasize the narrative and quite simply also by the predominance of vision: the preferred sensory supplement to the struggle of gaining access to the story or the myth: a domain outside the reach of music.

Music, film music and music in film

Music in film holds a unique position within musical phenomena, whereas music in advertising does not often distinguish itself from music in general as it draws directly on established socio-cultural codes associated with particular current or established styles of music and also on well-known musical icons, like the evergreen or last year's hit song. For one thing, it is not meaningful to talk of a particular film music style. All music styles can appear in film, thus film music is delimited solely as a particular genre comprising any kind of musical structure and sound, any kind of style or genre, exposed within the workings of film; in this way film music forms a genre in the broadest sense of the concept. However, at the same time and quite paradoxically, film music is in comparison to non-film music deeply rooted and tied up in signifying processes, obviously serving as a conveyer of meaning. Notably, it does so in a way that exceeds the mere ideological and cultural reproductive – or canonical – purposes that can be said to characterize non-film music, and it even seems reasonable to claim that film music (can) produce reductive and almost parodic understandings of idioms peculiar to music within a specific culture or subculture. Unless it is very 'avant-garde' non-film music – like music of the Baroque, Balinese gamelan, country & western, be-bop, thrash metal, contemporary, etc. – it is generally constructed and performed by means of and in accordance with (stylistic) norms and rules that are typical for the music in question. Insofar as a piece of music respects specific norms, it can not only be said to belong to the relevant culture or sub-culture but it also often takes part in the construction and continuous upholding thereof and furthermore can serve as a reference to whoever participates. Although film music, as I will try to show, is actually identifiable even though it is as a kind of negation, it never refers to itself or to film as a cultural product or phenomenon. The questions I am about to discuss are whether film music is really a particular kind of music, and whether it is truly possible to distinguish between sound and picture – and even between sound and music – in (sound) film. Is film music, at least to the film watcher, simply an integrated constituent of film as a multi-media aesthetic phenomenon, thereby distinguishing itself fundamentally from other kinds of music?

The main hypothesis behind these questions is that it is only rare – if ever – meaningful to talk of music in film, commercials and the like, since the use of musical means of expression in multi-media contexts generally appears as part of the field of sound in a text/picture-sequence and not as genuine musical expressions. This understanding of film music is considered to be valid no matter if the music is diegetic or non-diegetic. Broadly speaking, the diegetic aspect seems overexposed in the efforts to outline and understand music in films and commercials. By and large, the notion and in particular the emphasizing of the diegetic is remarkable as it obviously is not really within – or inside – the film but only in the understanding of the film that a diegetic element can emerge. What is articulated in the dichotomy between diegetic and non-diegetic music could seem to be the assumption that the film watcher is constantly looking for ways to legitimize the presence of the music. This is hard to imagine; to the film watcher, film music is always diegetic – heard or unheard.

Whether the music is written especially for the film or not and whether it appears to be a part of the environment and the surroundings within which the players are acting and, as such, is meant to be understood as belonging to the 'inside' of the pictured scene or not, is really of little importance. Music in film is always contributing to the unfolding and the dramatizing of the narrative; it is never outside – and never neutral – just as the overtures and the intermezzi are not to be understood as detached from the play during the performance of the opera. They belong to the play and entirely operate as part of the play.

Thus I support Kassabian's view that a film is not something you primarily see or watch, films are also heard (Kassabian 2001: 5). But I do not share the understanding that music brings (its own) specific meaning to the film. Instead, music must be understood as one – mostly unrecognized[1] – 'voice' in a 'dialogical polyphony' that makes up the multi-medial entirety that constitutes sound film and other similar cultural products. This voice being in itself a dialogical polyphony in the Bakhtinian sense, as the voice is put together by different types of musical expression that interact dialogically. As such, the meaning of film music is continuously negotiated in relation to all other elements: text, pictures, sound and narrative as well as inner and outer context.

Every element or 'dialogical voice' is just as constituting to the film as any other. None of them are separate entities and none of them can be left out at will without rendering the film either meaningless or thoroughly altered.[2]

In most cases, music accompanying or integrated in moving pictures stands out solely as a means, not as an objective. Already in this respect, it is not appropriate to talk about music in film, just as it does not make sense to claim that works of art – pictures, sculptures, architecture and so on – that appear in film are works of art in effect and expression. No matter if they are part of a specially designed setting or if they belong to the location that the movie is filmed in, they appear only as part of the film. They are but roles or props symbolizing works of art.

When we talk about the role of music in relation to moving pictures, it is precisely the role of the music we shall look for, not the music as music or the 'musicness' of the music. By virtue of its role as a role or a prop, film music does not take part in the discourse of music or its cultural space. Instead, within the discourse of film, it forms a musical domain of its own, which of course falls inside the definition of 'musicking' as does almost every kind of cultural sound[3], but which is at the same time otherwise fundamentally different from 'common music', comprising performed, broadcasted, distributed and other kind of principally one-way-communicated music as well as every kind of participatory music like dance music, 'unconsciously generated music', work songs, community singing, etc. Consequently, film music manifests a series of characteristics that delimits it from other kinds of music namely:

- Film music is not tied to its own time. It is timeless, asynchronous, ahistorical and capable of crossing any historic boundary at will
- Although particular forms of musical expression at least to some film watchers are related to specific cultures, film music is only referring to a certain culture by way of the universe of the film and it is not or does not need to be rooted in a specific music culture or subculture
- Film music does not form a particular musical style or genre[4]
- Film music is situated outside the circuits of traditional music styles and genres
- Film music can at will make use of and refer to traditional music styles and genres
- Film music is a one-timer; it is not repeated and it hereby separates itself fundamentally from the repetitive praxis that characterizes the conditions of traditional music. If film music is repeated, it leaves the domain of the film and becomes non-film music – possibly referring to the film[5]
- Film music is referential and non-essentialist[6]

Furthermore, film music seems unaffected by the characteristic high-low dichotomy that bourgeois culture continuously insisted upon and sought to maintain through its institutions throughout most of the 20th century. This is probably the main reason why there are remarkably few studies on film music before the rise of a new practise within musicology that focuses primarily but not entirely on popular music and seeks to integrate cultural theory deeply into the core of musicology, and it certainly seems to be the reason why "until relatively recently, academics have mobilized primarily aesthetic discourses in examining music for film, especially in the art cinema." (Gorbman 2004: 14).

It has to be noted, that music in advertising differs from the suggested characteristics of film music on at least two major points. One is, that in order to avoid providing the advertised product in question with a sense of the outdated and corny music in advertising needs to be much closer tied to the time and place of its presentation than film music has. For this reason it will often work either as a deliberate travesty or as an iconic symbol when it does not as we shall see later. Another point is that it cannot be restricted to work as a one-timer. On the contrary, it has to have sufficient musical quality and significance needed for continual presentation and repetition without being worn out; a situation that resembles the demands that charge music and other momentary cultural products – which it often has to be able to work alongside – has to meet.

However, in the subsequent discussion, I will generally focus on music in film seeking to investigate the relation between film music and other forms of music, mainly by evaluating the relevance of various means and methods for the description of music when applied to film music.

Film music perceived as music

In the following, film sound is generally left out, as sound alone, and the discussion will concentrate on the organization of sound within the perspective of traditional musical structuring principles. In other words, the discussion is as widely as possible restricted to the prevailing temporal structuring of primarily instrumental and vocal pitches and durations traditionally associated with music, referred to above – and generally – as 'common music' or 'non-film music'.

Taking this point of departure, obviously reveals an open flank, as the implied limitations can easily be criticized; especially today where, on the one side, sound design, sound production, etc. have become common, thus gaining increasingly larger cultural importance, and where, on the other side, the borders between the structuring and designing of sound and the composing of music, be it in the studio, on the computer or even on stage, are rather undefined.

However, as the goal is to discuss relations between film music and non-film music, it is music, in an essentialist understanding in which the definite piece of music is central, and also music's path into other media that is reflected. Thus, film sound as a whole is not included, regardless that the use of foley-techniques, acoustics, spatialization, shaping, etc. are very often characterized by a design that gives witness of a musical way of thought. Later, I shall however return to these matters.

There can be no doubt that in a technical and music-theoretical sense, film music is a legitimate and genuine form of music. It is made of elements we traditionally expect to find in pieces of music: organized pitches, chords and chord progressions, rhythms, dynamics and various repetitive patterns that stand out through combinations of these elements allowing for the emergence of themes, melodies, motives, sequences, etc. But whereas every other kind of music is restricted and obliged to follow inner logics and constructive principles that secure adequate (inner) coherence necessary for the establishment of meaningful syntactical and structural entireties, film music is not submitted to the same kind of logics. Formal demands that traditional musical pieces of work have to meet in order to be recognized and appreciated as such are generally either only relevant for title music and similar musical elements in film, or on a small-scale 'local' level. Film music usually emerges and fades away at will, leaving only vague hints of a music that could have been, or excerpts of passages from musical sequences whose beginning or end is never heard. In this respect, film music is fragmented and syntactically uncompelled.

Concepts of music and forms of description

The peculiar absorption that often characterizes listening to music without the simultaneous watching of moving pictures, be it the concentrated listening, the two-sided integration or participation, music while working, or merely the distraction we experience whilst doing the dishes or driving the car, is fundamentally distinct from the way we listen to or, rather, hear film music. Whereas film music as 'film music' is inextricably linked to the universe of the film and the complex of interpretations that is contained within the interaction between the narrative, the music, the articulations, the conceptions, etc., non-film music is linked to the participant, the listener, and eventually to a mental sculpting of the musical structures and aesthetics or, maybe, even to a visualization of the musicians performing the music if it is mechanically reproduced.

Aside from the recent widening of the concept of film music towards a general concept of music as simply audio or sound, it seems common to many criticisms and understandings of the complex interaction between film and music that they are generally reluctant to reflect upon the concept of music that lies behind the discussions (Prendergast 1992, Gorbman 1987). Music is ostensibly understood as a commonly acknowledged definite phenomenon, a given fact, and in this way it appears implicit in the performed examinations.

Furthermore, music is often sorted out in a kind of implied system making it appear as if it can be enrolled into forms of description that are as firm as those available regarding the visual and the narrative. This understanding – that can be summarized in a concept of music as formal and objective – appears untenable and difficult to substantiate, especially considering film music.

The referentiality of music – and film music – as well as its objectivity is essentially different from what characterizes the pictures. Whereas it is possible to distinguish between operative categories as outside and in-door-shootings, camera angles, various perspectives, types of lenses, lightning conditions, etc. in the case of pictures, it is not possible to refer to objective and exact conditions and situations to the same degree when dealing with music, and most certainly not in such a way that it becomes broadly understood.

On the contrary: The declarative concerning music is very difficult to accomplish with just a limited degree of significance for everything else but the kind of music in question (this is also true if it is the sound production of the music we wish to describe). No single tone, chord, timbre, rhythm or beat and no multiplication or combination of either is ascribed to – or can take on – just one particular, unambiguous meaning, function or character. And the same piece – or more often extract – of music can even perform very different, frequently contradictory tasks in different films (e.g. Samuel Barber's *Adagio for Strings* or Johann Strauss Jr. *An der schönen blauen Donau* that both are used in numerous films, some of which oppose each others' descriptions).

Contrary to most other agents of film, music apparently cannot be neutrally described 'from the outside', so to speak. In itself, this cannot imply that film music falls outside the domain of 'common music', quite the contrary; it could support the idea that it has to be evaluated and described from inside a musical discourse. As we shall see this does not seem to be true.

Technical or system specific description

It goes without saying that the generally system-dependent methods for the description of music that have been developed and continuously refined within musicology by and large are inadequate when striving for commonly understood descriptions of the forces evoking the emotive and psychological responses generally associated with music. It is even more so if the description is supposed to consider how the music affects and maybe contextualizes a particular film scene. Whereas there is absolutely no difficulty in describing how the film camera's selection significantly affects our experience of a scene, it is quite different when it comes to describing the way the music influences the scene in similar, objective terms.

None of the traditional musicological methods for the description of music are capable of showing and explaining how the character and the significance of a piece of music in a particular scene work internally and externally. Furthermore, even on the expert-level, the methods are in principle only capable of describing how music obtains meaning internally, how it works or makes sense in a particular theoretical perspective that is exclusive to music. What is described in this way is music's mere denotative capacity or syntactic meaning[7] referring to e.g. "the manner in which individual notes relate to one another melodically, harmonically and rhythmically." (Shepherd & Wicke 1997: 103).

Towards the 'inner' signification of music, the methods are more or less irrelevant and one does not get far with the technical description at least not without outlining where, how and to whom the music in question is 'functioning'. Analyses and descriptions of the music's technical composition are in themselves only capable of showing how the music is composed. In addition, it can only do this within a framework of understanding whose categories and terminology is determined in advance – and is known to all who participates in the communication. To the uninformed, they are of no use at all.

If it is not determined in advance what tasks the music is carrying out in the culture in which it belongs, the technical description only makes sense as far as music is acknowledged as a self-enclosed phenomenon, as pure aesthetics. A position that is rarely relevant towards film music.

Technical descriptions are generally irrelevant for the understanding of film music in its context. It may even act to obscure or derail in the same way as the technical description of the engineer's accomplishments behind the building of the scenery or the setting of the lights will hardly contribute to the understanding of the drama, and certainly will not support the theatrical experience.

The minute we try to understand film music on the premises of non-film music by applying traditional methods for music analysis and description, we are obviously neutralizing the music's filmic element. However, this does not imply that descriptive forms that focus on the music are automatically inadequate. They can only exclude descriptive procedures that primarily concentrate on normative structural features and elements.

CATEGORICAL DESCRIPTION

Categorical descriptions of genre and style are compilations of complex concepts or conceptualizations, which on a kind of meta-level contain relatively detailed information on the form, structure, character, origin and use or function of the music. As such, categorical descriptions also give hints to implications regarding signification, on at least a general level.

Form typologies and genres such as ballade, symphony, schlager and waltz, may, as well as style designations as punk, romantic, electronica and bebop, anchor and contextualize a scene deeply into sub-cultural, historical and ethnical milieus and situations. But they bring only little help to the understanding (and workings) of the specific music in the concrete scene. Of course, in many ways, they yield loud and clear signals but they are on the level of headlines and, furthermore, just as the usefulness of applying technical descriptions depends upon theoretical understanding, categorical descriptions also require knowledge of the cultures to which they refer.

Categorical descriptions are learned descriptions. They are meaningless to the unqualified, that is, to the one who stands outside the culture in question. From a Western-European viewpoint, this is well known from the encounter with exotic music styles and genres: besides the exotic and maybe a sense of the geography implied they do not tell us anything specific unless they are accompanied by pictures. And in these cases, we have to trust the authenticity of the combination. Is the music we hear actually related – or at all relevant – to the events depicted? We are in the hands of the picture and filmmakers.

Behind this scenario lurks one of post-modernity's most disturbing consequences: Does it really matter if we accidentally – or deliberately – mix the categories? To the informed, it can be entertaining to mix, and to the outsider it is merely a coincidence if it has or ever will have any importance at all.

Insofar as categorical descriptions are nevertheless considered to be viable means of explaining musical signification in film, it has to be taken into account that this kind of signification is also defined dialectically in the exchange between the music and the 'rest of the film'. Seen in this way, it is hard to ignore that film music, for instance, supports or may even have become one of the generators of the notion of historical époques and thus of époques in the history of music. If we are not specifically taught in advance, it is hard to see how we should be able to connect the music of Lully with the court of the Sun King, Louis the XIV, or just to the 17th century, without the special settings, the rhetoric of the mediated presentation. Film can produce a totality of information, a specific discourse, inside which all elements interact leading to a kind of mutual signification. And even musical means of expressions that fall outside traditional categories can, as we shall see later, form a category of their own.

As strong as categorical definitions may work, they are dependent upon signification processes that are continuously negotiated and ever transient. They can never deal with the 'musicness' of the music and they tend to provide an understanding that allows for interchangeability and negotiation to a degree that minimizes or overrules the importance of the specific piece of music in question, thus generally excluding music's capacity to form the *Barthenian* 'punctum' (Barthes 1993) to a scene, a situation that does not seem advisable.

METAPHORICAL DESCRIPTIONS

More objective or at least objectively sounding descriptions such as fast, slow, loud, weak, and well known dead metaphors – which however in certain cases may have a denotative non-metaphorical content through the principle of homology – such as light, dark, heavy, seem – through what appears to describe universal conditions – characterized by a sort of neutrality. This apparent neutrality seems, however, highly questionable. What do metaphors like these really imply?

Almost every metaphor that is used in connection with music takes off outside musical discourse – stating this is practically a tautology – and as such they stand out as external descriptions: "The music is gloomy" or "the quick ornamental runs in the accordion endow the piece with a carefree and light atmosphere," etc. However, what is considered 'gloomy' seems relative and very possibly ethnocentric, and this also seems to be the case when it comes to metaphorical descriptors such as 'ornamental', 'carefree' and 'atmospheric'. In the end, metaphorical descriptions are culturally determined, too, and they are to a great extent developed inside distinctive discourses belonging to certain historical and cultural spaces. The kind of understanding they bring forward is situationist and intimately dependent upon the participant's pre-understanding.

Metaphors are not objective or independent. They require familiarity with both the current musical code (or idiolect) and with the use of metaphors within the given socially, technologically, historically and culturally determined field of communication.

Culture, and especially the professional traditions that establish themselves towards music, develop certain forms of description based on metaphors that add up as musical types of character: a jolly song, a happy melody, a mournful ballad, a burden march, etc., paving the way for the notion of musical archetypes.

Towards sound or timbre it is common to use descriptive metaphors very often organized in contrasts of hard/soft, sharp/hollow, etc., and going a bit further it is well known that musical instruments can be endowed with certain spirits or even anthropomorphized; thus, the individual instruments are associated with specific animals or types of human beings.

Technical, categorical and metaphorical descriptions based on their use in non-film music do not present themselves convincingly as candidates for an adequate approach to the understanding of film music. Categorical descriptions probably stand out as the most informative followed by the metaphorical, but to work they both require a distinctive degree of familiarity with cultural practice and tradition and all three turn out to be ethnocentric and in case of at least the technical to a certain degree even elitist. However, this discussion gives a hint on one of the difficulties in dealing with film music as a distinctive form of music: the whole investigating apparatus discussed hitherto is tied up in practices that are closely entwined with non-film music. On the other hand, if film music is fundamentally dependent upon the existence of non-film music as a reference, then clearly the problem is to decide whether its signification, or coding, is inherited from the socio-cultural coding of the music in question, or has been taking place outside a filmic discourse – suggesting a coding established in a musical discourse – or if it is generated primarily in the encounter with the film.

However, no matter how the coding takes place, film music forms a fragmentary nature as a result of its primary conditions being closely entwined with the narrative and the pictures and it can only be analyzed in concordance with the film, as the pictures can only be meaningfully analyzed in tandem with the narrative, the music and so on.

Coding and signification

The complex of technical, categorical and metaphorical descriptions and their foundation within a certain culture, sociality and time also seem to govern the musematic notion of musical composing that, above all, is known from Philip Tagg – and to a certain extent but in a less indexical form from Asafjev. The musematic approach and understanding describes a great referential framework whose permutational capacity appears to be inexhaustible, but whose status and significance as basis, defining the conditions for musical communication on the whole, works as a matrix – a matrix that could be understood as an imprisonment, as references that fall outside the matrix cannot obtain status as musical expression.

The musical work, or actually the composer, can take an oppositional position towards this imprisonment by challenging or breaking down the borders. This is well known within the classical tradition as well as within the popular. Film music is, however, prevented from pointing out the imprisonment as it has been determined as referential. The imprisonment is the conditional basis for film music but film music itself is outside this imprisonment, thus actually confined in another: a negation of the imprisonment.

This is, of course, a very awkward way of defining why film music cannot gain genuine denotation or primary signification, only secondary.[8] It points towards signifying processes that fall outside the specific film music itself, but eventually towards other forms of music, and – in a non-concrete temporal understanding – also before the music. Film music can thus be seen as continuously dependent upon music that has been.

While traditional music is playing into a cultural space, where music materializes as music in a reflected articulation of the cultural space's technological systems, a gesture; film music – as long as it remains film music and aspires to be comprehended *as* music – is playing into an already established musical space that it stands outside and cannot influence. It is in the negation of that space that it is imprisoned. And if film music breaks out of its imprisonment, it really *breaks in* and shifts position; it becomes part of traditional music.

In consequence thereof, the signification or connotation that music is supposed to bring into or contribute to the film has to exist either as a cliché or a potentiality. In order to be considered film *music* and not just film sound, the musical code in play has to have been established previously – at least to a certain degree. No matter if the music is supposed to contradict or support the pictures and scenes it escorts, it can only do so if it is sufficiently coded beforehand.

Doing so, film music is dependent upon the practices and coding of non-film music and upon the coding and re-coding that film music and pre-existing music has undergone as they have been exposed in other, earlier films.

Although the coding is not entirely acknowledged by every film watcher – and does not need to be – almost every musical expression, any musical sound that occurs in film, is in a way already coded. The only other possible coding of the music is the one taking place inside the framework of the film, its pictures and narrative.

Coding is not limited to specific musical works, styles and genres. It also encompasses general voice leading principles, orchestration, instruments etc. not surprisingly in close relation to the practices and technologies that belong to Western-European culture.[9]

A single musical entity, like a note from a cembalo or the sound of a distorted electric guitar, is to many Western-Europeans a sufficient indication of a level within a specific social structure in a particular historical époque, to contextualize and characterize a dramatic situation.[10]

At the same time, and as already touched upon, it has to be considered that, to many filmgoers, the specificity of music's signifying content may as well have been generated within film discourse as within a musical pattern, meaning that the sign value and signification of, say, old music forms has been established in close relation to film. If the affinity between specific music forms and certain historic periods, cultures, social classes, etc. is maintained continuously, it will most likely be within generative media practices and not as much a result of educational efforts. Thus, the cultural learning process that entrusts us with the ability to distinguish between different types of music could in this way be seen as partly taking place within a filmic discourse. Within postmodernity's hyperrealistic modus of simultaneity, this observation is trivial. Still, it may be difficult to retain these relations or associations inside the filmic practices in the present, as film also makes use of music in asymmetrical ways, for example the well-known use of music by Rossini and Beethoven in Stanley Kubric's *A Clockwork Orange* (1971) – the apparent conflict is dependent upon the knowledge or a sense of the music as prerequisite (see later).

Returning to the question of coding, non-film music can be seen as shaped and developed through dialogical (inter-textual) processes, whereas film music is doubly monological: non film music inflects monologically upon film music as an external source. At the same time, the dialogical field that relates to film music is sterile: any exchange between the expressive means of film music unavoidably takes place in a context that includes and prioritizes the film. Hence, any dialogically based exchange is encapsulated within the universe of the film and the music is tied up as a single voice in the complex multi-media polyphony that constitutes the film.

Film music is as such excluded from the circuits of traditional music, leading an aesthetically unique existence and forming a separate idiosyncratic realm, which nevertheless is based upon structural and expressive techniques and methods that constitute what could be summarized as the rhetorical means of the circuits of non-film music. To a large extent, film music is seen in a similar way as rhetorical effect by Jon-Roar Bjørkvold (1996) a viewpoint, supported by Claudia Gorbman (2004).

However, contrary to what Bjørkvold – with references to Plato and a respectful reflection upon the theorizing of Eisler and Schönberg – suggests, film music is not able to unfold inner, structural qualities of music in a rhetorical way that calls for rational appreciation. No matter if the music is of the highest compositional complexity or plain trivia, there is no way it can escape being judged almost entirely on an emotional level. Film music – just as music in advertising – is always pathos, and even forms of expression that are traditionally considered to be mainly rational like Serialism and Elektronische Musik stand out as pathos, articulating, for instance, the dispassionate, cold and estranged nature of a scene appealing to emotionally determined response and signification.

MISSING LINK

Present signifying processes in relation to music become increasingly blurred and difficult to deduce. Whereas musical meaning as a social construction traditionally seems tied to the uses, knowledge and reception of music in various forums where music has been in the centre in one way or another, secondary signification emerges in close interaction with late modernity's almost omnipresent sound-picture-relations and within the practises that surrounds these. The coding that is traditionally imprinted upon music within specific practices – the club, the work, the concert hall etc. – in accordance to which musical expressions are perceived and eventually understood as codes and signs, is now taking place outside dedicated musical forums. Instead, secondary signification increasingly emerges in relation to practises and norms that are established inside the complex dialectics that characterize media in which pictures and music converge, eventually in what stands out as a synthesis, an enclosure that cannot be split up into separate entities. The extreme consequence being that music will only exist as (a kind of) film music.

Film music exists in its own domain that is obviously related to and dependent upon the current music-domain but does not belong to it. No matter if the music is written exclusively for the film or if it is either pre-existing or written as a contribution to the film, or released simultaneously on its own as potential chart-material; the inclusion into the film implies that it is installed as an element alongside dialogue, sound-effects, voice-over, text, and so on. Hence, it always appears as if it existed in advance, like the ready-made. And like the ready-made, it inevitable takes on a new form or presence.

For this reason, it is hard to support and substantiate the idea of identification as a function of association, a process of affiliation, in the case of non-film music used in film, as brought forward by Kassabian (2001). Whatever piece of music the film watcher could associate the 'local' or 'individual' discourse of the music in question with, its exposition in the film will almost certainly lead to a re-coding of its significance.

READY-MADE

The situation is comparable to that of the ready-made. When Marcel Duchamp, in 1917, exhibited a urinal under the title *Fontaine* at The Independent's Exhibition in New York, the urinal was transformed into a work of art. It ceased to be a urinal. Even if someone should decide to use it as such that action would in itself become a part of the work of art, or transform it into a new, a happening. It would never (re-)reach the trivial or mundane: a man relieving himself.

The aesthetic status of the ready-made can seem arguable but it certainly questions the authority of the artwork pointing towards its elements of intentionality and associative measures, not towards its inherent qualities. As Lars Qvortrup points out, this is basically a Kantian observation and not as much a modernist move as one might expect given that Kant acknowledged that the quality of a piece of art does not originate from qualities in the work itself, but from the observation or recognition of the work (Qvortrup 2001: 231).

The essential determination of the ready-made manifests itself through contextualization or rather re-contextualization. It is not as much the conferring upon the status of art on a urinal by exhibiting it as the element of entrusting an artefact with(in) nonnative coordinates, evoking a conflict or dialectic space as the ready-made challenges the surroundings. Hereby, the object acquires new values, which profoundly deprives it of its original qualities and uniqueness. The conferred object enters a kind of situationist dialogue in which it becomes a single voice in what can be acknowledged as multi media and polyphonic.

The idea of transforming existing (everyday) artefacts into artworks by the mere act of transformation appears to be a specific move and the parallelism is obvious, music exposed in film cannot be considered a traditional piece of music, it becomes film music. And neither is it of any importance here whether the music is diegetically integrated or not. In other words, music that is included in film will always become a kind of ready-made no matter if it is made for the film or not. The mere process of being installed into filmic context or employed in commercials renders the music transformed and functionalized.[11]

Stanley Kubrick's use of Beethoven's Ninth Symphony as the musical accompaniment for the dystopian highly misogynistic brutality depicted in *A Clock Work Orange* turned the music into a ready-made. The transformation was further intensified by the fact that the piece was performed by means of synthesized sound, outlining the determination of the operation. Even without the film, this brilliantly orchestrated synthesized version[12] of the piece is in itself a kind of ready-made in an almost true Duchamp sense: in a way, the sound of the synthesizer resembles Duchamp's contribution to, for instance, Leonardo's *La Gioconda*, the moustache and the goatee, dragging the emblematic anthem of European culture[13] out of its traditional field and entrusting it with the characteristic electrified timbre of the 20th century.

However, whereas the Duchampian ready-made rearticulates the well-known – be it a work of art or a plain everyday artefact – this way bringing an object into the foreground forcing the spectator to consciously (re-)interpret the object, the musical ready-made dissolves in the process and submerges into the film. The music is not accentuated and it does not stand out as a 'mis-placed' or re-contextualized object.

As it becomes tied up in the dramatizing of specific actions and values, the musical ready-made gains a metaphorical quality that music cannot else acquire. This is why for instance the (theme of the) second movement of Mozart's 21st Piano Concerto can serve as a reference to the sentiment of (ill-fated) love affairs as the piece was used as signature music in Bo Widerberg's film classic *Elvira Madigan* (1967). The kind of metaphorical signification goes way beyond the metaphorical quality music can achieve on its own even if it is put forward as (part of) a programmatic piece or a tone painting since the music is closely associated with specific narratives and pictures that are generally shared in a given culture.

FUNCTIONALIZATION AND MUSICALIZATION

Music installed in film is in this way functionalized sound that has ceased to be music. It is functionalized as a consequence of the way in which it contributes to the current story. It can be a picture or a reflection of music but it does not stand out as a piece of music anymore; the circumstances deny what it has been or what it refers to. It may be perceived but not received as music. The functionalization of the music implies – besides possible references to a specific original work – that generally merely the aesthetic and rhetorical 'elements' of the music stand out. Any reference to the inner logics of the work never becomes active except in the cases of specific music film,[14] a film that is entirely shaped and cut in accordance to the music, or of a film that only makes use of a single piece of music.

Luchino Visconti's use of the Adagietto, the 4th movement of Gustav Mahler's 5th Symphony (1901-02), as signature music (strongly leaning towards a genuine *leitmotiv*) in *Death in Venice* (1971) the filming of Thomas Mann's novel of the same name (1912), exemplifies a typical kind of functionalization. The sombre but enchanting, alluring piece serves as a deepening of not just the qualms and yearnings and at the same time joyous longing of the main character, Gustav Aschenbach, but also of the painful gravity of the decline of the romantic-bourgeois culture. Here, the pathos of Mahler's music is almost literally turned loose by the convincing interplay between the narrative, the pictures and the music, inducing a strong emotive sensation almost insisting upon the spectator's identification and leaving the austerity and transparency of the score behind. As the music is thus turned into a vehicle, the logic of the narrative overrides that of the music. Instead of being drawn into the music's meticulously neatly woven spatiality, the spectator is firmly taken even deeper into the psychological drama of the film.

In a way, Mahler's music is deprived of its authority and autonomy as a work of art. It is far away from the concert hall and the participation of the educated audience it was aimed at. It is not even performed but simply reproduced just as it is detached from the context of the symphony, making it appear as a piece of its own in the form of a ready-made installed in a montage. But the case is tricky, as the leading role of Aschenbach could be built upon Mahler's person and character, suggesting that the music is to be understood as heard by Aschenbach's inner ear. As such, the status of the music changes from simple underscore to what can be referred to as inner-diegetic, thus making room for the music's presence as a 'real' piece of music.

However, even if the setting is interpreted in this way, the music is still functionalized. It has merely shifted from one structural level to another, from that of an effect deeply integrated in the setting of the scenes to that of a role exposed on the stage.

In order to understand the Adagietto in either of the ways suggested here, the first obviously being integrated in the second, one has to have some kind of knowledge or at least vague idea about romantic music of the 19th century, and its aesthetic and ideological implications. And, in the second case, one even has to know the music in question and also have a notion of the life of Gustav Mahler. To the uninformed, who were never introduced to or took any interest in European cultural history and romantic music or who simply were brought up in another culture, the historical contextualization is maybe not lost but it can only appear as yet another example of heavy symphonic music in film, true to the idiom of classical film music. Mahler's music does not form a special case in the history of film, although maybe the film does.

Whether film music is compiled of pre-existing music, or composed solely for the film, it cannot escape its dependency on non-film music and it will continuously stand out as ready-made one way or another. It is however possible to talk of a particular form of music that is altogether exclusive to film although it seems to be closely related to certain areas within the field of electronic music and also to installation art. This particular kind of music stands out as a result of a process that could, with a term borrowed from Julia Kristeva (1987), be called musicalization,[15] and it comprises the hidden, almost secret music that emerges as the sound space is forced into systematic mapping.[16] This is, of course, also based on ready-mades as the sounds and effects in question are developed as effects symbolizing unfamiliar typically unearthly cultures, technologies, ages, etc.

The organization and distribution of effects, samples and concrete sounds by means of tempering into pitch and temporalizing into rhythm renders musical structures and forms of expression that are in many ways unique to film or at least to mixed media.

Since it is applied in order to qualify diegetic noise, the use of Foley-technique as a procedure that resembles musicalization is obvious. However, musicalization goes much further as the sound space is thoroughly organized according to given music systems that have dominated Western European music since the late middle ages. It is tempting to suggest that this approach is chosen because it produces a kind of familiarity – a Schein des Bekannten – that is or is considered to be vital to the fullness and narrative of the film.

An example of this is found in Eric Serra's music to Luc Besson's *The Fifth Element* (1997), a science fiction action movie with an impressive amount of amusing and subtle references to other films. The soundtrack presents a number of passages that utilize well-known space sound allusions that have been continuously developed and apparently stand out as a peculiar bricolage of heavily processed sounds generously trimmed with reverberation and echo.

The example shows a thoroughly composed – musicalized – sound setting, which discreetly but efficiently forms the atmospheric ambience surrounding the dialogues and environmental sounds of the scene. The montage is neatly put together by a number of highly different sound syntheses and possibly samples. Some, like the "giant foot-steps" which stems from the foley-effect that serves to illustrate the controlled dignity and weight of the good Mondoshawans as they walk, are collected from the soundtrack, while others are more indefinite effect sounds, supporting the gigantic size of the space-station, the space hotel *Fhloston Paradise*, as well as the impression of a remote location.

It is remarkable that almost all sounds of the setting, even the many concrete sounds, are organized in accordance with the common Western-European pitch system and temporalized in the meter of 4/4, tempo 72 BPM. In this case, it is not just the sound-sources that become a kind of ready-made, so does the tonal system and temporal organization into well-known rhythm patterns – a practice that could find its way into the realm of advertising insofar as the ongoing approaches for sound setting are liberated from mirroring the aesthetics of current popular music and the well established codes of musical articulation.

Furthermore, musicalization can also be understood as 'sonic decoration' implemented to 'colour up' the scene very similarly to the way that the visuals are pre-interpreted and charged by means of lights and camera lenses and angles. Within a strictly musical sense, the tonal quality of the 'sonic decoration' as transcribed in Fig. 1 builds a highly complex chord – a cluster – and give no evidence of any form of melody or harmonic progression. The absence of a musical syntax – apart from the continuous, Tintinnabula-like arpeggios in the electric piano – implies that the film watcher never becomes aware of the musical organization of the sound-design. Because one does not hear or reflect upon the sonic decoration as a musical expression – a reference to a musical idiom – this harsh and in a musical sense highly avantgarde structure is never judged or processed as anything but the 'sound' of (or) the sonification of the environment.

Fig. 1. Graphic mapping of a selection of pitched sounds in Eric Serra's sound scenery for Luc Besson's *Plavalaguna*, 1997.

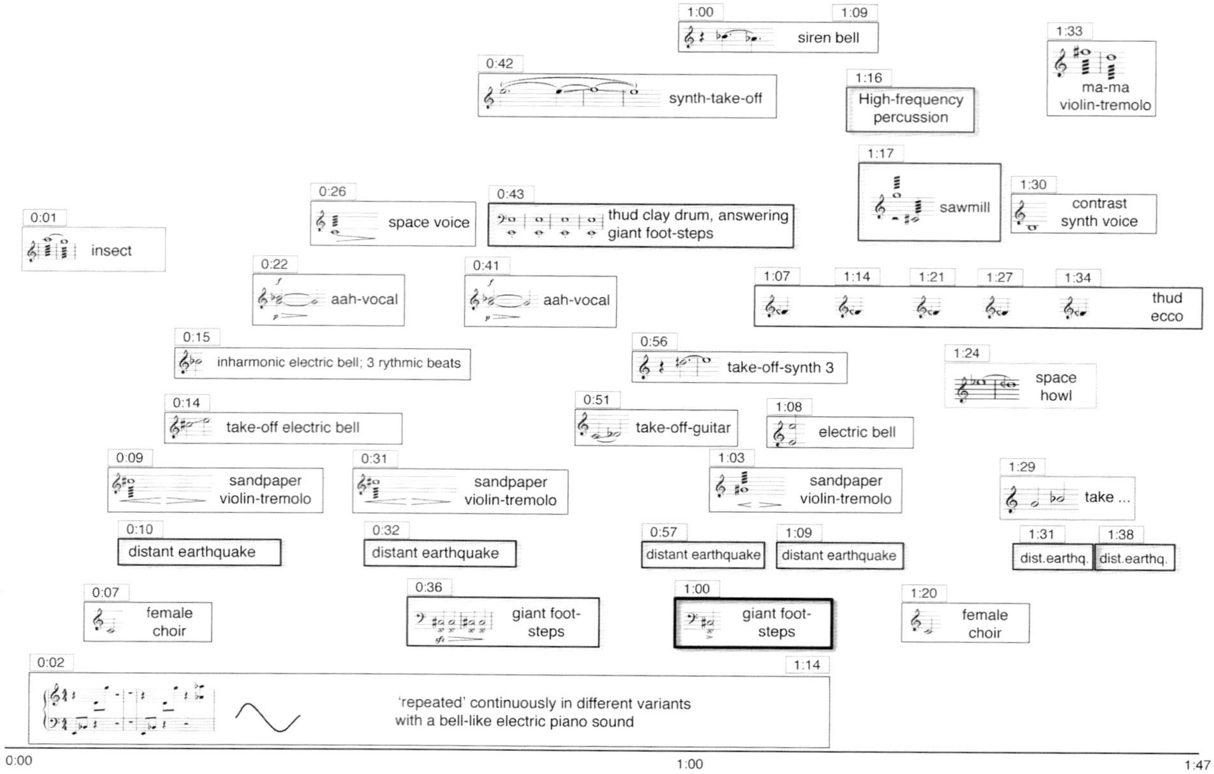

Among the many remarkable proportions in the small piece, please notice the use of the falling third at 1:33: A true European icon symbolizing the worried child's plaintive call for Mama.

Applying a similar procedure towards another axiomatic system such as language would produce a montage of words, word-like utterances, sounds – and even letters – with no inner coherence. However, unless we find a way to produce these sounds that did not call for human or human-like voices, this could not lead to a similar unrecognized result, as the film watcher would immediately appreciate the sound's origin in a humanly constructed communicative system and thus would continue to 'interpret' the decoration as a kind of reference. This does not happen in the case of musicalization, as it is a very sophisticated and obscured application of music as "… a system of signifiers without signifieds." (Tunstall 1979: 62, DeNora 1986: 87).

When musicalization is implied, the whole principle or 'Ge-stell' of the musical system is at hand as a ready-made. But it never stands out as such by itself. The ready-madeness is shrewdly hidden. The lack of motives, significant musical elements as well as familiar musical sounds implies that the average film-watcher never hears anything but 'the sound' of the setting or scene; its musical organization remains unacknowledged. And the unrecognized familiarity of the sonorous environment, the musicalized design of the decoration, ensures that a subliminal sense of confidentiality, vitality and (aesthetic) 'well-formedness' can emerge allowing for identification and regression. It is tempting to claim, that this is actually the way music generally works within film and possibly even in most other multi-media contexts as well.

SIGNATURES AND JINGLES

Signatures and title-tunes are often exposed in what seems to be full length at the beginning and/or the end of a film or a TV-series. At these positions, where the narrative is typically either no longer or has not yet become the core of the event, they seem to stand out as 'complete' music pieces forming a link between the universe of the film and the real world, as just another tune in a continuous sequence of tunes available everywhere and at all times in the modern world.

Placed at the beginning, they form an escape or gateway – a 'sesamic' sign – into the realm of the film. In the case of a TV-series or a film-sequel, signatures can even signify the well known and reassuring like the tolling of the church bell requiring or allowing you to let everything else go and attend the church service. Placed at the end, they can form a kind of relief letting the soothing familiarity of music come into focus as the end-titles starts rolling thereby building a bridge out of the filmic universe into 'reality' helping the film watcher to comfortably 'step back' to reflect upon the experience of the film. Musical instances like these constitute a kind of middle-form between the ready-made and the autonomous piece of music. As such, they can enter a recursive loop as far as the motives and passages from the signature are used as sonic decoration throughout the film or the episode whereby the ready-made actually becomes a kind of own-breed. This is the case in numerous films and also TV drama series like the British *Midsomer Murders*, where motives and short arrangements derived from the characteristic signature-theme in many episodes brilliantly formed the entire musical decoration of the series' inconsistent postcard-like universe.

The signature-tune for the American sitcom *Friends*, *I'll Be There For You* performed by The Rembrandts, forms a somewhat special case of the ready-made. For one thing, the song is obviously a pastiche, a revival or rehash of the aesthetic practices from the Sixties on both sides of the Atlantic giving strong allusions to early Beatles and Hollies songs in Britain and to songs by the Byrds and The Monkees in the US. Furthermore, the song only became a hit after the series had its debut (1994) implying that its primary reference was the (universe of the) series and not 'itself'. The song was actually written for the series, so although it stands out as ready-made in the sense that it can point towards and this way re-introduce – but not converge with – a carefree and juvenile atmosphere of – the myth of – the sixties, it does so by being a pastiche and not a known and authentic number from the sixties. *I'll Be There For You* is as such freed from specific associations and distinctive values except for its link to the series, and it takes on the form of a paradox pointing towards a historical construction by bringing references to aesthetics and values from another époque than that of the series whose setting is obviously contemporary. This way, the choice of music, the ready-made, stresses the series' deliberate lack of 'true' realism, its senselessness.

In Cooks study of a 1992 commercial for the Citroën ZX 16v, he suggests that the alignment of a specially segmented version of the opening of Mozart's overture to *The Marriage of Figaro* with the advertized car form a composite dialectical message making the car stand out as "the ideal synthesis of art and technology" (Cook 1998: 6). However, Mozart's music is not really presented or performed. It is present in the form of a reference, pointing towards the highly esteemed symbolic value of the work – or of the classical genre as a whole – it maintains in present time and not towards (definite values of) the work. As such, it is merely a kind of second-order signification.

In a recent commercial for the Danish financial institution, Danske Bank, the first 37 seconds of Isaac Albéniz' *Asturias Leyenda*[17] is performed by a female harpist who, from about a third into the commercial and onwards, is accompanied by a male so-called 'Human Beatbox'. The performance takes place on a stage in an apparently empty music theater and, at first, only the harpist is seen (and heard). Therefore the viewer is not able to decide whether this is a presentation or rehearsal of a musical performance or something different. However, the concentric moving of the camera encompassing the harpist (having completed half a circle as the Human Beatbox becomes visible just before joining the music) quickly makes it clear that this is not a (documentation of a) performance. This recognition unavoidably weakens the viewer's attention towards the music and its performance in favour of the complete presentation, pictures, progression and all. Even before the introduction of the Human Beatbox, the music has become an installation in a compound communicational event and the addition of the percussive sounds not associated with the otherwise familiar piece of music merely stresses this determination. To complete the picture – and the marginalizing of the music – commercials produced for Danske Bank have reached over a longer period of time a unique style or sub-genre, presenting apparently 'real' people in situations doing "what they are best at". So, the music is not only present as a ready-made by definition, so to say; this element is actually stressed by the doing-what-you-are-best-at-theme of the commercials, focussing on the element of human action not on the 'product'.

Conclusion

Given that "the picture fills the music with meaning and the music fills the pictures with meaning" (Bjørkvold 1996: 57) music obviously looses its own unique meaning in the interaction with pictures. Insofar as music brings "musical meaning" to the pictures, this meaning is either dependent upon music that exists before the film, or upon the meaning the particular piece may have (gained) in advance. In both cases, there is talk of a sign, a ready-made that is exposed and re-contextualized in a foreign discourse; this is even true if the music is exposed in cultural and historical settings with which it is traditionally affiliated. However, it probably stands out most strongly when historical, cultural, social discourses are mixed as in the use of The Dies Irae from Verdi's *Requiem* (1874) in Hans Alfredson's film *The Simple-Minded Murderer* (1982) about the life of a mistreated farmhand in Sweden in the late 1930s. Contrary to music in advertising, which can seem to draw heavily on the conventionalized significance that is attributed to music – be it the use of a classical idiom as a signifier of distinguished elegance and class (Den Danske Bank, Anthon Berg, Citroën), or the use of jazz-like music and setting to signify a relaxed intellectual and refined atmosphere (Den Danske Bank, Smirnoff, Schweppes) or the use of popular music signifying youth, power and freedom (Den Danske Bank, Mentos) – thus profiting from music's pre-contextualization, it's culturally ascribed values and codes, film generally redefines the significance of music through re-contextualization.

Music becomes pure connotation – or secondary signification – and is deprived of its capacity as self-contained communication. It looses its primary signification – its syntactical and semiotic coherence – and, at the same time, its secondary signification deviates from that of non-film music. The situation seems to closely resemble the ontology of music within the ancient Greek concept, mousiké, in which musical expression only forms one inseparable component alongside poetry and dance.

Just as the musical elements of the ancient Greek mousiké are 'processed' as established entities exposing or symbolizing specific, commonly acknowledged values and characters, it is precisely because music, consciously or unconsciously, is perceived as ready-made that it can work the way it does in film. If this were not the case, music would steal the picture and muffle or invalidate the film's fundamental polyphony.

The circulation of film music in culture is given in advance: It is introduced and distributed as part of the film. And it is in this particular context, its meaning emerges. By virtue of its dependency on non-film music, it stands out as a double parasitic construction contrived from non-film music and the film itself, its pictures and narrative. If, however, film music escapes the film, it becomes part of the musical domain. It is transformed.

To modern culture, film music is a prominent reading of the musical phenomenon. It may be referential towards traditional music but it articulates its references in a sort of twisted artistic almost anarchistic form. As proposed, this is closely related to film music's fundamental but hidden otherness but it also has to be a product of the absence of historicity in post-modernity.

At the same time, film music has a life of its own, which in certain cases leads to exceeding the traditional limits of musical articulation – at least on the surface.

Michel Chion (1982: 12f) insists that there is no such thing as a sound track, except for the material or physical layer in the media. Film music and film sound cannot be separated from the film implying that both the picture and the music would otherwise degenerate. The film will literally fall apart. And not only that: Neither the pictures nor the sound can survive the separation without being transformed. Published as a sound track, film music forces its way into the music domain and ceases to be film music thus stressing that, as far as the aesthetical significance of music goes, it is in a way definite while its rhetorical and cultural meaning is inconsistent and negotiable.

However: as pointed out, one can speculate if the non-existing sound track sets the agenda for the larger part of the cultural signification that is attributed to music. And maybe this seemingly awkward kind of external signification is even unavoidable to music. If this is true, we are facing a double negation: The ready-mades that pound out of loudspeakers everywhere do not originate anymore from music. They arise in the sound settings of Tinseltown's exclusively light-wave carried scenarios and they are continuously redefining the works of the music domain. The light-wave carried music thus becomes the ultimate reference, an insuperable perfect negation casting the musical setting of the modern world.

Notes

1. Surveys from the first half of 1990s strongly suggest that "filmgoers are typically unconscious of most film music" (Cohen 2000: 366).
2. Although silent movies have been very influential to modern film – and almost any kind of contemporary audiovisual media communication – they form a specific genre that distinguishes itself from other kinds of film not just with respect to the lack of sound and music but certainly also in terms of pictures, epic style, and the drama as a whole.
3. Small 1998.
4. As far as film music can be considered a particular genre, it is in the broadest sense of the designation namely precisely as film music.
5. Music in advertising, TV-series and similar reoccurring audiovisual artefacts do not comply with these characteristics – and others on this list. Quite to the contrary, music installed in these repetitive forms generally relies on elements of recognition and consequently on identification patterns.
6. By describing film music as referential, I only mean to suggest that it refers to conventions ascribed to non-film music and that it is dependent upon such references in order to 'communicate' or work. In brief, film music is dependent upon non-film music and non-essentialist.
7. The use of the term 'denotation' is motivated by the need for its opposition 'connotation'. As it is pointed out by a number of scholars (e.g. Middleton 1990, Shepherd & Wicke 1997) denotation in a literal sense is absent in music, as music and musical structures do not have specific meaning in the linguistic sense. Middleton suggests the use of the terms 'primary signification' and 'secondary signification', which without being identical correspond to a distinction between syntactic and semantic levels.
8. The distinction between primary and secondary signification is depended upon Middleton's clarification (1990 and 2000). Broadly taken primary signification concerns how intramusical coherence and 'meaning' is gained through the observation of specific structural means whereas secondary signification refers to the fact that music gives rise to complex associations and connotations of extra-musical observation.
9. The dominance of the aesthetics and techniques of Western-European music within film music is massive. It may be related to the fact that many German composers were forced to leave Europe and came to USA at a time when the practices of sound film were established. As a counterfactual exercise it is interesting to consider what classic film music would have sounded like if the composers who 'populated' Hollywood had mostly come from Japan.
10. See for instance Walser 1993.
11. The only exceptions being concert and music film. They like music video, form a special case where the music is the film's guest, its possessive – or a subordinate part given that the musician is often considered the leading actor – thus the music is not a part of the film as form. Here, music is not a part of the film's communicative structure, but the subject for the communication. It falls outside the definition of film music.
12. The orchestration was done by Wendy Carlos, who also performed the piece.
13. The fact that the piece later became the hymn of European Union seems to support the element of montage.
14. Film versions of for instance musicals and operas.

15 Hroar Klempe called my attention to this in his paper Mediatekstenes flertydelighet – et musikalsk anliggende? held at the seminar on *Music, Media and Meaning* at Aalborg University, 2000: http://www.musik.aau.dk/musikogmedier/2000Seminar/Seminarprogram11.htm

16 Donnelly (2005) uses the term 'musicalising' as a, as I understand it, more general description of the developments within sound design.

17 The piece that derives from the Suite Española (1886) for piano solo to which it was added in 1898, is probably best known as a transcription for Spanish guitar.

REFERENCES

Altman, R. (1992). Four and a half film fallacies. In R. Altman (Ed.), *Sound theory sound practice*. New York: Routledge.

Barthes, R. (1993). *Camera lucida: Reflections on photography*. Reading: Vintage Classics.

Berendt, J.-E. (1988). *Vom Hören der Welt* [On listening to the world] Frankfurt am Main: Network-Medien-Cooperative.

Bjørkvold, J.-R. (1996). *Fra Akropolis til Hollywood. Filmmusikken i retorikkens lys* [From Acropolis to Hollywood. Film music in light of rhetorics] Trondheim: Freidig Forlag.

Chion, M. (1982). *La voix au cinema* [The Voice in Cinema]. Paris: Cahiers du Cinema Livres.

Chion, M. (1994). *Audio-Vision: Sound on screen*. New York: Columbia University Press.

Cohen, A. J. (2000). Film music: Perspectives from cognitive psychology. In J. Buhler, C. Flinn, & D. Neumeyer (Eds.), *Music and cinema* (pp. 360-377). Hanover: Wesleyan University Press.

Cook, N. (1998). *Analysing musical multimedia*. Oxford: Oxford University Press.

DeNora, T. (1986). How is extra-musical meaning possible? Music as a place and space for "work". *Sociological Theory, 4(1)*, 84-94.

Donnelly, K.J. (2005). *The spectre of sound: Music in film and television*. London: Bfi (British film institute).

Gorbman, C. (2004). Aesthetics and rhetoric. *American Music, 22(1)*, 14-26.

Gorbman, C. (1987). *Unheard melodies: Narrative film music*. Bloomington: Indiana University Press.

Jensen, K. B. (2006). Lyd som kommunikation – En tværfaglig forskningsoversigt og dagsorden for medieforskningen [Sound as communication – A cross disciplinary research overview and agenda for media research]. *MedieKultur, 40*, 5-13.

Kassabian, A. (2001). *Hearing film: tracking identifications in contemporary Hollywood film music*. New York: Routledge.

Klempe, H. (*in press*). *The role of music in the experimental psychology of Wilhelm Wundt*.

Kristeva, J. (1987). *Soleil noir. Dépression et melancolie* [Black sun: Depression and melancholia]. Paris: Gallimard.

Middleton, R. (1990). *Studying popular music*. Buckingham: Open University Press.

Middleton, R. (2000). Popular music analysis and musicology: Bridging the gap. In R. Middleton (Ed.), *Reading Pop*. Oxford: Oxford University Press.

Prendergast, R. M. (1992). *Film music: A neglected art*. London: Norton.

Qvortrup, L. (2001). *Det levende samfund*. København: Gyldendal.

Shepherd, J., & Wicke, P. (1997). *Music and cultural theory*. Malden: Polity Press.

Small, Ch. (1998). *Musicking: The meanings of performing and listening*. Hanover: Wesleyan University Press.

Tagg, Ph., & Clarida, B. (2003). *Ten little title tunes*. New York and Montreal: MMMSP.

Tunstall, P. (1979). Structuralism and musicology: An overview. *Current Musicology, 27(5)*, 51-64.

Walser, R. (1993). *Running with the devil*. Hanover: Wesleyan University Press.